"The intellectual depth and breadth of this volume commends it to all those interested in figuring out ways for organizational entities to become more robust and resilient, for society to be more inclusive."

Daniel Daianu, *Professor of Economics, and President of the Romanian Fiscal Council*

"This is a book for anyone passionate about understanding our contemporary knowledge economies, connected deeply by technology, networks, people and places. It provides a hopeful theoretical underpinning as well as practical inspiring models to help develop fairer, sustainable, and resilient futures."

Carola Boehm, *Professor of Arts and Higher Education, Staffordshire University*

"This book provides valuable insights into the nature and importance of the interaction between public and private actors in enabling sustainable regional development. The theoretical considerations along with the four case studies offer a structure for developing community resilience."

Prof. Mihaela Lutas, *Universitatea Babes-Bolyai, Romania*

RE-CONSTRUCTING THE GLOBAL NETWORK ECONOMY

This book looks at how to build more resilience into socio-economic networks within local communities. Understanding the relationships between attachment to place, complex systems and patterns of knowledge creation is not straightforward, but these relationships are emerging as the challenges that we face in bridging the gap between the social worlds that we inhabit and an emerging digital world.

These issues have been brought into even sharper focus through changes resulting from the COVID-19 pandemic. On the one hand, forced familiarity with communication technologies is driving globalisation forwards, whilst on the other, the crisis has created awareness of dependencies and heightened desires for more local solutions. Plenty of books have been written about the rise of digital networks and the decline of local communities. This book takes a radical approach by identifying how these trends fit together and provides examples of how digital networks can be made to work for the local as well as the global economy. Using a case study approach, the book offers a clear-sighted view of the role of relational capital in specific places and organisations and shows the transformational impact that they can have at a micro level.

The book deliberately seeks to shake up preconceived ideas and is ideal for strategy practitioners and policy makers within governments and NGOs involved in connecting local to wider network economies.

Andrew Taylor has co-authored three books about people, place and economy. He leads the management consulting firm Connect CEE and the NGO Transilvania Executive Education. Andrew has a PhD in environmental politics from Cardiff University.

Adam Bronstone works in the non-profit sector and serves as an adjunct lecturer in the area of Politics and International Relations. Dr. Bronstone received his doctorate in political science from the University of Hull, UK.

RE-CONSTRUCTING THE GLOBAL NETWORK ECONOMY

Building Pathways to Resilience in Local Economies

Andrew Taylor and Adam Bronstone

Routledge
Taylor & Francis Group
LONDON AND NEW YORK

Cover image: Megan Collante and Xingbei-Li

First published 2023
by Routledge
4 Park Square, Milton Park, Abingdon, Oxon OX14 4RN

and by Routledge
605 Third Avenue, New York, NY 10158

Routledge is an imprint of the Taylor & Francis Group, an informa business

British Library Cataloguing-in-Publication Data
A catalogue record for this book is available from the British Library

Library of Congress Cataloging-in-Publication Data
Names: Taylor, Andrew, 1972– author. | Bronstone, Adam, 1969– author.
Title: Re-constructing the global network economy : building pathways to resilience in local economies / Andrew Taylor and Adam Bronstone.
Description: Abingdon, Oxon ; New York, NY : Routledge, 2023. |
Includes bibliographical references and index. |
Identifiers: LCCN 2022014273 (print) | LCCN 2022014274 (ebook)
Subjects: LCSH: Online social networks. | Communities. |
COVID-19 Pandemic, 2020—Social aspects. | Globalization
Classification: LCC HM742 .T38 2023 (print) | LCC HM742 (ebook) |
DDC 302.30285—dc23/eng/20220505
LC record available at https://lccn.loc.gov/2022014273
LC ebook record available at https://lccn.loc.gov/2022014274

ISBN: 978-0-367-70257-1 (hbk)
ISBN: 978-0-367-70259-5 (pbk)
ISBN: 978-1-003-14529-5 (ebk)

DOI: 10.4324/9781003145295

Typeset in Joanna
by codeMantra

Andrew Taylor
I would like to dedicate this book to the city and people of Hull. A place that represents so much to me and has all the ingredients described in this book to fulfil its potential. In the words of Andrew Marvel 'a city that is in the world, but sufficiently on the edge of it to have a different resonance'. To all of the left behind people and places in the world, may you flourish in your difference.

Adam Bronstone
There are countless people across the world who love where they live. They were born there, grew up there, married their high school sweetheart or beau, have lovely friends and for all those reasons wish to stay in those communities. These people should not be made to feel that they must uproot their lives to have a life that is productive and can support themselves and their loved ones. We can make it possible for these people to be able to stay in the community that they love and be productive. Modern technology is such that this is possible, now more than ever, and it is through these dedicated people that these opportunities are growing daily. I, personally, want to dedicate this work to the Educabs and like organisations of the world so are working hard to combine the global with the local, for the benefit of the local and the global!

CONTENTS

ILLUSTRATIONS

Figures

Tables

ACKNOWLEDGEMENTS

Andrew Taylor
First and foremost, I would like to thank the interviewees from my case studies that gave their time generously, without which this book would not have been possible. For their inspiration and encouragement, far beyond this book project, I would like to thank Prof. David Collins and Prof. Andrew Flynn. For introducing me to the world of complexity, I must give thanks to Prof. Yasmin Merali. Nancy Rice, our proofreader, is the sole reason that my writing is readable and for her patience I am very grateful. Last, but by no means least, I would like to give thanks to Oana and Elena for tolerating my interest in such projects.

Adam Bronstone
On behalf my parts of this work, I want to thank all the people who agreed to personal interviews and whom I also came back and back and back to for more questions and greater clarity about the respective case studies. I also want to thank Megan Collante, a very talented young adult who I have dragged into helping me with respect to designing the cover for the book. I want to thank Xingbei-Li, Megan's friend, who also worked on the cover. Of course, I want to also thank a few other people, including my co-author, Andrew Taylor, who inspires me, pushes me and does on his own brilliant work; our publishing team from Routledge, a group of people who are very

helpful to us; and our 'checker', Nancy Rice, who makes sure that even if the material is not great, we at least sound good! Finally, and as always, I want to thank my wife, Valorie, who constantly puts up with my fascination in this project, the late nights at a computer and at times the early morning Skype calls with Romania. She married an academic, and at times I am sure she wonders about that! Thank you for your support!

1

SETTING THE STAGE

Introduction

The convergence of technology and globalisation is transforming both the creation of value and the societies from which its value is derived. It is this convergence of technology and globalisation that is usually referred to in shorthand as the 'new' economy (Tapscott, 1999; Henwood, 2003; Kennedy, 2012). Our previous book, *People, Place and Global Order* (2019), mapped out how this is taking place, along with the related social and political consequences, at strategic and societal levels. We then offered examples that showed how commons and community enterprises can utilise digital networks to enrich people and places rather than simply exploit them. This book is the next step in the evolution of our research into how more people and places can flourish with an emerging global digital network economy while being able to remain in 'place'. In this work, we will take a deeper dive and look under the hood, both theoretically and through case studies of existing places and organisations, to see how connections between people and places can thrive in a networked world.

DOI: 10.4324/9781003145295-1

Recapping Our Story

Before venturing into new territory, however, we should summarise our previous work (Taylor & Bronstone, 2019), since it provides a foundation and a lens through which we seek to view an emerging world. We describe a shift in value creation from Porter's early call to use technology to capture value (Porter & Millar, 1985) within internal business processes more effectively to Hammer's (1990) desire to use technology to obliterate business processes completely. Back in the days before the internet, strategy was about securing value creation within business processes, products and brands. However, Prahalad and Hamel recognised that technological change requires a focus on core competence to be able to adapt a business to market evolution (Prahalad & Hamel, 1990). As the internet started to take hold, Hammer (1990) realised that global connectivity would wipe whole layers of processes and people from organisations. To prove his point, he cited how Ford salespeople now entered purchase data such that they could reduce accounts payable staff by 75%! This led to a noisy fad for so-called business process re-engineering (Taylor & Bronstone, 2019).

By the mid-1990s, Arthur (1996) provided a prescient insight into the key characteristics which were re-shaping not just strategy, but economics itself. He argued that wherever technology disrupts markets the law of diminishing returns no longer applies. In fact, the 'law' becomes the law of increasing returns where those that are ahead move further ahead and those that are behind are left behind. So-called network effects, or feedback loops, lead to market equilibrium at a monopolistic state of competition (with 1–3 major players), rather than closer to perfect competition (many players within a market). This takes place, Arthur (1996) says, because of 'groove-in' which can be technological or social. Technologically, 'groove-in' captures the idea that to collaborate with technology we need to agree to a technological standard and that whoever controls that standard captures market lock-in. Examples of this include controlling the VHS standard, where Sony dominated the video recorder market or the .doc format which continues to give Microsoft a monopolistic share of the office software market. Social 'groove-in' refers to the idea that it is hard to learn to use new technology and we are resistant to learning to use multiple technologies to do the same things. This is why companies such as Facebook are so successful and MySpace and Friends Reunited were not. Arthur argues that where this takes place, management shifts from a search for order and optimisation to become a search to catch the next big wave. In this world, adaptability and critical thinking are what define success.

Evans and Wurster (1997) showed how technological change and the forces of globalisation were converging to enable companies to achieve richness and reach. Historically, companies had to choose to sell in mass markets, competing for high volume and low margins, or go for niches where volumes were lower, but margins higher. However, in the digital economy companies could have both. As Amazon and eBay enabled global access, the tiniest niches became viable and the days when companies could simply offer a limited range of mass-market products ended. This situation has opened up the whole world to smaller companies and simultaneously a world of choice has made redundant the idea of simply marketing to consumers in specific geographic or sectoral markets.

In such a world, the boundaries of the firm are breaking down as value is leveraged through communities of practice (Wenger & Snyder, 2000) that are located within digital networks and aggregated by those controlling data platforms, such as Amazon, Facebook and Google (Owens, 2019). This world requires a whole new approach to business that is based on flexibility, adaptability and what Argyris calls double-loop learning which has greater emphasis on cognitive ability and associative thinking (Gavetti, 2011) than previously thought. Mason (2015) then showed how such disruption is driving the marginal cost of distribution (and in some cases even production) close to zero. Think, for example, how much it costs Apple to send you a track from iTunes. He then showed how the Wiki model provides a template to use collaboration to remove capitalist logic from markets entirely. Whilst we do not share Mason's belief that capitalism is about to crumble, we do recognise that network economics opens up opportunities for commons and community-based organisations to flourish. However, for that to happen we need to understand more fully some of the dynamics that drive network economics. The forces described above explain how the rise of the network economy is moving market dynamics towards a Pareto curve, a world where monopolistic competition is the new normal. This was captured in the idea of a so-called long tail model by Chris Anderson (2006).

The growing concentration of wealth because of this new economic trend has led to a dual approach to managing people. While those deemed able to adapt and deliver profit from this new world benefit from a renewed focus upon performance (Sparrow, 2015), those not central to value creation are increasingly exposed to a harder approach to Human Resources (HR) (Bloodworth, 2018). The network economy is simultaneously enabling the outsourcing of jobs to cheaper locations around the world, whilst e-commerce is undermining traditional retailers. What started with the moving of so-called non-core staff into call centres is currently expanding to include the traditionally value-added functions, including HR and accounting (Dragan, 2018). Meanwhile, town centres are being hollowed out by departing large retailers and turning many high streets and regional shopping malls into a blend of charity, betting and payday loan shops, if those uses of these locations exist at all anymore (Kingsnorth, 2008; McGarvey, 2017; Hubbard, 2017; Maconie, 2017; Welby, 2018).

A European example of this new economy is seen in some of the newer member-states of the European Union (EU), where these countries have attracted considerable investment based upon their lower labour costs, engineering experience and younger people's English language skills. Starting in the 1990s with investments by car companies in production facilities in Eastern Europe and by the time Romania joined the EU in 2007, the reach of the network economy led to a rapid growth of both outsourced IT and wider business services.[1]

The fuel for our previous book was anger with an editorial for *The Economist* that described people in northern towns of England as 'scroungers', because they did not want to move somewhere more economically successful. It argued that:

> governments should not try to rescue failing towns. Instead, they should support the people who live in them. That means helping them to commute or move to places where there are jobs
>
> (The Economist, 2013)

The notion that people should, as the editorial board of *The Economist* (2013) argued, just pick up and move from their homes, without consideration of identity-related issues, was a defining illustration of the primacy of profit over everything else. It was as if place and identity and history should mean nothing. For however poor the economics of a place appear to be, for those attached to that place they 'are not trading preferences, but safeguarding the things that cannot be traded' (Scruton, 2012, p. 201).

A Twenty-First-Century Gospel of Wealth

In the US and as a response to the growing inequality found in the US (OECD, 2021), and in a manner that appears to be unlike that of The Economist's editorial board, Darren Walker, the President of the Ford Foundation, who fashions himself as a modern-day Andrew Carnegie, wrote that 'perhaps it is time for a reimagined gospel of giving' (Walker, 2015). Walker's thoughts were not only inspired by Carnegie, but also by Dr. King, who wanted to reconstruct the very nature of economic society in a systematic manner.

In response to Walker, even the Business Roundtable came out with a 'Statement on the Purpose of a Corporation' (Business Roundtable, 2019). This document starts by stating that 'Americans deserve an economy that allows each person to succeed through hard work and creativity and to lead a life of meaning and dignity' (Ibid.). The statement continues by asserting that the members of this organisation 'believe the free-market system is the best means of generating good jobs, a strong and sustainable economy, innovation, a healthy environment and economic opportunity for all' (Ibid.) Yet one commentator asserted that Walker's position that capitalist benefits can be spread and used for the purpose of justice was one that 'defies the laws of capital formation. Neither good intentions nor window-dressing designed to fool the ignorant can overcome those laws. Either capital concentrates or capital (as in the less competitive enterprise) fails' (Leland, 2019). The reader further comments that it is because of this position, which he (the reader) considers contradictory, that the 'Ford Foundation and Mr. Walker base themselves on deception and fantasy. If Mr. Walker is serious, he should leave the Foundation and become a socialist' (Ibid).

Whilst our first book sought to understand the forces that are leaving some people and places behind, simply raging against the idea that capitalist logic is all defining may have populist appeal but doesn't change things.

We deliberately sidestepped overtly political choices and proposed to learn from Pioneers of the nineteenth century, such as the Cadburys, Rowntrees and others like them who realised that profit without principle was never going to be a successful path. For those so-called Merchant Princes (Kennedy, 2000), gaining the commitment of their workforce and surrounding community was more valuable than their compliance. This mode of thinking formed the basis of a wave of innovation (Kennedy,

2000), the development of urban planning, widespread healthcare provisions, education and much more. In short, that philanthropic approach to business proved to be not only profitable but also a catalyst for the transformation of people and place.

In face of this critique, we, in our 2019 work, hinted at several instances of modern-day entities that appear to operate on a motivation that is like that of The Merchant Princes (Kennedy, 2000), beyond profit; that encompasses profit but seeks to define people and place as sources of competitive advantage. Principles, in these instances, appeared to also matter.

The examples brought forward in 2019 were glimpses and were never intended to be full case study examinations. The intention of this work is to do that – to examine the interaction of people, organisations and places with the network economy to explore what are the drivers of both sustainable economic success and wider participation. In the context of renewed interest in so-called 'levelling up' the gap between London and the Northern cities of the UK (Smith, 2021), such a work is both timely and relevant.

Looking Under the Hood

Each of the places or organisations studied in our first book has narratives and myths which both describe how those living and working within them perceive themselves and how outsiders perceive them. These perceptions are sometimes congruent and sometimes contradictory or oppositional. However, it is mostly not the representation of 'place' itself which is of primary interest to us. Rather, it is the relationship between the importance attached to place and sense of agency that we seek to explore. Whilst all the case studies reveal a sense of pride in the city or organisation, not all have been able to convert that pride into economic success. How have some places and organisations succeeded, and others not, in using a cherishing of people and place that Scruton calls oikophilia (2012, 2017) not only as a badge of pride, but as a means to differentiate and to be a fulcrum around which to organise, develop and grow commercially and collectively?

This book, therefore, seeks to examine, using Rose's (2011) seminal work, the extent to which motivational states (mindsets) are both enabling and limiting participation in a global digital economy. Some people are more naturally comfortable with change, have a greater sense of agency, are less tied to place and hence are more positively predisposed emotionally and intellectually toward ambiguity than others. Put simply, the first question that we seek to respond to is, how, and with whom, do you create an environment that uses connectivity to enable a place or organisation as a whole to flourish and not just the elite groups.

The use, by Taylor and Bronstone (2019), of Rose and Goodhart's (Rose, 2011; Goodhart, 2017) characterisation of people into different groups, as a means of describing the broader consequences for political economies of this new dual-speed economy, links strategy to politics in developed countries. Rose describes three groups of people with different values that create what he calls motivational states that have a significant impact upon not just their ability to drive change, but also how to and for what purpose:

> For Settlers, the deep forces draw people to seek out safety, security, identity and belonging. For Prospectors, it is the yearning for success, the search for the esteem of others and self-esteem, while for Pioneers, the constant drive is for new ideas, the quest for connections waiting to be made, and living a life based on ethics.
>
> (Rose, 2011, p. 1)

Settlers crave a sense of certainty about their place in the world. In short, they desire stability over adventure (Taylor & Bronstone, 2019). Whilst Settlers' sense of stability may be as imagined as it is real, that only serves to underline the importance of symbols of continuity and change in driving their behaviour. This is something that few politicians have yet understood, but Nigel Farage, the leader of the UK Independence Party (UKIP), has fully grasped and exploited. A man in the pub, as the centre of a community, having a pint of traditional beer with the locals, is not the defining image of Farage by accident!

Using the same source data as Rose (2011), Goodhart (2017) says that the convergence of technology and globalisation has divided developed countries between those who see the world from *Somewhere* and those who see it from *Anywhere*. Those that remain attached to a sense of place as central to their identity and those that have broken free of that anchor. Goodhart's Anywheres value autonomy, openness and are comfortable with social change. Somewheres are, instead, less educated, more rooted in specific places and attached to symbols of tradition and continuity.

The terminology that we employ can be, at times, confusing. Let us make the following clear: Rose's Settlers and Goodhart's Somewheres are, we believe, broadly interchangeable terms, as are Rose's Prospectors and Goodhart's Anywheres. Goodhart's names point to the importance of place as a point of attachment, whilst Rose's names point to the importance of change. Both have merit, but, purely for the sake of clarity, henceforth we will use Rose's names. Taylor and Bronstone (2019) showed how Rose's Settlers or Goodhart's Somewheres are being left behind economically by outsourcing and socially by the rise of e-commerce. In both cases, these forces are assisting in hollowing out the sense of place that defines them.

With respect to Settlers, there are two groups of people we wish to discuss (Taylor & Bronstone, 2019), who are united by their lack of agency and fear of change. The first group are the Economic Settlers. This group of people are finding their productive spaces diminished as the convergence of technology and globalisation outsources and automates their jobs. As outsourcing progresses up the value chain, it is now moving jobs in HR, accounting and other functions from developed economies to cheaper locations such as Romania or the Philippines. Outsourcing is no longer a strategy reserved for production and customer service employees but is increasingly impacting upon roles that we would have once described as more executive than clerical. Automation, which first took a hold upon the public imagination during the 1980s, is also widening its impact far beyond production lines as digital technology advances. Contemporary discussion of automation is mostly defined in terms of the rise of artificial intelligence (AI) (Fountaine, 2019, p. 61) and how it is fulfilling Hammers (1990) prophecy to not just improve business processes but obliterate them and their human supports entirely. Whilst outsourcing and automation may reduce costs, they also embed the idea of work as a transactional relationship for remaining staff and they are self-evidently a zero-sum game for those at risk of redundancy.

Social Settlers are the second type of Settler we are interested in. People in this group may be rich or poor, working, middle or upper class but are united by a sense of loss of their consumptive space. As predicted by Evans and Wurster (1997), their shops are being closed by the rise of e-commerce. It is no longer just the odd retailer here and there, but the rapid decline of the entire British High Street that has brought about the collapse of brands as diverse as House of Fraser, BHS, Jessops, whilst giants such as Marks and Spencer and Boots are in serious trouble. Pressure upon retail rents is so intense that the shopping mall palaces of the 1980s are now targets of vulture funds (Shah, 2019). The visible result is high streets across the UK dominated by a depressing mixture of vacant shops and charity shops. This change is also happening at a rapid pace in the US with the ever-increasing rise of online shopping and the concurrent closing of large chains in every sector of retail (Butler, 2021). The pandemic has merely fast forwarded this process of decline.

Digital change is happening in more subtle ways too. To avoid the political furore that flowed from branch closure programmes, banks are increasingly converting remaining branches into screen-only experiences with staff purely there to help you utilise the software provided, in much the same way that supermarkets have created the self-checkout experience. This shift to shopping as a screen-based activity denies the human and social contact that it historically was associated with. It is no longer a means to share a common sense of place, behaviour, customs and culture where, to use a phrase from the American show Cheers, everyone at the bank did 'know your name'. Rather, it is becoming an individualistic and purely utilitarian experience based upon the goods, their price and not an investment of self in place or people.

Both Settler groups share a sense that their ability to resist change is being limited by declining social status and the rise of hegemonic discourses that disenfranchise them (Taylor & Bronstone, p. 70). However, Cowley asserts that 'a large constituency of working-class voters feel that not only has the economy left them behind, but so has the culture' (Cowley, 2018). Growing social (and increasingly legal) limits on language, with charges of racism, xenophobia, homophobia or just plain ignorance (Scruton, 2012) being used to restrict expressions of opposition to more permissive values. For liberals who doubted the power of political correctness, the dismissal of Roger Scruton from his role as a government housing adviser, based purely upon a quick reading of a philosopher's words taken out of context, was a wake-up call (Weaver, 2019). It did not come as a great surprise to Settlers, who had become used to the tearing down of statues representing great figures from America's confederate past or those associated with slavery from the UK (Murray, 2020), whilst the appropriate use of language to discuss issues of race, gender and sexual orientation by academics at Oxford and Cambridge became a subject of public debate, such that it was clear to all that failure to conform would be career limiting (Pells, 2017). As we write, in both the US and the UK, we are witnessing very public clashes between Settlers defending established views of the history of their country, region/ state and local place and Pioneers demanding a progressive revisionist history. As noted, such struggles matter to Settlers because they are symbolic of a fear that they are losing control of even the language with which they can relate to each other, their place and thus their identity. There is a 'close connection between a sense of disempowerment and a sense that people's identities are under siege' (Cowley, 2018). As the philosopher Scruton put it, we 'cannot question this publicly without risking charges of racism and xenophobia' (Scruton, 2012, p. 4).

Both Rose and Goodhart show how the convergence of technology and globalisation is undermining the Settlers sense of place and identity, whilst their internal lack of agency limits their ability to adapt:

> A Society without aspiration that is embedded in the virtues of community will become inward looking and complacent. It will become disposed to protect the status quo at the expense of desirable change for the common good.
>
> (Welby, 2018, p. 45)

However, for businesses to survive they, Settlers, need to be able to move with market needs. In a world of rising complexity (Snowden & Bone, 2007) and rapid change, critical questioning and a search for the right things, rather than doing things right, are becoming central to an organisations' ability to adapt (Argyris, 1991).

Undoubtedly, a shift away from the value being intimately tied up with measurable order and optimisation and towards management that rewards adaptability and ability to cope with ambiguity, rewards Rose's Prospectors and Pioneers. Work that is based upon facilitating the technological capture of networks that know no boundaries (Zhu & Iansati, 2019) to create value is, by definition, not tied to place and its fluid form repels Settlers.

Whilst Rose's Prospectors and Goodhart's Anywheres are surging ahead and, in their almost complete capture of the heights of capitalism, their political economies have created both governmental and business elites that are wholly unrepresentative of their own societies. The failure of Rose's Pioneers or the (rather poorly described) Inbetweeners of Goodhart has failed to step up and bridge the gap between Somewheres and Anywheres with some form of inclusive model of political economy that utilises global digital networks to enrich, rather than simply exploit, the local networks.

Thus we now seek to explore how Pioneers, with the capacity to prospect, yet attached to ideas that business is a means and not just an end in itself, construct business models that bring the global to enrich the local. To this end, how can Pioneers construct business models, in a digital world, that Settlers can participate in and flourish with as they reproduce specific local identities given their attachment to a specific sense of place and people? Pioneers' efforts would need to be rooted and attached.

Questions

Having identified that the convergence of technology and globalisation is leaving many people and places behind, the purpose of this book is to explore the central question of *how do we enable more people and places to flourish within the network economy?* Within this very large question there follows several key sub-questions, which enable us to examine the question in a more detailed and meaningful manner:

1. What are the key characteristics that underpin the success of small places and organisations to thrive within complex global networks?
    a. What role can entrepreneurialism play in the development of networked forms of stewardship?
    b. What role do shared values and experiences have in both constructing identity and economic development?
2. How do models of development inform our understanding of local flourishing?
3. Is there a new model of development that we can identify from our research?
4. Is there any evidence of polycentric modes of development and governance and, if so, how far do they reach?

To explore these questions, we will examine existing models of development and explore how historic models of stewardship may interact with contemporary models emerging from systems and complexity thinkers. We will do so through the lens of four case studies that provide insight into both the challenges and the opportunities of the network economy. For whilst the concluding chapter of our previous book identified examples of companies that appear to be following in the footsteps of Cadbury and others that, in the past, enabled Settler communities to flourish, much more in-depth work was and is required to 'understand how the engagement of people and place with global networks can both create value and enrich the local.

Having sketched out the big picture in our previous work, this book is all about induction: viewing perceptions of reality through the eyes of Settlers or Somewheres embedded in their locales; Prospectors or Anywheres devising strategies for surfing the digital wave; and those Pioneers and Inbetweeners who may be able to bridge the gap between these two.

The case studies include two organisations: a Kansas brewery, a Romanian NGO and two cities: Jacksonville, Florida and Cluj-Napoca, Romania. They were chosen for their experience in trying to develop patterns and use models of engaging with network economies. We seek to learn from the experience of those involved in such efforts about what works, why it seems to work and what does not. The extent to which such lessons can be applied elsewhere is inevitably bounded by the limitations of qualitative research. Nonetheless, we aim to identify patterns and trends that are worthy of further investigation elsewhere.

The Plan

This book, again, working as a 'next phase' to our first publication, will consist of the following chapters:

Section I

Chapter 2 will be a critical review of classical ideas of regional development and how they have had very mixed results, followed by introducing the idea of entrepreneurship as a catalyst for wider socio-economic transformation and locating that within specific local networks. The chapter will examine contemporary models of local/regional transformation, including Transition Towns, Transformational Entrepreneurship, The Preston Model and the Foundational Economy, and the intriguing possibility of systemic polycentrism.

The next chapter, Chapter 3, will explore the impact of network effects and their relationship to different network structures in terms of externalities and resilience. Resilience is both a question of structure and cognition, so this chapter will also explore how key conceptual models of the new economy, such as Argyris' (1991) learning loops and Snowden's (2007) Cynefin model can be useful tools to abstract how Pioneers connect ideas of stewardship and attachment to place in order to internalise externalities and thrive within global networks.

Section II

This section will be dedicated to the in-depth exploration of four case studies. Chapter 4 will be an outline of the case studies that we will use to illustrate our thought process with respect to how, in this networked world, Settlers can be engaged in an authentic manner as much as other groups in society. We will outline the reasons why we use these case studies and not others. Our method is broadly ethnographic, but certainly qualitative, using interviews and participant-observation to gather empirical data and induct perceptions of reality. Chapter 5 will be an investigation of the case studies and will include the sustainable development model of Boulevard Brewery Company (US), the attempt to replicate the Cleveland/Preston community wealth building model in Jacksonville, Florida, the economic success story of Cluj, Romania, and the NGO EduCab (Romania), which seeks to develop networks of socio-economic development between successful metropolitan centres and struggling small communities.

Stepping outside of the case studies and understanding the important lessons learned, as they relate to the overall purpose of the book will be the task of Chapter 6. In this chapter, the authors will pull together the empirical data from the case studies to map out what structures, concepts, people and tools have proven key to engaging Settlers, such that people and place have more widely flourished economically and socially. Key discoveries will be the extent to which they are locally specific or can be applied more broadly along with comments on what we might learn in order to construct a more inclusive political economy.

Finally, Chapter 7 will pull together the ideas and empirical discoveries from this research and set out a future research agenda for others to examine the extent to which the discoveries and insights found here are more widely applicable. Beyond opening the possibility for others to examine the wider validity of our findings, we will also set out where we intend to take our continuing research project next.

What's Next

The next chapter of this work will frame the challenges of socio-economic development facing people and places within established and emerging models of local and regional development.

Note

1 Companies as diverse as Kellogs, Deloitte, Deutsche Bank, Emerson and Michelin have outsourced HR and/or accounting functions to Romania, for example.

References

Anderson, C., *The Long Tail: Why the Future of Business is Selling Less of More.* New York: Hyperion, 2006.

Argyris, C., 'Teaching Smart People to Learn', *Harvard Business Review*, May–June 1991.

Arthur, W. B., 'Increasing Returns and the New World of Business', *Harvard Business Review*, July–Aug 1996.

Bloodworth, J., *Hired: Six Months Undercover in Low-Wage Britain*. London: Atlantic Books, 2018.

Business Roundtable, 'Statement on the Purpose of a Corporation', 2019.

Butler, S., 'Great Britain's High Streets Lost More Than 17,500 Chain Store Outlets in 2020', *The Guardian*, Mar 14, 2021.

Cowley, J., *Reaching for Utopia: Making Sense of an Age of Upheaval.* Norwich: Salt Publishing, 2018.

Dragan, A., 'Bucharest vs. Cluj-Napoca: The Transylvanian City Tops the Capital in the Main Economic, Social and Demographic Indicators', *The Business Review*, Dec 10, 2018.

Evans, P., & Wurster, S., 'New Economics of Information', *Harvard Business Review*, Sep–Oct 1997.

Fountaine, T., 'Building the AI-Powered Organization: Technology isn't the biggest Challenge. Culture is', *Harvard Business Review*, July–Aug 2019.

Gavetti, G., 'The New Psychology of Strategic Leadership', *Harvard Business Review*, July–Aug 2011.

Goodhart, D., *The Road to Somewhere*. London: Hurst and Company, 2017.

Hammer, G., 'Reengineering Work: Don't Automate, Obliterate', *Harvard Business Review*, May–June 1990.

Henwood, D., *After the New Economy*. London: New Press, 2003.

Hubbard, P., *The Battle for the High Street: Retail Gentrification, Class and Disgust*. London: Palgrave Macmillan, 2017.

Kennedy, C., *The Next Big Idea*. London: Cornerstone Digital Press, 2012.

Kennedy, C., *The Merchant Princes*. London: Hutchinson, 2002.

Kingsnorth, P., *Real England*. London: Portobello Books, 2008.

Leland, J., The Man with the $13 Billion Checkbook', *New York Times*, July 12, 2019.

Maconie, S., *Long Road from Jarrow: A Journey through Britain Then and Now*. London: Ebury Press, 2017.

Mason, P., *Postcapitalism: A Guide to Our Future*. London: Allen Lane, 2015.

McGarvey, D., *Poverty Safari: Understanding the Anger of Britain's Underclass*. Edinburgh: Luath Press, 2017.

Murray, J., 'Four Charged Over Damage to Colston Statue in Bristol', *The Guardian*, Dec 9, 2020.

OECD, 'Income Inequality', 2021, https://data.oecd.org/inequality/income-inequality.htm.

Owens, J., 'The Tech Giants Dominated the Decade: But There's Still Time to Rein Them In', *The Guardian*, Dec 2019.

Pells, R., 'University "Safe Space" Policies Leave Academics in Fear of Losing Their Jobs, Claims Professor', *The Independent*, June 20, 2017.

Porter, M. & Millar, V., 'How Information Gives You Competitive Advantage', *Harvard Business Review*, July–Aug 1985.

Prahalad, C. K. & Hamel, G., 'The Core Competence of the Corporation', *Harvard Business Review*, May–June 1990.

Rose, C., *What Makes People Tick: The Hidden World of Settler, Prospectors and Pioneers*. Leicester: Matador, 2011.

Scruton, R., *Green Philosophy: How to Think Seriously About the Planet*. London: Atlantic Books, 2012.

Scruton, R., *Where We Are: The State of Britain Now*. London: Bloomsbury, 2017.

Shah, T., 'Vultures Prey on Bombed-Out Shopping Centres', *The Times*, Dec 30, 2018.

Smith, D., 'Fix Our Cities First, Or We'll Never Level Up This Country', *The Times*, Nov 28, 2021.

Snowden, D. & Boone, M. E., 'A Leader's Framework for Decision Making', *Harvard Business Review*, Nov 2007.

Sparrow, P., Scullion, H. & Tarique, I., *Strategic Talent Management: Contemporary Issues in International Context*. Cambridge: Cambridge University Press, 2015.

Tapscott, D., *Creating Value in the Network Economy*. Boston, MA: Harvard Business School Press, 1999.

Taylor, A. & Bronstone, A., *People, Place & Global Order: Foundations for a Networked Political Economy*. London: Routledge, 2019.

The Economist, 'Britain's Decaying Towns', *The Economist*, Oct 12, 2013.

Walker, D., 'The New Gospel of Wealth', Ford Foundation, 2015, https://www.fordfoundation.org/just-matters/just-matters/posts/toward-a-new-gospel-of-wealth/.

Weaver, M. & Walker, P., 'Government Sacks Roger Scruton after Remarks about Soros and Islamophobia', *The Guardian*, Apr 10, 2019.

Welby, J., *Reimagining Britain: Foundations for Hope*. London: Bloomsbury, 2018.

Wenger and Snyder, 'Communities of Practice: The Organizational Frontier', *Harvard Business Review*, Jan–Feb 2000.

Zhu, F. & Iansati, M., 'Why Some Platforms Thrive and Others Don't', *Harvard Business Review*, Jan–Feb 2019.

2

THE OLD AND THE NEW

Regional Development and Transformational Entrepreneurship

Introduction

Thinking about why some places are more successful is hardly new. It has been the basis of much economic geography, geopolitics, economics and planning literature for many years. This chapter aims to summarise the major theories that have been used to explain both regional disparities and models for enabling greater economic success of cities and regions. These models are important because some of them have been used as frameworks for policy and investment decisions whilst others offer templates of how to construct more sustainable or successful economies. Yet all of them are attempts to identify patterns between people, places and resources that define societal change. In the context of growing complexity arising from the convergence of technology and globalisation in business, health and environment, understanding the key ingredients of successful adaptation is important. The emergence of a fast-growing network economy is changing the way that we think about production and consumption and our interactions with them in place and space. If the future of people and places are

DOI: 10.4324/9781003145295-2

not to be driven by the emerging giants alone, we would be wise to consider how different factors can influence their own futures.

The History of Regional Development Theory

Many theories of regional development arose between the end of World War II and the 1970s which were applied within both developed and developing countries as models of growth. We have sought to provide summaries of the more influential models before examining how the EU has used regional development as a key plank of its strategy towards supporting areas suffering industrial decline before the accession of poorer new members and as a more general support for its emergent single market. In response to neoliberal challenges to the idea that the State can and should intervene to redirect economic activity, technological change and emerging interest in sustainable development, a series of newer, more bottom-up models have recently gained the interest of policy-makers, academics and practitioners. These newer models emphasise the role of social capital, local entrepreneurship or local enterprise rather than central or local planning. Given the continued rejection of globalisation and distant authority by Rose's (2011) Settlers across developed countries (Taylor & Bronstone, 2019) and the interest in de-globalisation (Shiva, 2020) flowing from the COVID-19 pandemic, they are of interest to us.

There is a long debate, especially within geography schools, about how to define regions as arrangements of people and space. Sometimes defined by physical geography, other times politically, economically or socially. As an introduction to geography, Rosenberg (2020) claims that regions can be formal, functional or vernacular. Yet this is to miss their dynamic socio-economic features. Losch (1954) saw regions as hierarchical systems of central places whilst Hoover and Giarratani (1985) defined them as internally integrated toward a single point, or node, that dominates the surrounding area. Still others emphasise historic and cultural relationships in defining regions:

> as a spatially contiguous population (of human beings) that is bound either by historical necessity or by choice to a particular geographic location. The dependence on location may arise from a shared attraction to local culture, local employment centers, local natural resources, or other location-specific amenities
>
> (Dawkins, 2003, p. 4)

Whichever definition one chooses, there is no perfect way to delineate regions. Furthermore, as technology and globalisation converge, the centripetal forces that tie peripheries to centres are being weakened. This process has been accelerated through work from home schemes during the COVID-19 pandemic. However, our purpose is not to limit individual places and spaces, but rather to explore how they thrive, or not, within global networks. Traditionally, theories of regional development, based upon David Ricardo's theory of comparative advantage (1817), have emphasised specialisation. Simply put, theories have asserted that 'regions specialize in the production of goods for which relative factors are abundant and export those goods, importing goods for which factors are scarce, both regions gain from specialization and trade' (Dawkins, 2003, p. 5).

Established Models of Regional Development

The Heckscher–Ohlin–Samuelson theorem and David Ricardo's theory of comparative advantage (1817) explain why comparative advantages exist which leads to specialisation and comparative advantage based upon resources of different regions. Dawkins (2003) argues that dynamic versions of these theories, drawing upon neoclassical growth theory, particularly the models proposed by Solow (1956) and Swan (1956), allow for conditional growth where regions do not grow equally and absolute convergence where growth is equal across regions (building upon the Heckscher–Ohlin–Samuelson theorem).

Whilst there are important differences between Heckscher–Ohlin–Samuelson theories and neoclassical growth theories in their belief in the causes of convergence, one can argue that 'most current theories of regional economic development can be viewed largely in terms of their criticisms and response to the convergence hypothesis and neo-classical economics' (Dawkins, 2003, p. 6.). That is to say that early ideas of how regional development would lead to economic convergence have not been supported by either empirical evidence or critical evaluation (Krugman, 2019).

Location theory (Alfred Weber, 1929; Edgar Hoover, 1937; Melvin Greenhut, 1956; Walter Isard, 1956) provided structured mathematical models to evaluate the optimal location of industry based upon logistical costs. This model is predicated upon the idea that firms will locate close to markets when the costs of final product logistics are high and close to raw materials when the cost of input logistics is high. However, writers such as Hoover (1937) argued that firms and industries may agglomerate for reasons other than cost. Losch (1954) argued that because logistics costs and economies of scale vary by product market size and that locational choice will vary, thus 'central places emerge in locations where market areas for different products overlap … [leading to a] hierarchically structured system of cities of different sizes and different levels of product diversity' (Dawkins, 2003, p. 7). Both location and central place theory have been limited in their application particularly because of their underlying assumption that labour is static. The one thing that we do know about economic relationships between people and places is that they are not static.

Export base theory developed by Tiebout (1956) and North (1955, 1956) is rooted in the idea that growth is a response to exogenous world demand which in turn leads to diversification and a blurring of regional identity as trade intensifies and, eventually, through positive feedback loops it converges across regions. In contrast to the demand side models of Tiebout and North, neoclassical exogenous growth theory, developed by Swan (1956), is a supply-side model which emphasises investment in regional productive capacity as the source of conditional convergence (Dawkins, 2003). Barro and Martin (1999) added labour migration as an additional factor in the model to ensure contemporary relevance.

Inevitably, models of convergence have been criticised for their failure to reflect empirical reality (Dixon & Thirlwall, 1975). Whilst there is some evidence for inter-regional convergence, this is less visible between regions in different countries (Dawkins, 2003). Thus cumulative causation theory from Myrdal (1957) was developed upon the idea that increasing returns to scale leads to clustering behaviour that outweighs the higher costs of labour. Myrdal argues that there is a spillover or 'spread' effect into slower growth regions which Kaldor (1970) developed to incorporate productivity of labour into the idea of an efficiency wage as a key economic variable.

Ideas of divergence were developed by Perrouz and were central to his growth pole model (1950) which identifies defined spaces as networks held together by centrifugal and centripetal forces. Writers like Darwent (1969) developed the idea that growth does not occur equally but is concentrated in some places that he called growth poles. Based upon Schumpeter's (1947) model of innovation, he showed how growth was a result of discontinuous spurts in economic activity driven 'by a race for monopoly control over the stream of rents from new innovations' (Dawkins, 2003, p. 17). Growth pole models tend to emphasise the idea of functional linkages between (especially large) firms which leads to innovation and multiplier effects (Kuan Yew, 2000). Agglomerations of firms or industries can act, therefore, as propulsive poles or centrifugal forces of attraction as it is asserted that 'dynamic agglomeration economies – defined as territorial advantages that act on the capacity of firms and regions to innovate – become the centre of most recent theoretical reflections in this field' (Capello & Nijkamp, 2009, p. 6).

Rather like Myrdals 'spread' and 'circular causation', Hirschman (1958) showed how growth poles may benefit their hinterland. As the cost of land, labour and other factors of production rise and/or become scarce, industry starts to shift activities away from the centre of the pole and the pole begins to de-glomerate. He argued that since growth poles are dependent upon linkages growth should be encouraged by focusing on industries with the most linkages. His model provides a more self-reliant approach based on the acceptance of unbalanced economic development. Friedmann (1966) noted, with his centre-periphery model (which is very related to growth pole models), that the emergence of growth poles can be heavily influenced by the activities of local political and entrepreneurial leaders. The model came under attack during the 1980s from the broad neoliberal retreat from Keynesian interventions and criticism that the model lacked defined processes for action and sufficient empirical evidence for it to be a reliable tool (Dawkins, 2003).

Structuralist models have grown up based upon staged theories of economic maturity, rather than push or pull factors, with the thought that 'regional economic change can be viewed as a progression, through long waves of growth and decline, that are distinguished from one another through the differences in the nature of the innovations that characterize each period' (Dawkins, 2003, p. 11). This model has influenced contemporary thinkers, such as Mason (2015), who draw upon the idea of so-called Kondratiev waves to argue that approximately every 70 years industrial capitalism goes through a structural adjustment which can be thought of as a systemic level of creative destruction. Vernon (1966) showed how stages of development were linked to product and firm growth cycles whilst writers such as Massey and Meegan (1982) showed how the geography of decline was linked to loss of jobs as corporate strategies to embrace intensification, rationalisation and technological change. Piore and Sabel (1984) captured the idea of a stage of 'flexible specialization' and Saxenian (1994) argued that dense entrepreneurial social networks are key to successful flexible specialisation.

The guru of strategy for many years, Michael Porter (1990), proposed a staged model of his own arguing that clustering can be utilised as an organising force to drive competitiveness. Cooke and Morgan (1993) take Porter's point and emphasise how networks use proximity to develop patterns of trust that enable governance whilst maintaining market flexibility, thus going beyond Porter's (1990) industry networks to emphasise local cooperation across industries as a form of organisational strategy on the one hand and regional development on the other (Cooke & Morgan, 1993). Such networks are based upon mutualities of interests that require some pooling of resources and thus norms of behaviour (Powell, 1990; Cooke & Morgan, 1993). As such the idea of networks introduces a qualitative element to development that is closely tied to values and locational specifics. Furthermore, as we shall see in the next chapter, growth in digital technologies and accompanying cultural shifts have, by expanding network boundaries, shifted the value of networks such that, as Handy put it (2002), small company fleas can now use digital networks to compete with existing corporate elephants. Cooke and Morgan (1993) noted how networks were not just opening opportunities between firms, but also within them as linear models of organisation, product development, etc. were challenged by a mixture of technological change and new models of business where customers and partners were brought into the value creation process (Cross, Liedtka & Weiss, 2005). Several writers have argued that whilst sales, strategic and financial networks can be scale free, it is production and design networks that require proximity (Chesanais, 1988; Johanson, 1991; Cooke & Morgan, 1993). As we shall see, our case studies suggest that this is not true and may in fact be the opposite.

The EU and Regional Development

EU regional policy is an attempt to move from theory to practice in the attempt to implement a regional policy process at a supra-national level of economic activity, not to replace national programs, but in addition to and in concert with these programs.

An explicit European Union regional policy, or as it is known today, Cohesion Policy, can be traced back to 1975 with the establishment of the European Regional Development Fund (ERDF). However, the idea of regional policy, for the sake of cohesion and economic growth within the European Union, dates back to the much earlier establishment of institutions such as the European Investment Bank and the lesser-known European Agricultural Guidance and Guarantee Fund. The goals of EU-based regional policy, as differentiated from that of national policies of the same ilk, are:

- The European Union (regardless of iteration) can at times be more efficient with respect to regional policy because the implementation can be concentrated in the areas where the need is the most.
- Efficiencies can also take place at the European level because there is the possibility for better coordination and lesser developed regions do not need to fight against each other in the area of economic development.
- There is also a 'common interest, insofar as it is in the interest of all member-states to have a union that is as economically prosperous as possible'.
- Regional disparities may inhibit the march towards an 'ever closer union' because of the lack of integration across regions due to these disparities.

Source: Armstrong (1989, pp. 134–135)

By making the case that there is a supranational role in the area of regional policy because of the ability for an organisation such as the European Union to coordinate and make decisions that are more efficient, those who believe in integration theory (as seen through the practical lens of the European Union) could make the case that there is, and should be, a public policy role in influencing the distribution of economic activity for the sake of lessening and, hopefully eradicating, economic disparities and inequalities across a political entity for the benefit of the citizens of that political entity and the ability of these citizens to seize opportunity in an equal manner. It is also clear that since national regional policy existed before 1975 and continues to exist today in the member-state countries of the EU, the importance of such a policy for the benefit of lessening economic disparities is not a supranational phenomenon in Europe. Many other western countries have similar policies. Canada, for example, tries to close the gap between the so-called 'have' and 'have-not' provinces through a system of 'equalization' payments.

In practice, ERDF policies have been centred on assisting with the promotion and development of 'lagging' regions; the conversion of regions in industrial decline; the combatting of long-term unemployment; increasing employment opportunities for younger people; and the promotion of the development of rural areas (Ibid., p. 140). There are hundreds of examples of these types of projects, with examples ranging from a major water and wastewater infrastructure upgrade for the city of Kaštela-Trogir in Croatia to the introduction of high-speed broadband across Martinique, all for the sake of boosting the economy. Other projects at the level of €50m or more have, from 2014 to 2020, been funded in almost every country of the European Union and are intended to directly benefit the citizens of the member-states by creating better infrastructure, a healthier environment, new jobs and new business opportunities (European Union, Major Projects, 2020).

In addition to the existing European-wide regional policy, the European Union spent considerable political capital in the mid-1990s in establishing and funding the European Bank for Reconstruction and Development (EBRD). In brief, the remit of the EBRD was to assist in the re-development of the economies of Central and Eastern Europe so that they could integrate into the broader European political and socio-economic landscape. Some of the early EBRD projects included the funding of the transformation of old military-industrial plants for civilian use (Bronstone, 1999) and for key economic infrastructure. Acting as a public investment bank the EBRD has had notable success with its private sector investments, such as Banca Transilvania, which has grown from a small regional bank to the largest commercial bank in Romania and, in the process, has both financed small scale entrepreneurship and provided an example in itself (Ibid.).

The reasons for a regional policy at the European level (ERDF policies in particular) have, over time, changed, evolved and achieved much, according to those who have spent much time studying this issue as part of their broader work on the European Union (Armstrong, 1989). For the European Union, regional policy is good in and of itself because it is meant to help those in the periphery to be able to stay in those areas through increased economic opportunities that, at some level, only the EU can bring to bear because of its size and influence. Regional policy also has a larger goal, which is to ensure the sustainability of the Union, for if those at the periphery lack the ability to see the benefit of having an entity like the European Union (what have you done for me lately, or at all, for that matter), then there may be the real possibility of the growth of dis-entachment in not only EU regional policy, but the European Union itself. Brexit can be seen as a recent example of this 'resentment' of decisions perceived to be taken at the European level of governance in comparison to the level of the nation-state. This is often thought of as the 'democratic deficit' of the European Union (Lord, 2017). This, of course, sounds highly self-serving, but let one remember the rationale for the EU (then ECSC and EEC) at the outset – which was not for Schumann and Monnet to line their pockets or win Nobel Prizes, but to ensure the survivability of the people of Europe by bringing countries together in a manner where war through military means would cease to exist as a logical course of action (European Union, Schuman Declaration, 1950), in comparison to the long history of Europe. While it is the member-states that are represented at the highest levels of EU decision-making, for its founders, the people, and their ability to have a life without the constant threat of war, was the overarching goal.

The expansion of the EU eastward, following the fall of Communism, may have been the tangible face of what Fukuyama (1992) infamously called 'the end of history'. However, the collapse of Communism and the disorienting impact of the triumph of capitalism has caused a pushback from both Marxists and those that emphasise the growing importance of networks in creating value beyond that of simple profit maximisation (Jackson, 2003; Fuchs, 2019).

Rejection and Reflection

Marxist writers, in the meantime, have rejected the convergence–divergence debate, arguing that capitalism progresses through stages, or modes, of production, interspersed by periodic crises triggered by the inevitable conflict between classes (Dawkins, 2003). Thus Smith (1984) argues that uneven economic development is an unavoidable consequence of the internal tensions within capitalism and its tendency to concentrate capital. Goodman (1979) even argued that capitalism is structurally predisposed to play regions and workers off, to drive accumulation.

Institutional economists have built upon the work of Coase (1937) to discuss the importance of transaction costs in determining levels of growth. Writers like North (1991) suggest that political elites that can reduce transaction costs are more likely to be able to catalyse growth.

Krugman (1991) has drawn upon several of these schools of thought to construct his 'new economic geography' model, which emphasises circular causation that both drives and is driven by increasing returns as the basis for regional growth. For writers in this school of economic geography, it is 'the location of production in space' (Krugman, 1991; Ottaviano & Puga, 2003) with the most striking feature being its agglomeration or concentration with clear evidence of increasing returns (Krugman, 1991). Writers following Krugman's approach 'developed abstract models to explain spatial concentration and specializations leading to persistent regional economic disparities [and has] ... put geography back on the map of economists' (Hassink & Gong, 2019).

Until recently most regional development models have worked upon the assumption of linear growth, doubtlessly legitimised by Porter's (1979) five forces model of strategy development which sought to capture value creation within production and processes. However, Capello and Nijkamp (2009) argue that endogenous growth flows from the increasing returns of innovations which are a function of geographic proximity, relational proximity of executives and institutional proximity (shared rules and norms of behaviour that enable trust and cooperation). These authors contend that 'the application of non-linear models to the well-known neoclassical and Keynesian models has shown that the deterministic and unique results achieved by the dynamic linear models are no longer guaranteed' (Capello & Nijkamp, 2009, p. 7). In a networked world, linear models that predict ordered outcomes are of marginal value (Snowden & Boone, 2007). As we show in Chapter 3, the growth of the network economy has shifted the capture of value into digital global hubs which have radical implications for socio-economic relationships between people and place (Taylor & Bronstone, 2019). Capello and Nijkamp (2009) note the importance of considering how people learn if knowledge creation and innovation are central to regional development. Furthermore, they emphasise the need for more interdisciplinary work on the topic and bemoan a shortage of critical thinking when utilising models from other disciplines. Yet, given the well-established importance of Argyris (1991) learning loops model to business writers and executives for transforming organisational performance, especially during disruptive times (Taylor & Bronstone, 2019), it is a surprising omission from most of the literature that we will address in the next chapter.

The Emergence of Local Models

Recently, and perhaps as a reaction to the growth of global digital networks, a series of models debunking one size fits all models (Tödtling & Trippl, 2005; Barca, McCann & Rodríguez-Pose, 2012) have emerged. Each is rooted in an emphasis upon specific places and people as sources of competitive advantage. Morgan (2019, p. 2) claims that 'innovative activity is not uniformly or randomly distributed across the globe but tends to be spatially concentrated'. The models are all based upon progressive values yet look to an entrepreneurial spirit as the source and driver of socio-economic change. They all seek greater local resilience in economic, social and, in some cases, ecological terms. Yet they differ significantly in their approach to questions of scale with some explicitly limited by scale and others seeking to transcend it. Transition towns have mostly been applied to smaller places, whilst the Preston model has and is being experimented with at city and regional scales and the transformational entrepreneurialism and foundational economy models aspire to influence national policies and strategies towards development. Some models offer structured models for change whilst others are used more as a lens for thinking about and co-joining actors towards action. However, they all share in common a sense of place as a source of collaborative entrepreneurship in the service of acting as a catalyst for wider change in society.

The models are all either structures, manifestos or patterns of behaviour for driving transformative change. Whilst they differ in the practices required to drive transformation, they can all be said to share a broad sympathy towards Wahl's claim that 'a transformative response would aim to increase community resilience through increased regionalisation of production and consumption' (Wahl, 2020, p. 26). Whilst some models are about circulating resources within a locality and others are about developing entrepreneurial infrastructure to compete globally, all models emphasise the idea and identity of place as a central source of competitive advantage.

Territorial Capital

Camagni (2009) argues that in a global marketplace internal regional demand is often not the driver of economic outputs or performance. The author asserts that

> in terms of international and interregional trade theory, regions do not compete with each other on the basis of a Ricardian 'comparative advantage' principle – which guarantees each region a role in the international division of labour – but rather on a Smithian 'absolute advantage' principle, similar in nature to Porter's concept of 'competitive advantage'.
>
> (Camagni, 2002)

In 2009, the author went further and contended that

> a cognitive approach is increasingly superseding the traditional functional approach to show that cause–effect, deterministic relationships should give way to other kinds of complex, intersubjective relationships which impinge on the way economic agents perceive economic reality, are receptive to external stimuli, can react creatively, and are able to cooperate and work synergistically. Local competitiveness is interpreted as residing in local trust and a sense of belonging rather than in pure availability of capital; in creativity rather than in the pure presence of skilled labour; in connectivity and relationality more than in pure accessibility; in local identity besides local efficiency and quality of life
>
> (Camagni, 2009, p. 118)

Competitive advantage is, therefore, something that can be shared as a means of expanding growth and acquiring multiplier effects. Key elements of territorial capital are:

- A system of localised externalities, both pecuniary (where their advantages are appropriated through market transactions) and technological (when advantages are exploited by simple proximity to the source).

- A system of localised production activities, traditions, skills and know-hows.
- A system of localised proximity relationships that constitute a 'capital' – of a social psychological and political nature – in that they enhance the static and dynamic productivity of local factors.
- A system of cultural elements and values which attribute sense and meaning to local practices and structures and define local identities; they acquire an economic value whenever they can be transformed into marketable products – goods, services and assets – or they boost the internal capacity to exploit local potentials.
- A system of rules and practices defining a local governance model.

(Camagni, 2009, p. 120)

Relational capital is described by Camaggni as existing where 'geographic proximity is associated with socio-cultural proximity – the presence of shared models of behaviour, mutual trust, common language and representations, common moral and cognitive codes' (Camagni, 2009, p. 127). Territorial capital describes how relational capital and milieu effects combine to drive local development that, with its basis in a known group of actors with agreed norms of behaviour, Camagni (2009) suggests is best interpreted as similar to a club (Camagni, 2009, p. 127).

Transition Towns

Few models have been more founded upon specific values, local norms and actors than the Transition Towns movement. Less a clear analytical model than a set of behaviours oriented around the idea of organising local resources towards greater ecological resilience – 'the idea of local resilience as economic development' (Hopkins, 2013). Felicetti (2013) notes how 'ideas underpinning localist reforms and the Transition movement seem to differ widely' (Felicetti, 2013, p. 559). Founded in 2005, the Transition Network claims that

> ... Transition is a movement of communities coming together to reimagine and rebuild our world ... reclaiming the economy, sparking entrepreneurship, reimagining work, reskilling themselves and weaving webs of connection and support

Progressive and in response to the perceived urgency and failure of either public or private actors to adequately respond to an emerging ecological, especially climate, emergency, the movement seeks to develop and share practices that contribute to the construction of local small-scale, inclusive and sustainable enterprise. Practical, rather than analytically rigorous, transition towns are a call to action that has grown in places such as Totnes (UK), to become examples of what is possible. There is a strong desire to define success in terms of a sustainable local economy that recycles as much as possible within the community. Hopkins contends that 'in a local and resilient economy, we regard the money that leaks out of our local economy as a missed opportunity' (Hopkins, 2013). The idea that 'businesses embedded in the local community … provide not just the goods that they sell but the social glue that holds communities together' (Hopkins, 2013, p. 27) offers the potential to engage Rose's Settlers who mourn the loss of such symbols of community life (Taylor & Bronstone, 2019). The transition movement thus represents an attempt to connect attachment to place with progressive values through specific tangible activity. However, Felicetti (2013) notes how those driving ideas of transition are often representative neither of communities nor of local councils and institutions. Clearly led by people that Rose would describe as Pioneers, transition towns do seek to cooperate as a 'movement' to provide a visible variant upon Ostrom's (2009, 2012) polycentrism (see section below). Yet, there is limited evidence of the movement demonstrating an unusual ability to engage Rose's Settlers (Felicitti, 2013). If, as Hopkins (2013, p. 64) argues 'a communities resilience is defined by the set of possibilities that the community believes it has at its disposal', the question of who participates matters very much indeed for defining the community, its interests and a sense of agency.

The Foundational Economy Model

The foundational economy is a relatively new model, developed by academics, mostly in Italy and the UK. Crucially it 'recognizes the value of innovation beyond a strictly economic value' (Morgan, 2019, p. 4). The model has gained considerable traction with policy-makers in Wales, where research and policy recommendations have been presented and are under discussion and development as we write.

Foundational thinking rests on two big ideas: social consumption and public policy through local actions, which break with established ways of thinking and that challenge taken for granted assumptions, about economy, society and politics:

(1) The well-being of Europe's citizens depends less on individual consumption and more on their social consumption of essential goods and services.
(2) The distinctive, primary role of public policy should therefore be to secure the supply of basic services for all citizens (not a quantum of economic growth and jobs).

(Foundational Economy, June, 2020)

The writers continue:

- The foundational economy is about collective consumption through networks and branches which are the infrastructure of civilised everyday life. The foundational includes the material infrastructure of pipes and cables which connect households plus providential services such as health and care which citizens rely on; outside the foundational, there is a mundane overlooked economy of haircuts and takeaways.
- The foundational economy is about universal basic services which are a citizen entitlement and it is therefore about politics as much as economics. From a foundational viewpoint, the distinctive role of public policy is not to boost private consumption by delivering economic growth but to ensure the quantity and quality of foundational services.

Rather like transformational entrepreneurship and transition towns, the Foundational Economy is as much a manifesto as it is a model. Frustrated with 'generic industrial and regional policy focused on next generation tradeable industries and attracting mobile inward investment through competitivity' (Foundational Economy, 2020). Researchers at Manchester University argued that:

> the foundational economy, which employs 40% of the workforce and is both private and public, is the sector of the economy that provides goods and services taken for granted by all members of the population and is therefore territorially distributed. At the same time, it depends on a kind

> of 'social franchise', either because it is directly or de-facto franchised by the state, or because household spending and tax revenue sustains its activities which are therefore sheltered. This reconceptualisation justifies a new kind of political intervention which would challenge public and private business models that privilege the point value of least cost and most profit and neglect the preconditions of national, regional, and local economic security and social sustainability
>
> (Foundational Economy Manifesto, 2013)

Morgan (2020) believes that the foundational economy provides a

> learning-by-doing process through which communities learn to become self-managing communities. Arguably, this could be conceived as the ultimate form of devolution, a form of civic devolution, in which communities assume more responsibility for governing themselves
>
> (Morgan, June 2020)

Whilst the idea of the foundational economy usefully shines a light upon the connection between the provision of basic services and quality of life, at this point, it lacks an entrepreneurial dimension that renders it, as a model of economic development, incomplete. We welcome its interest in the local and the mundane, but the Transition Towns, Preston and transformational entrepreneurship models, contain ideas that emphasise the need to take responsibility, even locally, for the income side of socio-economic needs. Noting the innovative potential of the public sector (Morgan, 2019) is welcome, but without structure, the foundational economy is not yet a model of development. Furthermore, the model lacks a specific nature because the 'working assumption is that 'social value comes from politically mobilising different actors to work together. This is not about top-down policy but about effective action after coalitions of disparate forces have been mobilised' (Earle et al., 2017). Morgan claims that the foundational economy is 'exemplified by community energy initiatives, sharing economy schemes and recycling workshops, as well as social innovations such as affordable housing initiatives, time banks and community currencies' (Morgan, 2019, p. 5). Yet the model falls far short of the structured nature of both the Preston model and to a lesser extent the transformational entrepreneurship model.

Transformational Entrepreneurship

Maas, Jones and Lockyer (2019) claim that transformational entrepreneurship

> refers to a holistic and heuristic orientation in terms of entrepreneurship promotion and combines the individual and other subsystems (such as society and institutions) interacting and collaborating to create a positive framework in which opportunities can be exploited beyond the local level
>
> (Maas, Jones & Lockyer, 2019, p. 1)

Furthermore, they argue that

> a new approach to the development of socio-economic development is required—a systemic process that is more heuristic and holistic in nature to accommodate both individualistic and societal needs ... [otherwise] the potential for socio-economic development will remain limited and only benefit a minority of individuals, businesses and nations
>
> (Maas, Jones & Lockyer, 2019, p. 2)

It is claimed that '*transformational entrepreneurship is to promote enterprise and entrepreneurship through a systemic approach, bringing about transformation in socio-economic development*' (Maas, Jones & Lockyer, 2019, p. 4 [italics in original]) which emphasises the local as a source of systemic change. Miller and Collier (2010, p. 85) are more explicit and define transformational entrepreneurship 'as the creation of an innovative virtue-based organization for the purpose of shifting resources out of an area of lower and into an area of higher purpose and greater value under conditions requiring an holistic perspective' (Maas, Jones & Lockyer, 2019, p. 6). Both definitions suggest that transformational entrepreneurship is a manifesto, as much as it is a model. Certainly, definitions of transformation require further definition. Nonetheless, it connects organisations to localities with defined developmental goals that are targeted without being universally prescriptive. The model leans heavily upon qualitative drivers of behaviour emphasising leadership and storytelling. For this reason, it can be

> argued that leaders need to create compelling narratives in terms of entrepreneurship development (or intrapreneurship development within larger institutions). These narratives are needed to create growth opportunities.

> The current dominant focus on cost-efficiency might blind leaders from being more opportunity orientated
>
> (Maas, Jones & Lockyer, 2019, p. 9)

Clearly linked to Argyris' learning loops (1991), Maas and Jones (2017) emphasise the role of adaptive thinking over optimal efficiencies as drivers of entrepreneurial innovation claiming that 'new approaches need to be devised that challenge default reactions and which create new frameworks for adaptive thinking' (Maas & Jones, 2017, p. 7). Closely related, Knickel et al. (2009) describe first- and second-order innovations. First-order innovation describes limited changes, and second-order innovation describes systemic change based upon challenging existing assumptions, beliefs and values. Just like Argyris (1991), Knickel et al. (2009) argue that this can create positive-reinforcing cycles of innovative change.

Interestingly, in contrast to models such as the Cleveland/Preston model or the Transition Towns model, Maas et al. (2016) have argued that entrepreneurial activity focused predominantly on individual entrepreneurs, or local regions, will mostly fail to have a positive effect on national socio-economic development. They argue that 'a balance should be struck between a focus on individual entrepreneurial activities and society-wide changes which may have a more positive impact on socio-economic growth' (Maas & Jones, 2017, p. 7). They argue that universities have a central role to play not just to develop individuals as entrepreneurs but to enable more systemic and scalable enterprise. It is an argument supported recently by Duncan (2021):

> Universities are not just for educating people. They boost productivity, something that we've been worryingly bad at in recent years, by generating skills and helping develop new and better ways of doing things; and productivity brings prosperity. Location matters: a university's effect is particularly strong in the surrounding area.
>
> (Duncan, 2021)

Maas and Jones (2017) criticism of existing approaches by higher education institutions is withering in its sarcasm, asking if university-based 'entrepreneurial centres [are] part of the enterprising agenda or are they only used as a marketing or income-generating tool?' (Maas & Jones, 2017, p. 11). They continue by stating that

> it is without question that a focus on individual micro-business start-ups is far easier than constructing and implementing an ecosystem allowing for transformation to occur on the socio-economic front and therefore not surprising that the latter are not well supported by universities
>
> (Maas & Jones, 2017, p. 7)

Thus, in the eyes of this model's proponents, universities have a key systemic linking role between individual entrepreneurs, places and wider social change because 'within an entrepreneurial university context … students should be exposed to entrepreneurial learning and through that achieve the goal of encouraging an individual's intention to act enterprising and/or entrepreneurially' (Maas & Jones, p. 12). It is certainly true that positioning business-focused education at the centre of an entrepreneurial socio-economic ecosystem has been very effective for places such as Singapore (Curtis Perry, 2017; Kuan Yew, 2000; Huat Chua, 2017), who have quite deliberately positioned higher education as central to their development strategies.

The Cleveland/Preston Model

Just like the transformational entrepreneurialism model, the Preston model recognises the importance of higher education institutions, but, unlike the previous model, the Preston model only defines them as a part of one pillar of the model, rather than the centrepiece of it. Learning from the US city of Cleveland, the City of Preston has sought to use the model of community wealth building (CLES & Preston City Council, 2019) to 'create a collective and inclusive economy kept in the hands of the city's inhabitants' (Jones, 2020).

Peck defines community wealth building as an 'aim at improving the ability of communities and individuals to increase asset ownership, anchor jobs locally by broadening ownership over capital, help achieve key environmental goals, expand the provision of public services and ensure local economic stability' (Peck, 2019). Whilst the website community-wealth.org defines it as

> a fast-growing economic development movement that strengthens our communities through broader democratic ownership and control of business and jobs. It builds on local talents, capacities and institutions, rebuilding capital to strengthen and create locally-owned family and community owned businesses that are anchored in place, that aren't moving
>
> (Community Wealth Building, n.d.)

This model is built upon the five core pillars of what the think tank and cities advisors CLES (2020) calls Community Wealth Building:

- Plural ownership of the economy.
- Making financial power work for local places.
- Fair employment and just labour markets.
- Progressive procurement of goods and services.
- Socially productive use of land and property.

The model offers an attempt to:

- Keep more procurement money circulating within a local economy.
- Encourage and enable cooperative and more democratic participation in the local economy.
- Consciously try to connect and overlap such local ecosystems.

CLES claim that figures showed that over the five years since 2012/2013, locally retained spending had increased within Preston from 5% to 18.2% and within Lancashire from 39% to 79.2% (CLES & Preston City Council, 2019). Reports in the *Guardian* make the more modest, but still impressive claim that expenditure spent locally increased from 14% to 28% between 2012 and 2016 (Sheffield, 2017) and caught the attention of mainstream media from across the political spectrum (Mudie & Cardy, 2017; Stubbington, 2017; The Economist, 2017). Councillor Brown has said that 'it's about keeping wealth in the local economy, instead of letting it all flow to big companies and their shareholders' (Stubbington, 2017).

CLES has identified five key strands, or pillars, to local wealth building:

1. Workforce: Anchor institutions are the largest employers and their approaches to recruiting and employee development can have multiplier effects.
2. Purchasing:

   > The purchasing power of anchor institutions is important and can be locally enriching, especially if it is used progressively to develop dense local supply chains of local enterprises, small and medium-sized enterprises, social enterprises, co-operatives and other forms of community ownership.

3. Land, property and assets: Developing under-used land, encouraging equitable development and influencing pension funds investments to transform communities.
4. Ownership of the economy: 'This is at the heart of local wealth-building. Co-operatives, mutually-owned businesses, municipally-owned companies and local banks enable the wealth generated in a community to stay local and play a vital role in counteracting the extraction of wealth' ('Community Business and Anchor Institutions', Feb 2019, p. 3).

It is argued that the community wealth building is both a policy approach and a way of working, in which the '"embroidery" of linking people, activities and processes within and across institutions is crucial to the advancement of community wealth building and the achievement of real outcomes' (CLES & Preston City Council, 2019).

Practically, Preston City Council has directed pension investment into student accommodation, has supported the development of a local IT cluster, has nurtured retail and renewable energy cooperatives and has begun tentative work towards a local mutual bank. Whilst the commitment of large employers has lifted many people's wages to at least a 'living wage' (CLES & Preston City Council, 2019.) In addition to the above activities

> research carried out by the accountancy firm PricewaterhouseCoopers and the think tank Demos, which used a range of measures including employment, workers' pay, house prices, transport, the environment,

> work–life-balance and inequality to rank 42 UK cities, found that Preston had improved the most in its 2018 Good Growth for Cities index
>
> (Partington, 2018)

There is considerable debate about how these actions might be taken between interested thinkers, policy-makers and practitioners. However, what we are interested in is the extent to which a structured approach makes a difference to overcoming the network challenges outlined in the next chapter, such that places and organisations can flourish. Furthermore, when we speak of being successful, a key question is: Does the model make any difference to the participation of Settlers? If not, it may be valuable for creative, tech-savvy hipsters, but failure to engage Settlers undermines any meaningful claim to resilience or sustainability.

Much research and thinking lie behind attempts to deliver the model in practice.[1] Indeed, a large part of the drive behind the so-called Preston/Cleveland model is the desire to develop resilience. In the context of the community wealth building model, Michael Lewis (2017) describes seven principles of Resilience for what he calls a Cooperative Economic Democracy (CED). These principles include diversity, modularity, social capital, overlap, tight feedback loops and ecosystem services. However, CED can, for some writers, go beyond pure common's regimes. Restakis describes CED's as follows:

> a form of cooperative commonwealth that is pluralist, in that it leaves room for small and medium firms that are privately owned, as well as for publicly owned enterprises. In other words, the term 'cooperative common-wealth' is not a hegemonic system. Rather, it describes the operating logic of the overall paradigm in which cooperative entities are actively supported and encouraged—not the requirement that all enterprises must be cooperatives or collectively owned
>
> (Restakis, 2016)

The Preston model is a response to the perceived widening of economic divergence that is about harnessing local resources to overcome perceived central indifference and then create partnered approaches to learning and cooperation with other locations on the same journey. We will return to the Preston Model in Chapter 5, when we examine the case of the attempted redevelopment of North Jacksonville in Florida.

The Pattern

Looking across the contemporary models there are a number of themes which repeatedly occur in some form or other:

Stewardship: The idea that attachment to and care for people and place is a source of individual and collective identity that blurs the boundaries between work and home. As such it has the potential to be a motivational force.

Resilience: Resilience is a contested term, but there is agreement that it describes a capability to not only resist (that would describe robustness), but also flexibly adjust and adapt to systemic change. Should such resilience be self-organising and emerge from within communities themselves, we can describe them as showing evidence of complex adaptive systems. The strength of resilience is related to the types of social networks it emerges from, how they connect (or don't) to other networks and the question of appropriate scale.

Social Capital: A resilient world would promote trust, well-developed social networks and leadership. The resilience of social-ecological systems is rooted in the capacity of people to respond effectively to challenges together, not separately. In other words, trust, strong networks and leadership are critically important.

Tight Feedback Loops: A resilient world would possess tight feedback loops (but not too tight). Feedback loops refer to the communication flow within a system. Information about the impact of a particular process or event is returned to the system to enable it to correct itself next time. Resilience is characterised by focused effort to maintain, or tighten, the strength of feedback so we can detect thresholds before we cross them.

Innovation & Entrepreneurship: A resilient world would place an emphasis on learning, experimentation, locally developed rules and embracing change. James Fallows, in his journey across the US to find liveable and sustainable communities, as was mentioned in our 2019 work, commented that such communities were marked by a high degree of self-starting motivation. The communities that we are concerned about will not survive without a strong dose of innovation and ingenuity. Without the injection of these traits, these places and the people who live there will die.

Modularity: A resilient world would be made up of components that can operate and be modified independently of the rest. In resilient systems, everything is not necessarily connected to everything else. Overly connected systems are susceptible to shocks that are rapidly transmitted throughout the system: witness the recent global financial crisis. The modularity of a resilient system enables it to mitigate or absorb the repercussions of disaster. Thus, whilst scale-free networks may offer economic robustness, the price is likely to be social uniformity and reduced modularity, variety and systemic resilience.

These characteristics of connected modular networks, grounded in forms of governance that breathe life into ideas of entrepreneurial stewardship, appear closely related to Ostrom's concept of polycentricity (2012, 2015).

Polycentricity

Ostrom (1990, 2015) defines common property regimes as having eight key characteristics:

1. Define clear group boundaries.
2. Match rules governing the use of common goods to local needs and conditions.
3. Ensure that those affected by the rules can participate in modifying the rules.
4. Make sure the rule-making rights of community members are respected by outside authorities.
5. Develop a system, carried out by community members, for monitoring members' behaviour.
6. Use graduated sanctions for rule violators.
7. Provide accessible, low-cost means for dispute resolution.
8. Build responsibility for governing the common resource in nested tiers from the lowest level up to the entire interconnected system.

Ostrom goes on to define Polycentric systems, at a simple level, as 'where [commons] systems exist at multiple levels with some autonomy at each level' (Ostrom, 2012, p. 82) which provides for systemic resilience. A more detailed and nuanced definition of overlapping commons is:

> ... Polycentric' connotes many centers of decision making that are formally independent of each other. Whether they actually function independently, or instead constitute an interdependent system of relations, is an empirical

> question in particular cases. To the extent that they take each other into account in competitive relationships, enter into various contractual and cooperative undertakings or have recourse to central mechanisms to resolve conflicts, the various political jurisdictions in a metropolitan area may function in a coherent manner with consistent and predictable patterns of interacting behavior. To the extent that this is so, they may be said to function as a 'system'.
>
> (Ostrom, Tiebout & Warren, 1961, quoted in Ostrom, 2009, p. 3)

Heikkila (2018) argues that 'polycentric governance involves multiple overlapping centres of decision-making, which interact within an overarching set of rules' (Heikkila et al., 2018, p. 207). The question is whether polycentricity reaches beyond examples, such as Smedby (2019), of overlapping layers of legislative authority, to confirm that a mosaic of local regimes can produce enhanced adaptive capacity (Carlisle & Gruby, 2018, Biddle & Baehler, 2018) that Snowden and Merali (2019) might well describe as a complex adaptive system. The extent to which diffused polycentric community commons can be an effective response to the problems of 'blame avoidance over problem solving, persistent power imbalances, large wealth inequalities, and deficits of social capital and leadership' (Biddle & Baehler, 2019, p. 344), such that polycentric governance could be described as genuinely sustainable remains an open question.

Polycentricity describes both the breadth of overlapping commons, but also a depth (Ostrom, 2015) that is, perhaps, usefully thought of as like the concentric rings of a tree trunk. Ostrom (2012) makes it clear that within polycentricity there is space for a variety of organisational forms, which does not exclude capitalist forms, limited only by scale and attachment to place. It is not a significant intellectual stretch to connect polycentrism to models like the Preston model, Transition Towns or transformational entrepreneurialism. However, what Ostrom usefully does that the aforementioned models do not, is to provide a coherence about how shared visions of the local thriving within global networks may cooperate without abandoning local difference or being subsumed under a central authority.

Conclusion

As stated previously (Taylor & Bronstone. 2019), the convergence of technology and globalisation is not only changing value creation and associated business strategies, but is leaving some people and places behind. Therefore the question is how can the various models described within this chapter inform efforts to enable people and places to flourish within global networks. Interest and debate about the nature of how and why growth takes place in certain places and regions has raged between faculties of geography, business, politics and economics, probably since their inception. However, in recent times there has been a shift away from top-down models of both Keynesian and supply-side economics or their Marxist critics. Contemporary models have tended to emphasise patterns of behaviour or values that are defined empirically. Furthermore, there has been considerable interest in entrepreneurship as a vehicle for systemic transformation of people and places. This has often been tied to both an interest in sustainability and the role of, particularly higher, education. The three have been tied together through an interest in the importance of networks of shared interests, experience and values.

We suspect that one of the reasons that there has been a shift away from top-down models is the pace and scale of change that is taking place as a result of digital market disruption and complexity. Such changes will only be exacerbated by the impact of the COVID-19 pandemic as the use of technology to change working experiences has been fast-forwarded even further. Thus, positioning models of development within the context of how such disruption is emerging is both important and the subject of our next chapter.

Next Steps

The next chapter will examine relationships between the network dynamics driving markets where technology disrupts and ideas of stewardship, in the context of tensions between robustness and resilience that go to the heart of economics, society and sustainability.

Note

1 See www.thenextsystem.org for a collection of detailed research papers.

References

Armstrong, H., 'Community Regional Policy', in Lodge, J. (Ed.), *The European Community and the Challenge of the Future*. London: Pinter Publishers, 1989.

Barca, F., McCann, P. & Rodríguez-Pose, A., 'The Case for Regional Development Intervention: Place-Based Versus Place-Neutral Approaches', *Journal of Regional Science* 52(1): 134–152, 2012.

Barro, R. J. & Martin, X., *Economic Growth*. Cambridge, MA: MIT Press, 1999.

Biddle, J. & Baehler, K., 'Breaking Bad: When Does Polycentricity Lead to Maladaptation Rather Than Adaptation?', *Environmental Policy & Governance* 29(5): 344–359, 2019.

Bronstone, A., *European Bank for Reconstruction and Development*. Manchester: Manchester University Press, 1999.

Camagni, R., 'Territorial Capital & Regional Development', in Capello & Nijkamp (Ed.), *Handbook of Regional Growth and Development Theories*. Cheltenham: Edward Elger, 2009.

Capello, R. & Nijkamp, P., *Handbook of Regional Growth and Development Theories*. Cheltenham: Edward Elger, 2009.

Carlisle, K. & Gruby, R., 'Why the Path to Polycentricity Matters: Evidence from Fisheries Governance in Palau', *Environmental Policy & Governance* 28(4): 223–235, 2018.

Chesanais, F., 'Technical Cooperation Agreements Between Firms', in STI Review, Nr. 4. Paris: OECD, pp. 52–115, 1988.

CLES (a) 'Community Business and Anchor Institutions', Feb 2019.

CLES, June 22, 2020, https://cles.org.uk/what-is-community-wealth-building/the-principles-of-community-wealth-building/.

CLES & Preston City Council, 'How We Built Community Wealth in Preston: Achievements and Lessons', 2019.

Coase, R., 'The Nature of the Firm', *Economica* 4(16): 386–405, 1937.

Community Wealth Building, n.d., www.community-wealth.org, retrieved June 2, 2020.

Cooke, P. & Morgan, K., 'The Network Paradigm: New Departures in Corporate and Regional Development', *Environment and Planning D: Society & Space* 11: 543–564, 1993.

Cross, R., Liedtka, J. & Weiss, L., 'A Practical Guide to Social Networks', *Harvard Business Review*, Mar 2005.

Curtis-Perry, J., *Singapore: Unlikely Power.* Oxford: Oxford University Press, 2017.

Darwent, D. F., 'Growth Poles and Growth Centers in Regional Planning: A Review', *Environment and Planning* 1(1): 5–31, 1969.

Dawkins, 'Regional Development Theory: Conceptual Foundations, Classic Works, and Recent Developments', *Journal of Planning Literature* 18(2): 131–172.

Dixon, R. J. & Thirlwall, A., 'A Model of Regional Growth Rate Differences on Kaldorian Lines', *Oxford Economic Papers* 27(2): 201–214.

Duncan, E., 'Britain Needs More Second-Class Universities', *The Times*, July 9, 2021.

Earle, J., Froud, J., Haslam, C., Sukhdev, J., Moran, M. & Williams, K., 'What Wales Can Do: Asset Based Policies and the Foundational Economy', A CREW/ foundationaleconomy.com report, June 19, 2017.

European Union, 'Schuman Declaration', Schuman declaration May 1950, europa.eu.

European Union, Regional Policy – Major Projects, 2020, https://ec.europa.eu/regional_policy/en/projects/major/#1.

Felicetti, A., 'Localism and the Transition Movement'. *Policy Studies* Vol. 34, Nr. 5, 2013, pp. 559–574

Foundational Economy, 'Manifesto', 2013, https://foundationaleconomy.com.

Foundational Economy, June 11, 2020, https://foundationaleconomy.com/introduction/.

Foundational Economy, 'Introducing the Foundational Economy', 2019, https://foundationaleconomy.com/introduction/, retrieved June 11, 2020.

Friedmann, J., *Regional Development Policy: A Case Study of Venezuela.* Cambridge, MA: MIT Press, 1966.

Fuchs, C., *Rereading Marx in the Age of Digital Capitalism*. London: Pluto Press, 2019.

Fukuyama, F., *The End of History and the Last Man.* Free Press: New York, 1992.

Goodman, Robert, *The Last Entrepreneurs: America's Regional Wars for Jobs and Dollars.* New York: Simon & Schuster, 1979.

Greenhut, M., *Plant Location in Theory and in Practise: The Economics of Space.* Chapel Hill: University of North Carolina Press, 1956.

Handy, C., *The Elephant and The Flea: New Thinking for a New World.* New York: Random House, 2002.

Hassink, R. & Gong, H., 'New Economic Geography', in Orum, A. (Ed.), *The Wiley Blackwell Encyclopedia of Urban and Regional Studies.* Oxford: Wiley, 2019.

Hirschman, A., *The Strategy for Economic Development*. New Haven, CT: Yale University Press, 1958.

Hoover, E., *Location Theory and the Shoe Leather Industries*. Cambridge, MA: Harvard University Press, 1937.

Hoover, E. M. & Giarratani, F., *An Introduction to Regional Economics* (3rd ed.). New York: Alfred A. Knopf Inc, 1985.

Hopkins, R., *The Power of Just Doing Stuff: How Local Action Can Change the World*. Cambridge: Green Books, 2013.

Huat Chua, B., *Liberalism Disavowed: Communitarianism and State Capitalism in Singapore*. New York: Cornell University Press, 2017.

Isard, W., Iwan, J. A., Drennan, M., Miller, R., Saltzman, S. & Thorbecke, E., *Methods of Interregional and Regional Analysis*. Brookfield, VT: Ashgate, 1998.

Johanson, J., 'Interfirm Networks in Swedish Industry', A Paper presented to the European Commission Conference Europerspective II: Visions and Actions, Namur, April, 1991.

Jones, T., *Utopian Dreams: In Search of a Good Life*. London: Faber & Faber, 2020.

Kaldor, N., 'The Case for Regional Policies', *Scottish Journal of Political Economy* 17(3): 337–348, 1970.

Knickel K., Brunori G, Rand S., Proost M., 'Towards a Better Conceptual Framework for Innovation Processes in Agriculture and Rural Development: From Linear Models to Systemic Approaches', *The Journal of Agricultural Education and Extension* 15(2), 2009, pp. 131–146

Krugman, P., *Geography and Trade*. Cambridge, MA: MIT Press, 1991.

Krugman, P., *Regional Economics: Understanding the Third Great Transition*, Sep 2019. https://www.gc.cuny.edu/CUNY_GC/media/LISCenter/pkrugman/REGIONAL-ECONOMICS-3rd-transition.pdf, retrieved July 29, 2020.

Krugman, P., 'The Role of Geography in Development', *International Regional Science Review* 22(2): 142–161, 1999.

Kuan Yew, L., *From Third World to First: Singapore and the Asian Economic Boom*. New York: HarperCollins, 2000.

Lewis, M., 2017, https://thenextsystem.org/sites/default/files/2017-08/MichaelLewis.pdf.

Lodge, J., (Ed.) *The European Community and the Challenge of the Future*. London: Pinter Publishers, 1989.

Lord, C., 'The Myth of Europe's Democratic Deficit', Princeton, NJ: Princeton University, May 2017.

Lösch, A., *The Economics of Location*. New Haven, CT: Yale University Press, 1954.

Maas, G., & Jones, P., (Eds.) *Entrepreneurship Centres: Global Perspectives on Their Contributions to Higher Education Institutions*. Switzerland: Palgrave Macmillan, 2017.

Maas, G., Jones, P. & Lockyer, J., *The Journey to Transformational Entrepreneurship*. New York: Springer, 2019.

Mason, P., *Postcapitalism: A Guide to Our Future*. London: Allen Lane, 2015.

Massey, D. & Meegan, R., *The Anatomy of Job Loss: The How, Why, and Where of Employment Decline*. London: Methuen, 1982.

Miller, R. & Collier, E., 'Redefining Entrepreneurship: A Virtues and Values Perspective', *Journal of Leadership, Accountability, and Ethics* 8: 80–89, 2010.

Morgan, K., & Coenen, L., 'Evolving Geographies of Innovation: Existing Paradigms, Critiques and Possible Alternatives', *Norwegian Journal of Geography* 74(2): 1–12, 2019.

Mudie, K. & Cardy, P., 'How One City Is Beating Tory Austerity with 'Radicalism on a Shoestring', *The Daily Mirror*, Nov 4, 2017.

Myrdal, G., *Economic Theory and Underdeveloped Regions*. London: Duckworth, 1957.

North, D., 'Exports and Regional Economic Growth: A Reply', *Journal of Political Economy* 64(2): 165–168, 1956.

North, D., 'Location Theory and Regional Economic Growth', *Journal of Political Economy* 63(3): 243–258, 1955.

Ostrom, E., 'A General Framework for Analyzing Sustainability of Social-Ecological Systems', *Science* 325: 419–422, 2009.

Ostrom, E., *Governing the Commons: The Evolution of Institutions for Collective Action*. Cambridge: Cambridge University Press, 2015.

Ostrom, E., *The Future of The Commons: Beyond Market Failure and Government Regulation*. London: IEA, 2012.

Ostrom, V., Tiebout, C. M. & Warren, R., 'The Organization of Government in Metropolitan Areas: A Theoretical Inquiry', *American Political Science Review* 55(4): 831–842, 1961.

Ottaviano, G. & Puga, D., 'Agglomeration in the Global Economy: A Survey of the "New Economic Geography"', *The World Economy* 21(6): 707–731, 2003.

Partington, R., 'Preston Named as Most Improved City in UK', *The Guardian*, Nov 1, 2018.
Peck, J., 'Putting Banking Back in the Hands of the People – RSA', Royal Society of Arts, July 15, 2019, www.thersa.org.
Perroux, F., 'Economic Space: Theory and Applications', *Quarterly Journal of Economics* 64(1): 89–104, 1950.
Piore, M. & Sabel, C., *The Second Industrial Divide*. New York: Basic Books, 1984.
Porter, M., 'How Competitive Forces Shape Strategy', *Harvard Business Review*, Mar 1979.
Powell, W., 'Neither Market nor Hierarchy: Network Forms of Organization', in Straw, B. & Cummings, L. (Eds.), *Research in Organizational Behaviour Volume 12*. Greenwich, CT: JAI Press, pp. 74–96, 1990.
Restakis, J., 'Cooperative Commonwealth & the Partner State', Part of a Series of Thinker Articles Commissioned, Dec 2016, https://thenextsystem.org website, retrieved June 22, 2020.
Ricardo, D., *On the Principles of Political Economy and Taxation*. London: John Murray, 1817.
Rose, C., *What Makes People Tick: The Hidden World of Settler, Prospectors and Pioneers*. Leicester: Matador, 2011.
Rosenberg, M., 'The 5 Themes of Geography', *ThoughtCo*, Feb 11, 2020, thoughtco.com/five-themes-of-geography-1435624.
Saxenian, A., *Regional Advantage: Culture and Competition in Silicon Valley and Route 128*. Cambridge, MA: Harvard University Press, 1994.
Schumpeter, J., *Capitalism, Socialism, and Democracy*. New York: Harper, 1947.
Sheffield, H., 'The Preston Model: UK Takes Lessons in Recovery from Rust-Belt Cleveland', *The Guardian*, Apr 11, 2017.
Shiva, V., 'One Planet: One Health'. *Resurgence & Ecologist*, Issue 321, July August, 2020, p. 10–12.
Smith, N., *Uneven Development*. Oxford: Basil Blackwell, 1984.
Snowden, D., 'The Cynefin Framework', July 2010 ((1) The Cynefin Framework – https://www.youtube.com/watch?v=N7oz366X0-8&t=288s).
Snowden, D. & Boone, M. E., 'A Leader's Framework for Decision Making', *Harvard Business Review*, Nov 2007.
Solow, R. M., 'A Contribution to the Theory of Economic Growth', *Quarterly Journal of Economics* 70(1): 65–94, 1956.

Stubbington, T., 'Buy Local, Hire Local: Preston Blossoms on Corbynomics', *The Sunday Times*, Oct 29, 2017.

Swan, T. W., 'Economic Growth and Capital Accumulation', *Economic Record* 32(44): 334–361, 1956.

Taylor, A. & Bronstone, A., *People, Place and Global Order: Foundations for a Networked Political Economy*. London: Routledge, 2019.

The Economist, 'Preston, Jeremy Corbyn's Model Town', *The Economist*, Oct 17, 2017.

Tiebout, C. M., 'Exports and Regional Economic Growth', *Journal of Political Economy* 64(2): 160–164, 1956.

Tödtling, F. & Trippl, M., 'Regional Innovation Policies for New Path Development: Beyond Neo-liberal and Traditional Systemic Views', *European Planning Studies* 26(9): 1779–1795, 2018.

Transition Network, https://transitionnetwork.org/about-the-movement/what-is-transition/, last updated Nov 2021.

Vernon, R., 'International Investment and International Trade in the Product Cycle', *Quarterly Journal of Economics* 80(2): 190–207, 1966.

Wahl, D., 'Building A New Normal', *Resurgence & Ecologist* 321, 2020.

Weber, A., *Theory of the Location of Industries*. Chicago: University of Chicago Press, 1929.

3

STEWARDSHIP AND RESILIENCE IN NETWORKED SPACES

Introduction

Understanding the relationships between attachment to place, scale, complex systems and patterns of knowledge creation is not straightforward, but they are emerging as the cornerstones of the challenges that societies face in bridging the gap between the social worlds that we inhabit and an emerging digital world. This chapter seeks to show how the use of models such as Snowden & Boone's (2007) Cynefin framework (Snowden) and Argyris' (1991) learning loops are key to making sense of emerging network economies. The capture of network effects as a source of value creation has grown network scale and integration, but negative feedback loops, outsourcing of jobs and hollowing out of communities have all caused a rejection of the liberal international order with the election of Trump, the bitterness of the Brexit debate and the rise of Le Pen as indicators of this breach in the robustness of the liberal international order. This chapter, therefore, will explore questions of robustness and resilience and how to

DOI: 10.4324/9781003145295-3

build more resilience into socio-economic networks. In doing so, we will look specifically at scale as a key factor in network sustainability and stewardship as a source of identity that both flows through some networks and affects network connectivity. This exploration will be grounded in our previous study of Rose (2011) and Goodhart's (2017) work on Settlers, Prospectors and Pioneers and the impact of network economics upon them.

Network Effects

There is no doubt that the context of business has changed. Value creation is shifting beyond the boundaries of the firm into network hubs and whoever controls these hubs captures more value. Thus, we need to understand in greater detail how network effects work and how they interact with existing social systems to understand how they affect people and places differently.

Network effects exist when the value of a product or service increases according to the number of others using it. Facebook, WhatsApp and other social media are based on the idea that as the number of users increases, the value of each increases. Importantly, as the network grows, its value to each user and to owners of networks increases exponentially:

> But while value is being created for everyone, value capture is getting more skewed and concentrated. This is because in networks, traffic begets more traffic, and as certain nodes become more heavily used, they attract additional attachments, which further increases their importance.
>
> (Iansati & Lakhani, 2017, p. 5)

As networks gain popularity, they develop positive feedback loops which is what often leads to them becoming so pervasive. The value of your mobile phone and even your computer is driven by its connection to networks, rather than having an inherent value in itself.

It is the capture of, or evidence of the capture of, network effects and control of network hubs that creates situations where technology companies are making heavy losses, but they still attract significant stock market valuations. This situation arises because 'there exist feedback loops, which are encouraging and pushing markets towards monopolistic, rather than perfect, competition' (Taylor & Bronstone, 2019). As Martin wryly observed 'although David Ricardo clearly identified the efficiency gains from trade, he did not anticipate the impact on Pareto outcomes' (Martin, 2019). That is to say, that, in our search for convenience, the need to collaborate around shared technological standards and the sheer cost of competing with established networks are turning the law of diminishing returns upside down (Arthur, 1996). Network effects are driving increasing returns and creating markets that appear to be in equilibrium when dominated by between one and three major players with all others left in the so-called long tail (Anderson, 2006). It is posited that 'modern digital technology enables the sharing of information at near-zero marginal cost' (Iansati & Lakhani, 2017, p. 5). Thus, the capture of a network is quite literally a license to print money as both the valuations of tech companies and the margins of companies like Amazon demonstrate all too well. However, not all networks, in the digital economy, are equal. An example of this is that nodes that can connect different networks together provide so-called bridging and such nodes are, from a network point of view, unusually valuable as they provide higher levels of connectivity. This is why YouTube vloggers that attract large numbers of followers appeal to advertisers and why you are drawn to connect to people on LinkedIn with more connections. Advertisers and ambitious executives are both, unconsciously, attempting to leverage network effects. The greater the connectivity a network can gain, the more powerful network effects become, which is why those that get ahead tend to get even further ahead (Arthur, 1996).

The Uber Example

Zhu and Iansati show, using the examples of Uber vs AirBnB, that 'the more a network is fragmented into local clusters – and the more isolated those clusters are from one another – the more vulnerable a business is to challenges' (Zhu & Iansati, Jan–Feb 2019, p. 5) (Figure 3.1).

The same authors also contend that 'platforms on global networks are much less vulnerable to challenges, because it's difficult for new rivals to enter a market on a global scale' (Zhu & Iansati, 2019, p. 5). It is easier, therefore, for incumbents to resist disintermediation and for tech competitors to challenge small local networks. Furthermore, local networks often connect customers with suppliers that they are likely to work with again.

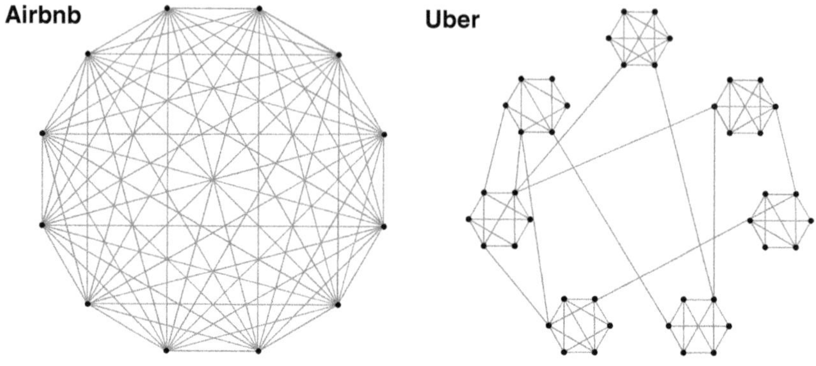

Figure 3.1 The Uber Example

Unlike hotels, for example, which are not mobile and that have customers that rarely return to the same hotel without ever needing others. Local transactions are often personal and there are incentives to bypass the hub. Local transactions, such as plumbers, electricians and caterers, if the consumer experiences with them are positive, are likely to be repetitive over a long period. Even worse, once a supplier has gained sufficient clients to fill their schedule, they will not need the hub (Zhu & Iansati, 2019). However, having gathered a significant number of positive customer reviews the hub needs exactly these suppliers to maintain its appeal. In other words, the more that a business model can aggregate trust and connectivity into a centrally controlled hub, and by implication create local dependence upon it, the more successful the business model is likely to be.

Network Resilience

Social systems are complex adaptive systems (Merali & Snowden, 2019), where the macro emerges from micro interactions and can transform rapidly. Some even argue that 'they are "complex evolving systems" that can change the rules of their development as they evolve over time' (Jackson, 2003, p. 115). Thus we, in this book, are interested in the relationship between structure and dynamics, not just structure – how do macro level phenomena arise from micro level changes. In no way do we, as authors, claim to be system thinkers and this is not a systems book. However, systems and complexity tools do enable us, as we have seen, to observe patterns of connection that are shifting the world and are thus worthy of further investigation.

Systems thinkers make a distinction between systems that are robust and systems that are resilient. Robust systems are strong, are mostly reliable and are able to survive without alteration until catastrophic change like that of a sea wall. Resilient systems survive with a continuity of identity over time (they change and adapt over time), for example, a salt marsh (Merali & Snowden, 2019). Liberal international network robustness has clearly been breached, in multiple places recently, as seen in the Brexit vote and the election of Trump, for example. Thus the question going forward is, when the robustness of the liberal order is failing, how can one develop network participation that is both more inclusive and resilient. The precise nature of the differences is sometimes disputed by scholars (Jackson, 2003; Senge, 2008; Snowden & Merali, 2019; Walker et al., 2004, etc.) yet in a world where the impact of distant change is rippling through networks faster, clearly social sustainability requires more resilience.

Resiliency

Ecologists Walker and Holling describe the key components of resilience as latitude, resistance, precariousness and panarchy (Walker et al., 2004).

1. Latitude: the maximum amount a system can be changed before losing its capacity to recover.
2. Resistance: the ease or difficulty of changing the system.
3. Precariousness: how close the current state of the system is to a limit.
4. Panarchy: the degree to which networks (or hierarchical levels) are influenced by other networks, as part of larger networks.

Although not the same, there are clear overlaps with the definition provided by Merali & Snowden (Cluj, November 2019) who describe the key characteristics of resilience as follows:

1. Permeable: [returning to the metaphor of a sea wall] there is a barrier, but it acts as a filter, rather than a wall.
2. Punctuated: the mechanism of change is driven by context.
3. Dark: I can see that there is a constraint, but I cannot see what it is and cannot explain why.

Stefan Hiermaier (2019) described resilience as a means of preserving functionality, ensuring graceful degradation and enabling fast recovering availability following the disruption. Cuthill (2008) describes social resilience as 'the way in which individuals, communities and societies adapt, transform, and potentially become stronger when faced with environmental, social, economic or political challenges' (Cuthill et al., 2008, 146). In comparison, Maclean, Cuthill and Ross (2014) argue that 'complex adaptive systems describe social resilience as the adaptive and learning capacity of individuals, groups and institutions to self-organise in a way that maintains system function in the face of change or in response to a disturbance'. More recently, Wahl argued that

> there are 2 types of resilience. Type 1 resilience is based on persistence in the face of disruption and adaptation in response to disruption in order to recover the old status quo. Type 2 resilience is based on an evolutionary or transformative response
>
> (Wahl, 2020, p. 25)

Wahl further notes that the reaction to the COVID-19 pandemic will have to be a Type 2 response.

Related to resilience is the idea of adaptive capacity (Jackson, 2003). Adaptive capacity in social systems describes the ability of people to use observation, learning and new interactions to cope with change (Folke et al., 2004). The adaptive capacity and resilience of social networks are clearly affected by the type of network being studied. Understanding these differences has been key to the development of Boisot's so-called I-space model (Boisot, 1995; Boisot & Child, 1988), as shown in Figure 3.2. Boisot uses a graph illustrating four different types of networks which reveal the extent to which they are able to codify and diffuse knowledge. Codification refers to the organisation of data into conceptual categories and diffusion refers to the ease with which knowledge is passed through social networks. In simple terms, the greater the codification and diffusion, the greater the ability to abstract and apply more widely. Management writers mostly concern themselves with market-based networks (as we have seen). However, growing interest in commons' approaches to business and environmental economics leads us to realise that socio-political contexts, especially at the local level, may not conform to either bureaucratic or pure market mechanisms. In fact, as we have seen, Settlers show preferences to resist both

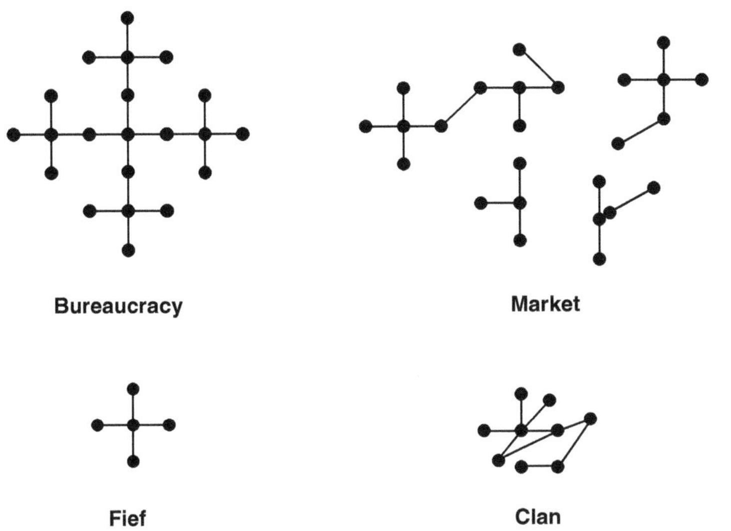

Figure 3.2 Bosiot Network Structures

(Rose, 2011). Thus, if the local is to participate and thrive (i.e. be resilient) in global networks, we also need to have a look at fief and clan-based networks where the closed nature of networks reduces codification opportunities.

Network Types

In simple terms, we can think of the network differences as follow:

- Bureaucracy: Highly codified information. Culture is predicated on the free diffusion of information.
- Market: Highly codified information. Culture is predicated on free diffusion of information.
- Clan: Free diffusion of information across members of the 'clan'. Information is embedded in tacit understanding and practices (so not highly codified).
- Fief: Ownership of information resides with an elite group (the 'fief'). Keeps its strategic knowledge closely held (unstructured and undiffused) (Wang & Buckland, 2016; Merali & Allen, 2017).

These differences are described in more detail in Table 3.1.

Table 3.1 Four Institutional Types. Based on Boisot (1998, p. 127), taken from Wang and Buckland (2016)

Bureaucracies	**Markets**
Documents diffusion limited and under central control.	Documents widely diffused, no control.
Documents are codified and abstract.	Documents are codified and abstract.
Relationships impersonal and hierarchical.	Relationships impersonal and competitive.
Submission to superordinate goals.	No superordinate goals.
No necessity to share values and beliefs.	Horizontal coordination through self-regulation.
	No necessity to share values and beliefs.
Fiefs	**Clans**
Documents diffusion limited by lack of codification to face-to-face relationships.	Documents are diffused but still limited by lack of codification to face-to-face relationships.
Documents are uncodified and concrete.	Documents are uncodified and concrete.
Relationships personal and hierarchical (feudal/charismatic).	Relationships personal nonhierarchical.
Submission to superordinate goals.	Goals are shared through a process of negotiation.
Hierarchical coordination.	Horizontal coordination through negotiation.
Necessity to share values and beliefs.	Necessity to share values and beliefs.

This understanding is important for developing learning and frameworks to help people make sense of network decision-making, as Snowden (2010) has acknowledged and we shall see further on. Clearly, understanding how networks codify and diffuse knowledge according to their connectivity and interconnectivity is key if we are to make more effective use of Rose (2011) and Goodhart's (2017) insights and learn how to construct more resilient network participation.

Drilling into Network Depth

Whilst the financial logic to the firm of an integrated global network makes perfect economic sense, we saw during the 2008 financial crisis that such monopolistic networks reduce the resilience of the system as a whole (Ownes, 2019). In this instance, the failure in a small number of key nodes within an integrated network can induce failures in neighbouring nodes creating a cascading failure or snowball effect that the algorithms of the digital world actually accelerate and amplify rather than dampen.

If one small local network fails, it is disruptive, but rarely catastrophic for the wider network that it is part of; whereas the failure of a dominant global network is disastrous at a systems level. Kohr (2001) describes this as the mattress effect; where pressing hard on one spring hardly affects the resilience of the bed as a whole. This effect matters since the tech firms that are able to aggregate such networks are no longer simply dominating markets; instead, they are actually developing their own ecosystems as they leverage network effects into growing numbers of markets – so-called network bridging (Zhu & Iansati, 2019).

We are not suggesting that we do away with large firms entirely. However, rather like the banks, we do need a few global players, but not many of them. In Chapter 2 of our previous book, we described how markets are moving from a bell curve to a Pareto curve wherever technology disintermediates. However, technology merely enables networks. It is the shift of value creation into the network that is the key driver towards a Pareto curve. If we are to avoid the failures and externalities of global networks (on a global scale), we need to recognise that from any perspective, other than a short term financial one, a plurality of smaller local networks will create greater resilience to a network system. As firms like Google and Amazon increasingly try to bridge networks, they are creating closed ecosystems and effectively capturing entire marketplaces (Zhu & Iansati, 2019). As Pentland (2013) and Bonebau (2004) have noted, if an individual or organisation's network of contacts, reference points or influencers is not diverse enough you end up trapped in an echo chamber. Thus, it is important that networks do intersect. We need to avoid the retreat of Settlers into angry fief-type structures as much as we need to avoid purely bureaucratic and pure market-based structures. However, this is where the logic of networks of connected networks, like the one shown to be Uber, is key. Whilst they may create a level of inefficiency, perhaps that inefficiency is a necessary price for overall system resilience (Martin, 2019) that we often term sustainability.

The logic towards global, over local, networks not only empowers rootless Somewheres and Prospectors, but it also actively undermines the richness and personal nature of local networks that are likely to be the key to the Settlers sense of place, the idea of oikophilia and hence their ability to flourish, and, finally, subsuming differences under a digital veneer of predictable uniformity. Random encounters, purchases and the surprise of the unexpected are, instead, being replaced by efficient algorithms. From a pure utility perspective this makes perfect sense, but it is exactly this sort of logic that leaves Settlers feeling robbed of virtue that flows from the human investment in specific people and places. Algorithms may be enabling e-commerce to gain economic efficiency and widen choice, but the price is the health of a community's productive and consumptive places, which are forced to compete on lower and lower costs or wither away. To put it bluntly, algorithms have got no soul! The social consequences of efficiency-focused data capture are effectively driving many people to reject globally integrated networks themselves and seek to escape connectivity beyond a defined and known group of local connections. Furthermore, in the immediate wake of the COVID-19 pandemic 'Globalisation was found wanting' (Aldrick, 2020). Capturing the rising sense of insecurity flowing from a networked pandemic, Aldrick (2020) further claims that enhancing sovereign resilience, however, involves moving from efficient [robust] 'just in time' supply chains to expensive 'just in case' ones. He may be right that resilience resides in the long tail (Aldrick, 2020) and that 'Resilience cannot be measured easily, so does not lend itself to economic modelling' (Aldrick, 2020). Recognition of the need for inefficiency noted previously (Martin, 2019) and value in the qualitative emerging from the experience of the COVID-19 pandemic is reconfirming Settlers of their worldview and convincing others that they might have a point.

Network Responses

Cross, Liedtka and Weiss (2005) show how there has been a mismatch between the challenges to the liberal international order, both within and between states, and the response of business and political elites. They show how customised network responses are required where both 'problems and solutions are ambiguous' (Cross, Liedtka & Weiss, 2005, p. 125). A modular approach to networks works best, as Cross put it, 'where components of a problem and solution are known but the combination or sequence of those components is not yet known' (Cross, Liedtka & Weiss, 2005, p. 125), whereas a routine response works best where 'problems and their solutions are well defined and predictable' (Cross, Liedtka & Weiss, 2005, p. 126). Although their work was aimed at organisational responses to problems, the diagram below allows seeing more clearly the relationship between network structure and effectiveness of actions (Figure 3.3).

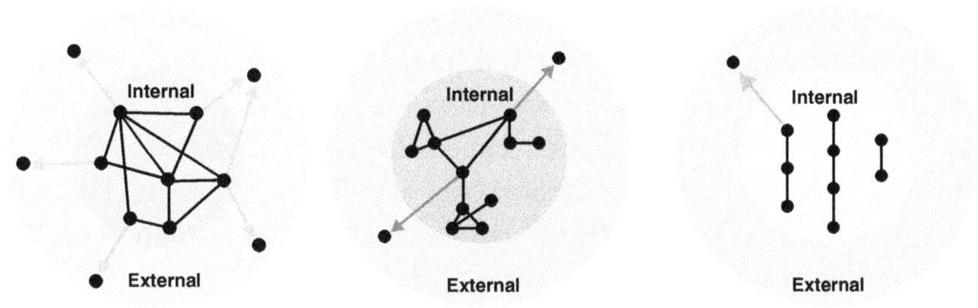

Figure 3.3 Cross' Network Responses

Cross, Liedtka and Weiss (2005) describes routine response networks as functioning 'through efficient, consistent responses to a set of established problems … external connections are limited … defined boundaries; embedded decision rights and information' (Cross, Liedtka & Weiss, 2005, p. 127). Although not the same as Boisot's network patterns, with the internal structure of networks shown by Cross clearly derived from business contexts, the broad patterns between the internal and external are very similar. Equally, the simplicity and closed nature of his routine network closely mirrors Boisot's (1995) fief network. The modular network is like Boisot's clan network and the customised is more like a market structure.

Furthermore, whilst Rose (2011) and Goodhart (2017) reveal how the growing absence of Settlers from elites (mostly replaced by Prospectors) has created a paradoxical situation, where the underlying assumption that the ambiguity of global networks is a good thing, has blinded them to the insecurity they create for those left behind. What we can see in Boisot (1995) and Cross, Liedtka and Weiss (2005) is the retreat of Settlers into closed, self-referencing networks with hardening boundaries. This situation has actively reduced permeability and created a spiralling cycle of disconnection. Thus, we need to better understand the nature of the spaces around the different network types captured by Cross, Liedtka and Weiss (2005) and Boisot (1995, 1998). Whilst the response needs to increase permeability and increase inter-network connection, as noted, Settlers fear and lack of agency mitigates against it.

If local networks are to flourish through their connections to other networks the bridging required will not come from Settlers who lack the agency required. Prospectors will likely follow the economic logic of developing closed integrated networks to capture value. Thus, we need to look to Rose's (2011) Pioneers and Goodhart's (2017) Inbetweeners to provide the bridge that enables distant networks to engage with and enrich local networks. This is very much what, as described in our previous book (Taylor & Bronstone, 2019), Cadbury did with their chocolate business. It is also what Triodos is trying to do with their crowdfunding business which enables small investors from anywhere to invest in specific community enterprises. If Pioneers are to do this, they will need to master a set of skills that are quite different from those required for the 'old economy'. Fortunately, Pioneers instinctive interest in new ideas and desire to drive ethical change (Rose, 2011) positions them well to do this. Thus, before moving on, we need to understand the key attributes that will be required by leaders of organisations to thrive in this new world and that will need to be learned by Pioneers (2011) if they are to bridge the gap between local and global networks, so that Settlers can flourish.

Culture, Cognition and Uncertainty

It is widely accepted that if optimisation was the key to value creation during the twentieth century, the rise of global digital networks has caused adaptability to be the driver of the new economy (Alexander 1983, Kennedy, 2002). As Zhu and Iansati put it:

> Ultimately, in a digital network business, the employees don't deliver the product or service – they just design and oversee an automated, algorithm-driven operation. Lasting competitive advantage hinges more on the interplay between the platform and the network it orchestrates and less on internal, firm-level factors
>
> (Zhu & Iansati, 2019, p. 5)

This occurrence has profound implications for what we think of as both good management and the sort of people that might be best suited for it. Zhu and Iansati (2019) raise questions of how managers should structure their activities and appropriate ways of thinking about the relationships between those activities and value creation itself. They show how managers need to contextualise their work differently if it is defined through the prism of a global social or digital network, rather than the linear internal flows within corporate boundaries.

Yet, it is only through thinking more critically that we can see that the fundamental challenge of the new economy is not just tactical, but that it represents a challenge to modernism itself. Traditional management has been about numbers and what is measurable as managers seek out truth and construct value that can be bounded and enclosed within the firm. Thus, the question is:

> Why do these approaches fail even when logic indicates they should prevail? The answer lies in a fundamental assumption of organizational theory and practice: that a certain level of predictability and order exists in the world. This assumption, grounded in the Newtonian science that underlies scientific management, encourages simplifications that are useful in ordered circumstances. Circumstances change, however, and as they become more complex, the simplifications can fail. Good leadership is not a one-size-fits-all proposition
>
> (Snowden & Boone, 2007)

Value creation in the network economy is far more about facilitating qualitative experiences through a network (Taylor & Bronstone, 2019). The use of algorithms and quantitative data in digital coding underlines that quantitative knowledge and tools will remain important. However, instead of being the source of value creation, they are increasingly being used as tools to support value flowing from qualitative insights, representations and choices directly from the diverse preferences of consumers. To this end 'complexity is more a way of thinking about the world than a new way of working with mathematical models' (Snowden & Boone, 2007). In the network economy, the ability to achieve richness (Arthur, 2006) and reach is enabling the smallest and strangest niches to be viable commercial opportunities. This ability makes management both more complicated and more complex. The Cynefin framework is an attempt to enable decision-makers to recognise the characteristics of the problems they face so that they react accordingly:

> The framework sorts the issues facing leaders into five contexts defined by the nature of the relationship between cause and effect. Four of these – simple, complicated, complex, and chaotic – require leaders to diagnose situations and to act in contextually appropriate ways. The fifth – disorder – applies when it is unclear which of the other four contexts is predominant
>
> (Snowden & Boone, 2007)

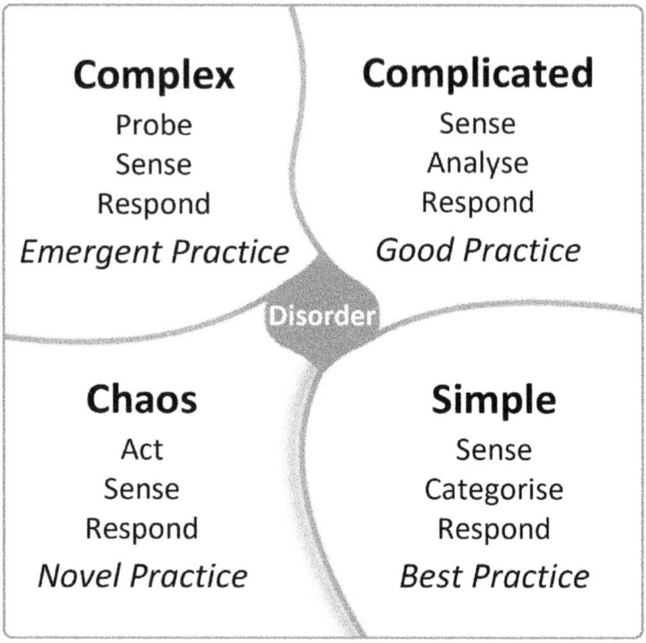

Figure 3.4 The Cynefin Framework

Cynefin opens up both a better understanding of the network types described by Boisot (1995, 1998) and Cross, Liedtka and Weiss (2005) and a means to structure thinking that is appropriate for engaging different network problems:

> Simple contexts are characterized by stability and clear cause-and-effect relationships...Here, leaders sense, categorize, and respond. That is, they assess the facts of the situation, categorize them, and then base their response on established practice.... Difficulties arise, however, if staff members are discouraged from bucking the process even when it's not working anymore.
>
> Complicated contexts, unlike simple ones, may contain multiple right answers, and though there is a clear relationship between cause and effect, not everyone can see it. This is the realm of 'known unknowns
>
> (Snowden & Boone, 2007)

Analysis paralysis, caused by the entrained thinking of experts, or a clash of egos between experts, are real problems in this complicated space (Snowden & Boone, 2007). Complex contexts are, however, different because they are defined by their dynamic state, where order is emergent and in constant flux, rather like an ecosystem. Trying to impose order in this domain is doomed to failure. It is better to observe patterns of emergence and bring in thinkers from diverse backgrounds to seek meanings that may be as novel as the emergence itself, to facilitate and channel emerging order. The key here is to encourage dissent, challenge existing assumptions and nurture emergent ideas without clear predetermined outcomes. In this space, the opportunities are neither obvious nor found in predictable places.

Chaotic contexts require leaders to act first to re-establish some sense of order and then provide meaning (Snowden & Boone, 2007). A good example might be the leadership of the US immediately after 9/11. In the short term, this can work well but can easily lead to perceptions of demagoguery as leaders start to believe in their own invincibility. The space in the middle of disorder is not knowing which box you are in and is, of course, the space we often find ourselves in (Snowden & Boone, 2007).

The Cynefin Framework Explained

Snowden's model (Snowden & Boone, 2007) is a powerful tool for both of us, as researchers, to structure how to think about what is happening, and for managers to apply appropriate methods. Table 3.2 provides a structure for recognising characteristics of each space and suitable reactions, within the context of Snowden's model.

It is important to recognise, however, that the Cynefin framework is a sensemaking model and not a categorisation model. That is to say that it is a tool of induction, rather than a drag and drop in the correct box type model. As such, and unlike many analytical models, it requires more critical thinking rather than removing the need for it. However, it does provide a structure for that thinking. Snowden and Boone (2007) argue that complexity is rising and organisations would do well to manage mostly in the complicated and complex spaces; responsive to deep knowledge and a capacity to coordinate and facilitate amidst ambiguity, respectively. Organisations should manage far less in the simple box, using best practices, based, as they are, upon a stable and predictable environment. This contrasts with the typical behaviour of managers and consultants which is to reduce as much as possible to establish best practices and procedures.

The further one moves away from the best practices space the greater the importance of questioning fundamental assumptions, that we will describe

Table 3.2 Decisions in Multiple Contexts: A Leader's Guide

	The Context's Characteristics	*The Leader's Job*	*Danger Signals*	*Response to Danger's Signals*
Simple	Repeating patterns and consistent events Clear cause-and-effect relationships evident to everyone; right answer exists Known knowns Fact-based management	Sense, categorise, respond Ensure that proper processes are in place Delegate Use best practices Communicate in clear, direct ways Understand that extensive interactive communication may not be necessary	Complacency and comfort Desire to make complex problems simple Entrained thinking No challenge of received wisdom Overreliance on best practice if context shift	Create communication channels to challenge orthodoxy Stay connected without micromanaging Don't assume things are simple Recognise both the value and the limitations of best practice
Complicated	Expert diagnosis required Cause-and-effect relationships discoverable but not immediately apparent to everyone; more than one right answer possible Known unknowns Fact-based management	Sense, analyse, respond Create panels of experts Listen to conflicting advice	Experts overconfident in their own solutions or in the efficacy of past solutions Analysis paralysis Expert panels Viewpoints of nonexperts excluded	Encourage external and internal stakeholders to challenge expert opinions to combat entrained thinking Use experiments and games to force people to think outside the familiar
Complex	Flux and unpredictability No right answers; emergent instructive patterns Unknown unknowns Many competing ideas A need for creative and innovative approaches Pattern-based leadership	Robe, sense, respond Create environments and experiments that allow patterns to emerge Increase levels of interaction and communication Use methods that can help generate ideas: Open up discussion (as through large group methods); set barriers; stimulate attractors; encourage dissent and diversity; and manage starting conditions and monitor for emergence	Temptation to fall back into habitual, command-and-control mode Temptation to look for facts rather than allowing patterns to emerge Desire for accelerated resolution of problems or exploitation of opportunities	Be patient and allow time for reflection Use approaches that encourage interaction so patterns can emerge

Chaotic	High turbulence No clear cause-and-effect relationships, so no point in looking for right answers Unknowables Many decisions to make and no time to think High tension Pattern-based leadership	Act, sense, respond Look for what works instead of seeking right answers Take immediate action to reestablish order (command and control) Provide clear, direct communication	Applying a command-and-control approach longer than needed 'Cult of the leader' Missed opportunity for innovation Chaos unabated	Set up mechanisms (such as parallel teams) to take advantage of opportunities afforded by a chaotic environment Encourage advisers to challenge your point of view once the crisis has abated Work to shift the context from chaotic to complex

Source: Snowden and Boone (2007, p. 7).

as double loop learning (Argyris, 1991), as below, due to the need for adaptability and critical thinking. Whilst a mixture of experience and established analytical models will suffice as the basis for expertise in the complicated space, this is not true for the complex space. The need to sense change based upon data, which either has not been or cannot be analysed using established models, requires the ability to recognise the critical meaning of patterns at an emergent stage. During a period of rapid and significant change double-loop learning provides:

> A culture of learning to question assumptions and think beyond the execution of tasks. It is a model which requires a high level of critical thinking and mitigates against process-based organisations in favour of a more agile, dynamic working environment that is well-suited to utilise communities of practices and adhocracy models
>
> (Taylor & Bronstone, 2019)

In an environment which is less predictable, more dynamic and less about reproducing order, where managers are expected to embrace change as an opportunity and be comfortable with ambiguity, the important questions to ask are how do they do it, what are the real challenges and how can this go wrong, as well as right, in the search for the next big wave (Kennedy, 2002) (Figure 3.5).

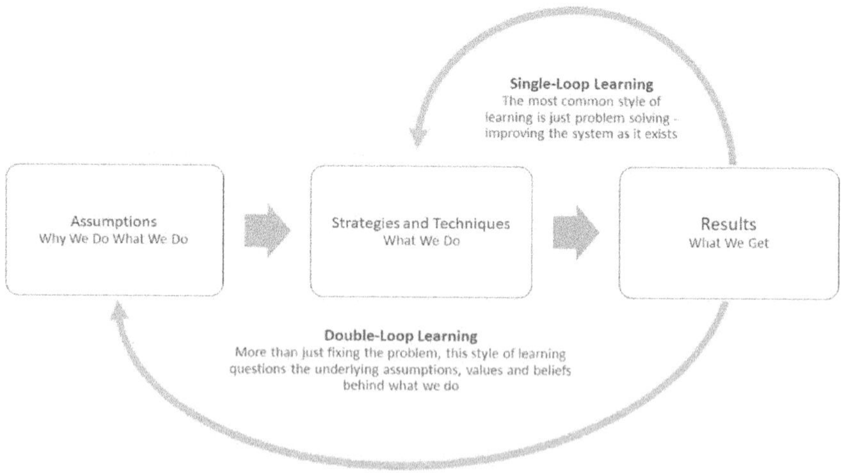

Figure 3.5 Learning Loops

Double Looping

Double-loop learning is about shifting from questions of how to do things right towards questions of what are the right things (Argyris, 1991). An example of organisational failure to grasp this is a global services company that one of the two authors of this book (Andrew Taylor) once worked with. Despite having a very high staff turnover, low productivity, a focus upon optimising internal flows and facing emerging technology companies offering similar services through cheaper automated agile platforms, the management insisted on continuing to both invest in processes to optimise and reward managers that 'could make the trains run on time'. When sales in their biggest market collapsed dramatically, they focused on cutting costs and delivering operational excellence. Despite this being, to the author in question, a clear case of an organisation trapped in single-loop learning and trying to manage an increasingly *complex* operating environment through *complicated* industry and functional expertise, the management continued to define the problem as a tactical failure of middle management to develop and coordinate sufficiently effective best practices. When a world-class complexity professor was introduced to the CEO and the Cynefin model used by the consultant to demonstrate that using experts to develop more best practices and processes was simply pushing the organisation closer to the cliff edge that divides the simple from the chaotic space, they were told to 'stop talking about strategy and work harder'. Needless to say, the problems of the organisation in question continue to grow and, if nothing changes, they are likely to fall over the cliff from the simple into the chaotic space where recovery is very expensive, if possible at all (Snowden, 2010). It will either fail, or be acquired. Either way, their failure to understand how value creation is changing continues to harm their present and undermine their future.

The above example shows the extent to which managers, in the real world, have often spent so much time learning how to master organisational bureaucracy that questioning it becomes very difficult and new additions to the organisation often find themselves being nudged, by longer-standing employees, into conforming, in order to fit in and be accepted. In our experience, it takes a lot of confidence and courage to invite others to question the assumptions which have defined individual and organisational success until now.

Critical Thinking

If double-loop learning is the key to individual and organisational adaptability that is central to the network economy, critical and associative thinking (Gavetti, 2011) becomes more central to value creation. Gavetti (2011) argues that managers need to learn to make cognitive leaps to leverage their core competencies into disparate markets, rather than focus on markets that are closer to their experience. Failure to do so will lead to the kind of failure that occurred at Kodak (Anthony, 2016). Managing complexity requires the ability to connect the abstract to the emergent, what Gavetti (2011) calls associative thinking, and mitigates against established knowledge. As we saw earlier, abstraction works well in markets, where codification and diffusion are high, but are more challenging in other network forms. This empowers those more naturally predisposed to be comfortable with ambiguity, fluidity and periods of change. For some this way of thinking is exciting, liberating and engaging, but for others these situations remove certainties and values change over order. As noted in our previous book, this significantly empowers Prospectors and Pioneers and disempowers Settlers (Rose, 2011). Double-loop learning requires a level of comfort with ambiguity that Settlers simply do not have. Furthermore, the idea that they will thrive in Snowden's complex space is absurd. As complexity frightens them, Settlers are far more likely to seek out leaders offering simple solutions and retreat into closed networks. Cynefin, therefore, allows us to see that the desire to appeal to Settlers is what drives those seeking absolute power to try and push periods of change towards the chaotic space. This is, of course, a big part of how extremists and populists do well during crises since they claim to know all the answers, a most comforting thought in a world of madness (Kohr, 2001).

Rooted in a specific sense of place, with lower educational experience, the natural space for action for a Settler is both based upon established norms and falls within their personal and/or professional experience. Cognitive leaps require a familiarity with, and practice of, abstract conceptualisation, which is most unlikely for most economic Settlers and which are unlikely to have been positive experiences for social Settlers who may understand the economics of restructuring, but hardly enjoy the unfreezing (Lewin, 1947) of certainties it entails.

Feedback Loops, Externalities and Property Regimes

Actions have unintended feedback loops (positive and negative), which are often magnified through network systems. In order to make sense of network dynamics, we also need to understand how socio-economic systems create incentives that lead to some of the impacts of human activities being externalised. This is important in digital networks because such feedback loops are heavily influenced by the systems from which they emerge. How such externalities occur, are transmitted, magnified, and either (in the case of negative externalities) dampened or (in the case of positive externalities) amplified will enable us to construct economies that are more sustainable socially, ecologically and economically. Thus, the following section is first an exploration of the problem of externalities and will lead into a study of stewardship and its role in moderating human behaviour.

The challenge with problems of externalities is how to align the interests of the producers and the consumers of externalities. Central to resolving problems of externalities is therefore about improving economic and social efficiency through innovative models of organisation and that, almost by definition, is related to regimes of resource governance that are usually referred to as property rights. If one was, therefore, able to limit only specific activities which have harmful external consequences, then one could at once prevent externalities from affecting those beyond the property boundaries without undermining the property right itself. Simply said, if we can restructure the property rights and obligations that underpin market transactions, we can create more sustainable outcomes. This is, Bromley (1993 [italic in original]) argues, because, contrary to popular belief, property:

> is a benefit (or income) stream, and a property right is a claim to a benefit stream that the state will agree to protect through the assignment of duty to others who may covet, or somehow interfere with, the benefit stream ... Property is not an object but rather is a social relation that defines the property holder with respect to something of value (the benefit stream) against all others. Property is a triadic relation involving benefit streams, rights holders and duty bearers

Thus 'it is *not* the resource itself which is owned: it is a bundle, or a portion of rights to use a resource that is owned' (Alchain & Demsetz, 1973, p. 17

[italics in original]). Rights to exploit land for activities such as agriculture, hunting, minerals and fishing were therefore often historically controlled by different parties. Where network markets prevail opportunities for unbundling and recommodifying benefits streams are that much greater, not least as it is the aggregation of access or connectivity that is the locus of value creation.

Bromley's (1993) argument means that not only may property be unpackaged by the owner, to divide and sell various benefit streams, but also that claims may be made on behalf of society over some of the benefit streams (Taylor, 1998), or, as we shall show, they may be shared. Historically, claims made by the state, on behalf of wider social or environmental interests, have been made through legislation to directly restrict an activity, or to introduce taxation to increase its cost. However, the emerging legitimacy of free markets as the solution to socio-economic problems, associated with neo-liberalism and the reforms of Thatcher and Reagan, gave rise to the idea that the state may be able to represent society's interests effectively by creating a value in reducing external costs and thus converting a negative externality into a potential benefit stream (Gillespie & Thomas, 1989). This process resulted in a new global marketplace, for example, for the trading of emission reductions with the Kyoto Protocol (Grubb, 1999) and associated European emission trading scheme (Taylor, 2004).

Whilst business always seeks entrepreneurial means to charge for accessing and/or consuming benefit streams, advanced forms of capitalism have sought to commoditise benefit streams, as a means to add value (Porter & Millar, 1985). As the former Communist countries of Eastern Europe were recast as emerging markets during the 1990s, the collision of Communist systems with unchecked market forces gave rise to new definitions of Bromley's (1993) triadic relationships. Infamously described by Fukuyama (1992) as 'the end of history', where market forces and private property rights were the outright winners and the interventionist state and ideas of society, rooted in Rousseau and Hegel (Ryan, 1984) lost. The failure of capitalist and Communist economic systems to internalise the full costs of industrialism's production and consumption through historic notions of stewardship has been widely documented (Jacobs, 1991; Peterson, 1993; Diamond, 2006; Grubb, 1999). However, the triumph of private property is only part of the story. The failure of state-owned property revealed that such regimes were not the same as common property; they were simply open access regimes (Boiler, 2014), and something that is owned by everybody is, *de facto*, owned by nobody and treated as a free good. Externalities are a product of feedback loops created by human activities and emerge out of socially constructed systems that govern, or fail to govern, productive and consumptive activities. Studies of externalities have mostly focused upon ecological and economic consequences, but they may be social also (Jacobs, 1992; Bromley, 1993). We also know that understanding how they function and creating regimes that avoid them is based upon the construction of social costs and benefits. Naturally, these flow from perceptions of network connectivity, which as we have seen, in the case of Settlers, are not always about economic rationality.

Scale leads towards externalities as it creates a separation, bureaucratic or geographical, between decisions and consequences. They are usually of three types:

- Common resources
- Public goods
- Future generations

The debate over externalities is often confusing, since the most famous work on the subject is Garret Hardin's *Tragedy of The Commons* (1968), which, whilst identifying the problems of externalities, erroneously confuses the problems of public goods with those of common resources. The absence of meaningful ownership rights is not the same as shared ownership rights that are common property.

Examples of common resources, therefore, might be grazing lands shared between a number of villagers, which still exist in the UK and Europe and which is common in parts of Africa or in the maintenance of an apartment building in Romania (see below). The challenge with common property regimes is to both develop socio-legal mechanisms that are effective in balancing the interests of rights holders fairly and in conserving the resource for the future (Boiler & Ostrom, 1990). Public goods are resources where either the state as a faceless bureaucracy notionally owns a resource, but it is *de facto* treated as a free good to be used and spoiled without meaningful restriction, or use of the resource lacks either meaningful agreements upon resource usage or punishments for those who act selfishly. Examples might be the world's oceans, or, more locally, the rivers and landscapes of Soviet

Russia which were unproductive, polluted and despoiled (Peterson, 1993; Scruton, 2012). One of the great problems of the Communist States of the Soviet Union and Eastern Europe was that something that was owned by everybody was effectively owned by nobody and thus remained uncared for. The essence of the problem of such resources, as identified by Hardin (1968), is that resource users are trapped in the classic prisoner's dilemma which encourages and rewards free-riding and mitigates against resource sustainability. For example, a sea, such as the North Sea, has fishermen from many nations active and where, for many years, there was no international agreement on how to share the resource. Everybody knew that the best thing to do was act with restraint to conserve overall fish stocks and ensure an income stream over the long term. However, fear that others would not restrain themselves led fishermen to take as much as they could before others did. The result was that fish stocks collapsed dramatically leading to the so-called 'cod war' over what remained and, ultimately, the near total demise of once great fishing fleets from cities such as Hull and Grimsby in the UK. Individual and short-term rational self-interest had led to a collectively disastrous collective long-term outcome. We see the same patterns emerging in conflicts over fishing rights in the English channel as we write (Dethan, Bremner & Courea, 2021). One of the key questions therefore, if we are to develop local resilience, is the relationship between connected local networks, compared to integrated scale-free networks and externalities. Simply put, can local networks reduce negative externalities and capture positive externalities in ways that larger scale-free networks cannot?

The importance of the social construction of local resource networks is revealed by residential water metering, in Romania, during the early part of the noughties. Described by Taylor (2004), the case illustrates the difference between public goods and common resources and the challenges of pooling resources to move from one to another despite the rationality of doing so. In this instance

> drinking water is provided centrally, consumed individually, but paid for communally – and thus treated as a free good. It therefore provided no incentive to restrain usage, and placed residents of apartment blocks in a prisoners dilemma, where everyone realises it is in the collective interest to reduce consumption, but a fear that neighbours will simply free

ride - and not reduce their usage, but still enjoy lower bills arising from the conservation efforts of others – maintains the status quo.

Following significant increases in prices for all utilities, during 2002, many residents of blocks took measures into their own hands and started installing water meters in a bid to escape the prisoners' dilemma and gain personal control over consumption costs of the resource. Unfortunately the seemingly reasonable demand by newly metered residents that they ought only to pay for the volume of water that they consumed was without legal basis and has created a raft of additional problems.

Back in 2002, block administrators were under no obligation to take account of the fact that a meter indicated that a family's bills ought to be lower than if calculated on the traditional communal division of costs. Yet even as the number of metered apartments grew geometrically the absence of meters provided by the water company at the entrance to each staircase (a defined communal unit within a block) meant that the water company could not assign unattributed consumption (losses) to a particular group of residents. The water companies have no interest in who consumes how much; rather they simply want the total amount leaving their plant to be paid for. Thus without stair meters they blocked the use of meters as well.

In Bucharest and some major cities the water companies have begun a programme of installing meters at the stairs of blocks. This has enabled block administrators to start using the meters as the basis of cost calculation. However, attempts to shift losses onto those without meters created huge disparities in bills and conflict between neighbours. The problem was compounded by the facts that there was no legal basis to discriminate against those without meters, and that the poorest members of society were those who could not afford meters and yet it was precisely those people that were being asked to shoulder all of the losses.

In the autumn of 2003 the government further embedded the emerging chaos, by allowing block administrators to use meters as the basis of calculation, without providing a clear indication of what should be done with the losses. Rather than address the root of the problem, the government had allowed those with some measure of wealth to offload some of their financial burden upon the poor. Now that meters are being fitted to stairs you might well ask where are the losses? Surely a system of metering would encourage residents to fix leaky pipes and reduce such wastage?

Many residents have discovered that if you leave the tap running at a very low level continuously the meter does not register the flow, thus enabling you to escape payment. However such usage is captured at the water company's stairs meter, thus creating "losses". In some blocks administrators divide such losses between all residents, thereby encouraging neighbours to monitor each other's behaviour. However the more common practice is to simply shift the costs to non-metered residents, who have no measurable means of defence. Such problems are compounded by a practice of meter readings being taken by residents themselves, inevitably leading to the creation of fictional losses that are being stored up as future debts and conflicts.

This case illustrates the economic and environmental inefficiency of state-controlled open-access property regimes, but also demonstrates the limitations of private regimes in improving equitable outcomes. The difficulties of residential housing in fact demonstrate that the challenge in Romania is often not so much how to replace state property with private property, but how to develop sufficient trust to be able to pool resources and formally, or informally, make common property regimes work. Key problems include trust and the tension between free riding and unequal abilities to pay. In the case study above, it appears that the number of participants is small enough for free diffusion of information between a defined group of people where 'information is embedded in tacit understanding and practices' (Snowden, 2019) and where it does not require a high level of codification to be successful. Thus, in this case, clan-based structures produce superior outcomes to bureaucracy or pure market-based structures (Boisot, 1998).

Ostrom (1990), who won a Nobel prize for her work on common property rights, defines common property as having defined boundaries, rules of governance, principles of what may be taken out (if it is a production commons) or put in (if it is a consumption commons), and a system of sanctions to punish rule breakers. Thus, if you want to manage the feedback loops that flow and are often magnified through networks 'the real issue is not technological but social' (Day, Schoemaker & Snyder, 2009, p. 286).

Despite early problems, as described above, the management of apartment block infrastructure has gradually, but inexorably, and almost universally, shifted from an open-access regime to a common property regime (Figure 3.6).

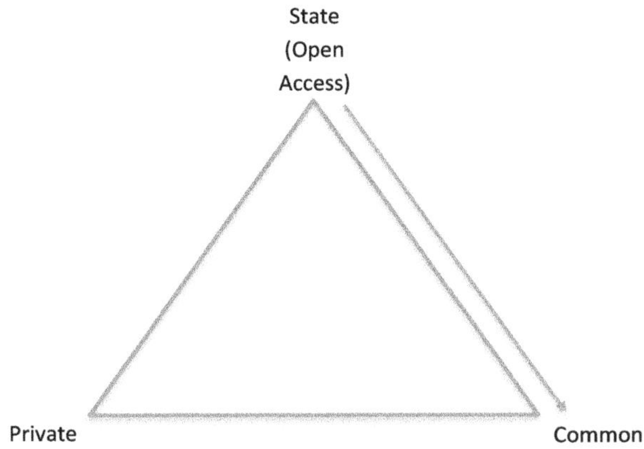

Figure 3.6 Romanian Residential Property Regime Change

Let us take the example of the physical condition of apartment buildings in Romania as another example. The entrances and stairwells were, for many years, in poor condition with plaster crumbling, paint peeling and smelling like a toilet. However, once residents placed access controls (intercom activated locks) on the exterior doors a dramatic improvement took place. Suddenly, the interior public spaces were repaired, painted and a different quality of living was created. Yet, in fact all that had really changed was a shift from an open access to a common property regime. The resource boundaries could be controlled and mechanisms to contribute to its maintenance could be developed. Nowadays almost all apartment blocks have such entrance locks in place and it is easy to forget how awful apartment buildings used to be.

The example of apartment blocks is an instructive one, for not only did it improve efficiency and overall outcome by internalising the costs and benefits of maintaining the resource to a defined group of commoners, but it invested commoners with a stake in their surroundings. The motivational impact of this cannot be overestimated. The development of property regimes, therefore, has a dramatic impact upon both behaviour and resource sustainability over the long term.

An interesting feature of studies of common property regimes is that they have been shown to create positive feedback loops, or beneficial externalities if you prefer, both in ecological and social terms (Ostrom, 1990,

2015; Bromley, 1993; Bollier, 2014). However, although less commonly noted, private property regimes can also create significant positive feedback loops that reach beyond the self-evident economic multiplier type effects. Examples might include superior customer service compared to state-owned enterprises, or in the case of carbon trading, a more efficient and effectively delivered environmental outcome. Whatever the nature of social governance, it is important to note that feedback loops exist, that they can be both positive and negative and that they may be quantitatively measurable (such as fish or pollution) or qualitatively important (like access to land or community health). Furthermore, because the management of feedback loops is primarily a social issue (Day, Schoemaker & Snyder, 2009) understanding the relationship between human preferences for action and network types is key.

In recent times, efforts have been made to use market mechanisms to create an economic interest in rights holders' internalising externalities. Examples include the development of carbon markets (Grubb, 1999; Taylor, 2004) to create a financial value from emission reductions and a financial cost from failure to do so. The idea here is to stop both the shifting of production costs to future generations (the greenhouse effect) and to do this by limiting the ability of large polluters to treat the skies as a public good. Indeed, such markets seem to have worked best when they have a defined boundary, such as the so-called EU bubble, with clear participants, effectively creating a proto common property resource as the basis for market transactions. Markets work best where there is a high diffusion and codification of knowledge since abstraction is key when trading a commodity as nebulous as 'hot air'. So-called cap-and-trade markets, such the EU emissions market, try to do this by creating an agreed maximum level of defined pollution, with planned reductions in that amount every year, which are then divided between market participants. As long as punishments for non-compliance are above the costs of compliance this will enable the market to search out the lowest cost emission reductions. Market participants can find internal efficiencies or purchase other participants surplus efficiencies, thus enabling what were externalities to become an internalised, networked search for the largest reductions at the lowest cost. In other words, what was a potential liability, pollution, has become a potential asset. Given that carbon markets include heavy polluters utilising capital-intensive assets, actors typically plan investments over the long term. Therefore, one of the keys to resolving externalities in public goods and common resources is having incentives that encourage actors to think about their role in a system over the longer term.

John Maynard Keynes famously said that 'In the long term, we are all dead' (Keynes, 1923). Human beings find it very easy to discount an unknowable and unpredictable future and, as a species, we have become adept at passing the costs of today's actions onto the shoulders of future generations. Externalities imposed upon future generations are insidious as the costs are not immediately visible. Large-scale examples include generous pension schemes for the baby boomer generation, paid for by their children, which are financially impossible to be provided when those children come to retire, or acid rain, the greenhouse effect and nuclear waste which all result from producing things for today that create legacy costs for future generations to deal with. However, most of us experience such costs more locally through the degradation of land quality and loss of public space for our children to play on. A specific example of social externalities that digital networks are creating is the closure of shops on High Streets that future generations could benefit from in order for us to enjoy the convenience and cost benefits of online shopping today. The loss of shops and high streets and town centres is keenly felt as a loss of points of connection between people and place (Silverman, 2019; Morris, 2020). Externalities, whether social, environmental or simply economic, flow from the utilitarian view, formed during the enlightenment, that the world is there for humans to exploit.

Stewardship

Rejection of utility as the basis of decision-making is usually based upon some sense of virtue that encodes a sense of duty to not exploit or place limits upon exploitation. This act is usually called stewardship and based upon the idea that 'the good things we inherit are not ours to spoil, but ours to use wisely and pass on' (Scruton, 2012, p. 216). Duties to not impose externalities have been defined as incumbent upon owners, as a corollary of their rights, culturally and philosophically, since the beginning of time. They exist to inject some measure of virtue into human behaviour, such that people do not confuse ends with means (Schumacher, 1993) and utility does not become an end without thought to its wider impact.

This relationship of duties that bind people to cherish their attachment to a place he calls oikophilia 'so as to embellish and renew the plot of earth, and the community, to which one is attached' (Scruton, 2012, p. 412).

At its core stewardship defines (often implicitly) a code of virtue that ties a group of people together around a specific place to create an identity that transcends both. Scruton (2017, p. 16) describes (the English) people as 'inseparable at every point from the attachment to the land and the desire to endow the land with the character of home'. It is attachment to identity that drives Settlers to reject change and the unknown. Yet, as Scruton (2017, p. 23 [italics in original]) so eloquently recognised '*Who we are is where we are*', it is the Settlers desire to conserve and protect that is a key component of any form of sustainability. For this reason alone, we should reject the views of Settlers as Luddites and idiots that were held by metropolitan Prospectors during the Brexit debates and the election of Trump (Wilkinson, 2017; Peck, 2018; Liddle, 2019). 'Oikophobes define their goals and ideas *against* some cherished form of membership' (Scruton, 2017, p. 89 [italics in original]).

In the modern age the founding father of property rights in Britain and the USA, John Locke, makes his belief in stewardship clear when he says 'nothing was made by God for man to spoil or destroy' (Locke, 1991, p. 131) and that 'at the heart of resilience is the determination to do what is right' (Welby, 2018, p. 53). The essence of stewardship is that acting with restraint upon purely utilitarian exploitation is how the idea of work becomes an act of virtue. As Shaiko puts it, the 'execution of stewardship was therefore the ultimate act of God's will on earth through his designated manager, man' (Shaiko, 1987, p. 244). For thinkers such as Schumacher (1993) and Scruton (2012), stewardship enables people to put aside the economic pressures and moderate their behaviour, such that socio-economic costs that might be economically rational to externalise and the interests of non-owners become real.

As fear of God declined, Godwin and others have tried to maintain the interests of non-owners as boundaries upon exploitation of rights (Taylor, 1998). This perspective was clearly stated by the Bishop of Oxford who argued that the justification for private property 'just depends upon no a priori principle, but upon its social effects' (The Bishop of Oxford, 1913, pp. X–XL).

With, or without, a religious component, the idea of stewardship acting as a brake upon utilitarian economics dates back to primitive societies. Despite the claims of Bentham and neoliberal thinkers from Hayek to Friedman, relationships between rights and duties are inherently political questions. To think otherwise is to ignore the role of power in the world and this is precisely why the network economy is so frightening to Settlers. For it is not globalisation or technology themselves, as sources of economic opportunity, that Settlers reject. It is the implicit and uniform utilitarianism that rides roughshod over respect for the stewardship which binds people and place together. In placing ends before means, the idea of community is lost.

At the time of Locke, stewardship created a sense of virtue to communities that were limited in their scale and reach and, through social norms, became an embodied part of identity that attached people to place. However, industrial progress widened connections whereby market networks overwhelmed many traditional elements of clan membership. Easily dismissed by Marxists as no more than a fig leaf to maintain class relations, stewardship has retained its appeal as a human virtue.

Kohr (2001) argues proximity is required for stewardship to be a meaningful component of identity that could serve as a brake upon utilitarianism. Cuthil contends that their research suggests 'that much of the passion and commitment to protect and preserve cultural and natural landscapes emanates from connection to place' (Cuthil et al., 2014). Proximity of relationships also allow us to cross networks and to recognise the differences with other networks without feeling threatened by the scale of the others. Organisations of people are most effective when they are large enough to fulfil functional needs but small enough for individuals to not be dominated by their bureaucracies (Kohr). Cuthill (2014) also posits that, based upon their research, sustainability:

> could involve facilitating the formation of and facilitation of actions by stewardship groups more deliberately, so as to enhance social capital. Stewardship groups might be fostered in areas needing stronger people-place connections and/or social capital. This suggests developing new, more engaged, governance forms
>
> (Cuthill et al., 2014, p. 153)

Thus stewardship, defined in the specific by Scruton (2012) as oikophilia:

> is a call to responsibility, and a rebuke to calculation. It tells us to love, and not to use; to respect, and not to exploit.

In the absence of alternatives, people will undertake work knowing that it is creating negative externalities. However, as employees, they are unlikely to do it with much enthusiasm since it turns work into nothing more than a necessary evil (Schumacher, 1993). Managers may get compliance but are unlikely to get much commitment (Taylor & Krouwel, 2013).

In contrast to the efforts of those such as Porter (1979, 1985) to create robust economic models, ideas of oikophilia (Scruton, 2012, 2017) and the cherishing of place as a source of identity emphasise resilience over a fixed robustness. In the network economy, this may well be both more valuable and more sustainable. Thus, we seek to explore how this might work and the way that leaders and organisations can make use of such models to embed social richness from economic reach.

The Scale of Work?

Settlers rejection of utility as an end in itself is not philosophical, so much as a recognition that the subsequent growth of scale creates a separation between people and between people and place that reduces both to a transactional relationship. As Kohr famously put it 'the world's one and only problem is not wickedness but bigness' (Kohr, p. 95). Scale really became important through the progress of the industrial revolution. As industrialism took hold, supported by the anthropocentric Cartesian belief in humans as the conquerors of nature, a separation took place between cause and effect that was unprecedented. Increasingly, industrialists and merchants could separate the places that they despoiled for work and the places that they could treasure as home. What both Soviet-style economics and the emerging digital economy illustrate is that it is not so much whether people are good or evil, but that growth in scale makes it progressively harder to move beyond utilitarianism and maintain a sense of virtue.

The network economy is proving transformative for a global elite of adaptive and bright executives whilst effectively externalising the consequences of those left behind. In the UK, zero-hours contracts, it is argued

(Fleming, 2015; Hutton, 2015; Bloodworth, 2018), are simply not sustainable without the state benefits which now act as a *de facto* subsidy to many tech and retail companies. As we noted previously:

> one of the contradictions of the new economy is that the networked ability to search out the lowest price is often no more than a global means of identifying the most exploitative means of production and distribution
> (Taylor & Bronstone, 2019)

Wherever value creation depends upon discretionary input, such as the use of knowledge, commitment starts to matter (Beardwell & Thompson, 2014). The more that discretionary input matters, the more that commitment becomes important to value creation. Hence, knowledge businesses typically apply so-called soft HR models designed to nurture commitment whilst more predictable process-driven businesses tend towards harder forms of HR where less commitment is needed. Thus, the employee-owned retailer John Lewis is an example of 'soft' HR and the budget airline Ryanair is an example of 'hard' HR. As organisations grow, reliance upon bureaucratic processes tends to grow and intrinsic motivation becomes harder to sustain. This matters because 'If our goal is excellence, no artificial incentive can ever match the power of intrinsic motivation' (Taylor & Krouwel, 2013, p. 97). It is not just network connectivity that matters, but also the intensity of connections that matters. This is especially true for both Settlers and Pioneers because 'they work because they love what they do' (Taylor & Krouwel, 2013, p. 97).

Work, for Settlers, is not just a transactional activity; it is a means to build connections with my people and this place. This is why the closure of mines, farming bankruptcies and the like are so devastating. For Pioneers, work is a means of driving ethical change of some kind. In both cases, work has a metaphysical value that goes beyond anything material. For both Settlers and Pioneers work offers 'man a chance to utilise and develop his faculties; to overcome his ego centeredness by joining with other people in a common task; and to bring forth the goods and services needed for a becoming existence' (Schumacher, 1993, p. 39).

Understanding how Prospectors are, by their very nature, driven by a utilitarian view of the world, while Settlers and Pioneers are not (Rose, 2011), is key to changing political economies. Settlers fear that the world may be, as Hobbes described it, a war of every man against every man. Whether it is, or not, Settlers fear that however we have escaped our evil nature for now, it will not last and we should prepare for bad days ahead. Pioneers believe that with the right nurturing, humankind can develop a better and more virtuous world and the forces of utility must be harnessed and channelled in the service of nurturing visions of virtue. Prospectors see the world in materialistic and utilitarian terms, and it is this worldview that underpins their desire for action. For Prospectors, virtue is interesting to the extent that it is a useful pull towards action, but holds little intrinsic value, whilst any tendencies towards the nurture idea are purely because it can be key to overcoming the inertia and lack of agency that holds Settlers back. However, as noted in our previous book:

> in terms of leadership an almost paradoxical situation is being created. On the one hand enormous effort is going into developing business knowledge, strategic thinking and soft skills of high potential employees. On the other hand, those that they are supposed to lead are being asked to make greater commitment to a deal which offers increasingly few benefits in long term development (company pensions gone, training now functional and not aspirational) and delivers a harsher reality in their material status and social standing
>
> (Taylor & Bronstone, 2019, p. 17)

Yet, small companies, with smaller resources, cannot afford to carry passengers. Furthermore, the proximity of action and outcome is such that mere compliance is not an option. Whilst small companies may not always be especially innovative, they do provide an active contribution to communities through the commercial life that they breathe into people and places (Taylor & Krouwel, 2013). If the network economy requires leadership that is adaptable enough to cope with complexity and ambiguity then this clearly disadvantages Settlers whose lack of agency and fear of change effectively handicaps them. Whilst this situation empowers both Prospectors and Pioneers, only Pioneers have sufficient interest in notions of virtue to think beyond opportunities for arbitrage and use these skills to bring the global to enrich the local. In short, the question is, provided with the correct tools, are Pioneers able to bring global network opportunities to enable the local to flourish, just as Cadbury and others did during the nineteenth century? Are they able to construct bridges between local networks that can enable the global to enrich, rather than simply exploit, the local.

If the gap between the global networks and local places is to be bridged it will require Pioneers. Goodhart's (2017) Inbetweeners, to create structures that provide security and practical incentives for Settlers to participate that enrich, but also enhance, their sense of pride in their values of oikophilia. In our previous book (Taylor & Bronstone, 2019), we provided schematic examples of this taking place, both historically and with more recent examples. The rest of this book will take an empirical look at how to construct structures where Settlers can thrive through global networks.

Conclusion

Whilst global digital disintermediation of markets is creating significant economic opportunities, the network effects which are driving those opportunities are also globalising the externalities that flow from market failures. Many of these are social and affect Settlers disproportionately. Whilst Prospectors may well have come of age, Settlers are being left behind, and not only by the pace of change. The need to think critically, conceptually, and to be able to adapt, that are all key in network economics, mitigate against Settlers. Furthermore, the implicit dismissal of the relevance of place and tradition, which is inherent in digital markets, is profoundly unsettling for Settlers. This is felt through the pressure of global networks upon the local clan-type networks that historically bound people to place. As Scruton (2017, p. 54) says 'it is surely apparent to all of us that we are in need of an inclusive first-person plural, one that unites both the mobile elite and the settled people'.

As noted in our previous book (Taylor & Bronstone, 2019), if Settlers are to be engaged and not left to be ignored until they use their political voice to reject globalisation out of hand, it will likely require Pioneers to create commercial bridges between local and global networks for them to feel sufficiently secure to contribute. The rest of this book is therefore about how, and with whom, to construct networks and network bridges that enable the commerce of place to thrive in global networks. The next chapters will explore case studies where Settlers have been successfully engaged to see how such tools might be employed by Pioneers to be sustainable.

The Next Steps

The next chapter of our research is to outline the method used to gather and interpret empirical data, such that we are able to induct from subsequently described case studies. This will enable us to examine the relative merits and utility of the models described and permit others to explore the extent to which our findings hold wider validity.

References

Alchain, A. & Demsetz, H., 'The Property Right Paradigm', *Journal of Economic History* 33, 1973.

Aldrick, P., 'Huawei Ban Strengthens Britain's Shift Towards Greater Self-Reliance', *The Times*, July 17, 2020.

Alexander, C., 'The New Economy', *Time*, May 30, 1983.

Anderson, C., *The Long Tail: Why the Future of Business Is Selling Less of More.* New York: Hyperion, 2006.

Anthony, S., 'Kodak's Downfall Wasn't About Technology', *Harvard Business Review*, July 15, 2016.

Argyris, C., 'Teaching Smart People to Learn', *Harvard Business Review*, May–June, 1991.

Arthur, W. B., 'Increasing Returns and The New World of Business', *Harvard Business Review*, July–Aug, 1996.

Beardwell, J. & Thompson, A., *Human Resource Management: A Contemporary Approach* (7th ed.). Harlow: Pearson, 2014.

Bloodworth, J., *Hired: Six Months Undercover in Low-Wage Britain.* London: Atlantic Books, 2018.

Boisot, M., *Information Space: A Framework for Learning in Organizations, Institutions and Culture.* London: Routledge, 1995.

Boisot, M. & Child, J., 'The Iron Law of Fiefs: Bureaucratic Failure and the Problem of Governance in the Chinese Economic Reforms', *Administrative Science Quarterly* 33: 507–527, 1988.

Bollier, D., *Think Like a Commoner: A Short Introduction to the Commons.* Gabriola Island: New Society Publishers, 2014.

Bonabeau, E., 'The Perils of the Imitation Age', *Harvard Business Review*, June 2004.

Bromley, D., *Environment and Economy: Property Rights and Public Policy*. Oxford: Blackwell, 1993.

CLUJ Business, https://clujbusiness.ro/business-support/education/universities/#:~:text=One%20of%20the%20most%20important, 219%20 students%2F1.000%20resident%20population.

Cross, R., Liedtka, J. & Weiss, L., 'A Practical Guide to Social Networks', *Harvard Business Review*, Mar 2005.

Cuthill, M., Ross, H., Maclean, K., Owens, K. & Witt, B., 'Reporting Social Outcomes of Development: An Analysis of Diverse Approaches', *The International Journal of Interdisciplinary Social Science* 3: 145–158, 2008.

Day, G., Schoemaker, P. & Snyder, S., *The Network Challenge: Strategy, Profit and Risk in an Interlinked World*. Upper Saddle River, NJ: Prentice Hall, 2009.

Dethan, M., Bremner, C. & Courea, E., 'Macron Gives Britain Ultimatum in Fishing Row', *The Times*, Nov 1, 2021.

Diamond, J., *Collapse: How Societies Choose to Fail or Survive*. London: Penguin, 2006.

Fleming, P., 'There's Nothing Good About the Rise in Zero-Hours Contracts – Ban Them Now', *The Guardian*, Sept 7, 2015.

Folke, C., Carpenter, S., Walker, B., Scheffer, M., Elmqvist, T., Gunderson, L. & Holling, C. S., 'Regime Shifts, Resilience, and Biodiversity in Ecosystem Management', *Annual Review of Ecology, Evolution, and Systematics* 35: 557–581, 2004.

Fukuyama, F., *The End of History and the Last Man*. New York: Free Press, 1992.

Gavetti, G., 'The New Psychology of Strategic Leadership', *Harvard Business Review*, July–Aug 2011.

Gillespie, C. & Thomas, J., *Property Rights and the Environment*. London: IEA, 1989.

Goodhart, D., *The Road to Somewhere*. London: Hurst and Company, 2017.

Grubb, M., *The Kyoto Protocol: A Guide and Assessment*. London: The Royal Institute of International Affairs, 1999.

Hardin, G., 'The Tragedy of the Commons', *Science* 162(3859): 1243–1248, 1968.

Hiermaier, S., 'Keynote Speech to the Global Resilience Research Network', *Freiburg*, Apr 2019.

Hutton, W., *How Good We Can Be: Ending the Mercenary Society and Building a Great Country*. London: Little Brown, 2015.

Iansiti, M. & Lakhani, K., 'Managing Our Hub Economy: Strategy, Ethics and Network Competition in an Age of Digital Superpowers', *Harvard Business Review*, Sept 2017.

Jackson, M., *Systems Thinking: Creative Holism for Managers*. Chichester: Wiley, 2003.

Jacobs, M., *The Green Economy*. London: Pluto Press, 1991.

Kennedy, C., *The Merchant Princes*. London: Hutchinson, 2002.

Keynes, J. M., 'A Tract on Monetary Reform', *The Economic Journal* 85(338): 249–271, [1923] June, 1975.

Kohr, L., *The Breakdown of Nations*. Croydon: Green Books, 2001 (Originally published by Routledge & Kegan Paul, 1957).

Lewin, K., 'Frontiers in Group Dynamics: Concept, Method and Reality in Social Science; Social Equilibria and Social Change', *Human Relations* 1: 5–41, 1947.

Liddle, R., 'What If the 'Village Idiots' Are Right About Brexit?', *The Spectator*, May 11, 2019.

Locke, J., *Two Treatises of Government*. London: Dent, 1991.

Martin, R. L., 'The High Price of Efficiency', *Harvard Business Review*, July/Aug 2019.

Merali, Y. & Allen, P. in Maguire, S., Allen, P. & McKelvey, B., *The Sage Handbook of Complexity and Management*. London: Sage, 2017.

Merali, Y. & Snowden, D., 'Mastering Complexity In The Networked World: Strategy & Leadership', Cluj, Romania, 2019.

Morris, S., '"It Came Out of Adversity": How Treorchy Became UK's Best High Street', *The Guardian*, Jan 24, 2020.

Ostrom, E., *Governing the Commons: The Evolution of Institutions for Collective Action*. Cambridge: Cambridge University Press, 1990.

Ostrom, E., *Governing the Commons: The Evolution of Institutions for Collective Action*. Cambridge: Cambridge University Press, 2015.

Owens, J., 'The Tech Giants Dominated the Decade: But There's Still Time to Rein Them In', *The Guardian*, Dec, 2019.

Peck, T., 'Theresa May Has Delivered an Idiot's Brexit, But the Idiots Will Not Stand for It', *The Independent*, Nov 22, 2020.

Pentland, A., 'Beyond the Echo Chamber', *Harvard Business Review*, Nov 2013.

Peterson, D. J., *Troubled Lands: The Legacy of Soviet Environmental Destruction.* London: Westview Press, 1993.

Porter, M., 'How Competitive Forces Shape Strategy', *Harvard Business Review*, Mar 1979.
Porter, M., 'Strategy and the Internet', *Harvard Business Review* 79(3): 62–78, 2001.
Porter, M. & Millar, V., 'How Information Gives You Competitive Advantage', *Harvard Business Review*, July–Aug, 1985.
Rose, C., *What Makes People Tick: The Hidden World of Settler, Prospectors and Pioneers*. Leicester: Matador, 2011.
Ryan, A., *Property and Political Theory*. Oxford: Blackwell, 1984.
Schumacher, E. F., *Small Is Beautiful: A study of Economics as If People Mattered.* London: Vintage Books, 1993.
Scruton, R., *Green Philosophy: How to Think Seriously About the Planet*. London: Atlantic Books, 2012.
Scruton, R., *Where We Are: The State of Britain Now*. London: Bloomsbury, 2017.
Senge, P., *The Necessary Revolution: How Individuals and Organizations Are Working Together to Create a Sustainable World.* New York: Doubleday, 2008.
Shaiko, R., 'Religion Politics, and Environmental Concern: A Powerful Mix of Passions', *Social Science Quarterly* 68, 1987.
Silverman, R., 'The British High Street that Became a Ghost Town', *The Telegraph*, July 16, 2019.
Snowden, D., "The Origins of Cynefin (Part 1)", Cognitive Edge, Mar 2010.
Snowden, D. & Boone, M. E., 'A Leader's Framework for Decision Making', *Harvard Business Review*, Nov 2007.
Snowden, D. & Merali, Y., *Complexity In a Networked World.* Cluj-Napoca, Transylvania Executive Education Workshops, Romania, Nov 16–17, 2019.
Taylor, A., 'Government Cackhandedness in Water Management Policy is Money – and Water – Down the Drain', Vivid, Nr. 63, 2004.
Taylor, A., 'Property Rights and the Differentiating Countryside: A Case Study in South West England', Unpublished Ph.D. Thesis, Cardiff, University of Wales College of Cardiff, 1998.
Taylor, A., *Taking Care of Business: Innovation, Ethics & Sustainability*. Cluj-Napoca, Romania: Risoprint, 2013.
Taylor, A., 'Trading Hot Air: Backwards, Forwards or Any Which Way You Like', *European Environment* 14, 2004.

Taylor, A. & Bronstone, A., *People, Place and Global Order: Foundations for a Networked Political Economy*. London: Routledge, 2019.

The Bishop of Oxford, *Property: Its Rights and Duties*. London: Macmillan, 1913.

Wahl, D., 'Building A New Normal', *Resurgence & Ecologist* 321, 2020.

Walker, B., Holling, C. S., Carpenter, S. R. & Kinzig, A., 'Resilience, Adaptability and Transformability in Social–Ecological Systems', *Ecology and Society* 9(2): 5, 2004.

Wang, L. & Buckland, M., 'From Fief to Clan: Boisot's Information SpaceModel as a Documentary Theory for Cultural and Institutional Analysis', University of Akron Idea Exchange, Proceedings from the Document Academy, Dec 2016.

Wilkinson, A., 'Leave Voters Are Not All Idiots – Some Londoners Still Don't Get It', *The Guardian*, Feb 14, 2017.

Zhu, F. & Iansati, M., 'Why Some Platforms Thrive and Others Don't', *Harvard Business Review*, Jan–Feb 2019.

4

A FORK IN THE ROAD

Exploring Space, Place and Method

Introduction

Theories of how and why people and places may flourish under differing conditions are interesting, but without consideration of how they apply in practice remain just theories. Thus we have selected four case studies through which to examine the characteristics that enable people and places to flourish within contemporary global networks.

Case studies selected for any work offer researchers insights into the stories that subjects tell so that they can consider what those stories mean and this ultimately enables them to create narratives of their own (Whyte, 1943; Collins, 2021). They are an empirical lens that causes us to think about how applicable insights may be beyond the case studies and thus informs our theories of the world (Hammersley & Atkinson, 1983; Wolcott, 1994). This work builds upon our previous work (Taylor & Bronstone, 2019) to tell a story of a select group of organisations and cities that have chosen, or in one case has attempted, to construct a future where attachment to place is

DOI: 10.4324/9781003145295-4

a vehicle for flourishing rather than being an impediment to growth. The lessons that can be learned and the extent to which they may be applicable elsewhere we will explore in the next chapters. This chapter sets out the means by which the process of discovery that underpins our claims to validity, and that lies behind our storytelling, was constructed.

Contextualisation of the Case Studies

Why These *Case Studies?*

It is always a good question – why choose those case studies in comparison to these case studies? Could you not have looked there instead of where you did? Do these case studies provide the author with enough substance so as to make the argument that one wishes to make? (Baxter, 2008). The selection was based upon a mixture of identifying case studies that both appeared to offer insights into the key issues we sought to explore and to offer access to key actors.

At times the decision is also based on what one already knows in comparison to what one does not know, and also what is accessible compared to what is not as accessible or is not accessible at all (McKenzie, 2015; Bloodworth, 2018). Certainly, given that this work was completed during the global pandemic, there were certain on-site limitations, some of which are described later in this chapter. Finally, and for those who have been through the process of selecting case studies for qualitative research, the search for access to valid representations precludes any scientific search for wider reliability (Collis & Hussey, 2014). This process is as much art as it is science (Hammersley & Atkinson, 1983). Nonetheless, we chose four case studies to examine the extent to which patterns of motivation, structure and behaviour might be discernible across the case studies without compromising their internal validity.

Selecting Case Studies

Understanding the extent to which local governance regimes can engage in questions of complexity is, as we have seen, key in thinking about their sustainability within digital networks. Thus, one of the key questions we will be looking at is what are the conditions that enable some places to thrive amidst complexity and others to struggle? Does it require certain types of people, such as Pioneers, as we argued previously (Taylor & Bronstone, 2019), to lead, or is it particular structures, norms of behaviour or some other external factors?

The case studies presented in this volume were selected on the basis of being useful for exploring our core themes of how people and places do and do not succeed in thriving within global networks. We have deliberately selected two cities and two organisations in order to be able to meaningfully compare and contrast. At the outset, we sought at least one case study that was perceived, by those involved, as successful and at least one where participants perceived failure. Equally, we sought case studies of places and different types of organisations. Thus, we have two very different cities (Cluj-Napoca and Jacksonville), a business (Boulevard) and an unconventional non-governmental organisation (NGO) (EduCab). Cluj was chosen because Andy had established relations in the city through his role in coordinating an MBA programme there and his work as a management consultant. Jacksonville is a place in which Adam had previously lived and Boulevard was a company that he knew through an NGO. EduCab was founded and led by a former colleague of Andy.

- Cluj-Napoca (Romania). The city of Cluj is an example of a city that has recently thrived as a centre of entrepreneurialism, despite poor economic beginnings, a dysfunctional national government and the relative absence of similar success stories in the same country. Led by an infamous nationalist Mayor during the 1990s, the city has, during the new millenium, experienced dramatic economic growth. Sectors such as IT, healthcare and engineering have expanded to the point where they have created shortages of labour. Cluj is home to several well-regarded Universities and remains the headquarters of, what has become, Romania's largest commercial bank. Both institutions which, as we saw in Chapter 2, CLES (2019) have identified as key pillars of community wealth building. However, there has been no collective effort to use the Cleveland/Preston model and none of the people that we met and interviewed were aware of the model.
- Boulevard Brewing Company. Boulevard is a local brewing company in Kansas City (MO) that through conversations with local environmental groups that work with the business community sought to

re-develop its manufacturing processes in a sustainable manner. From that initial decision, the company has embarked, since the late 1990s, on a substantive sustainable development journey, which has included programs that continue to reach beyond the company itself. Indeed it has even spun off a waste business that grew out of no more than an attempt to internalise the hidden costs of their production.
- EduCab is an NGO network of volunteers that seeks to connect volunteers from economically successful urban centres with less successful smaller towns and villages. Started in Romania in 2015, the 12 countries that they operate in have significant rural to urban migration and often international outward migration. Thus, EduCab tries to bring entrepreneurial people to develop programmes and partnerships that enrich small places and enable individuals and communities to flourish economically and socially.
- Jacksonville, Florida, made an explicit attempt to develop a Cleveland/Preston-type model of polycentric community wealth building. We will learn about why the project came about, the expectations from those involved in the initial formation of the work and, over time, the successes and failures of the project.

Our prior knowledge of the case studies has self-evidently provided us with insights and knowledge that we otherwise would not have gained. Yet simultaneously prior knowledge risks a level of bias that may skew data or its interpretation. There is no conclusive answer to the problem of bias, beyond acknowledging the problem and doing our best to constantly question our own assumptions, preferences and attributions of meaning (Hammersly & Atkinson, 1983; Collis & Hussey, 2014). In the search for validity, problems of bias and interpretation are an inevitable aspect of qualitative investigation (Hammersly & Atkinson, 1983; Walcott, 1994; Mckenzie, 2015).

The 'How' of Our Research

Some writers have analysed questions of development on the basis of a positivist worldview, applying quantitative methods (Gartell & Gartell, 1996) and certainly this was historically popular in business and management research (Gray, 2017), whilst others, more recently, have tended to adopt a more interpretivist view (Larrain, 1979; Newby, 1985, 1988; Hammersley, 1992; Walcott, 1994). We have no fixed ontological or epistemological position and we are open to the possibility of an objective reality. Yet we know that motivations, social systems and complexity are driven as much by perception as any objective truth (Hammersley, 2006). As Tett (2015) says:

> the patterns that we use to organize our lives are often a function of nurture, not nature. That makes them fascinating to analyze.
>
> (Tett, 2015)

Given that it is the interaction of people and constructions of place that is of primary interest, what was sought in this research was validity over reliability. Thus, an interpretivist paradigm has been assumed as the basis for data collection. Quantitative data have informed research, but ultimately provided no more than the background.

The general approach to the empirical research can broadly be described as qualitative, using a mixture of interviews and participant-observation. Some may even characterise this approach as somewhat ethnographic (Hammersly, 2006; Tett, 2015), although the shortage of time in empirical data gathering and our exploration of specific issues limits any claims we might make for our ability to induct perfectly. We have sought to produce data that has validity and not reliability. This may sound strange, but all we mean is that we seek to capture the subjective reality as perceived by those we have studied, rather than any objective reality, in order to understand and explain behaviour rather than measure it in any objective way. A reason for this methodology is, as Harari states, because 'the subjective is something that exists depending upon the consciousness and beliefs of a single individual' (Harari, 2011, p. 131). Thus, the role of qualitative researchers is to discover how people construct reality in their individual heads and share these constructions socially between them (Harari, 2011; Tett, 2015). Understanding the tacit knowledge that enables people to cooperate, collaborate and pool capital, that is central to our empirical research is difficult to define:

> tacit knowledge has an important cognitive dimension. It consists of mental models, beliefs and perspectives so ingrained that we take them for granted, and therefore cannot easily articulate them.
>
> (Nonaka, 1991, p. 98)

Yet as we have seen from the work of Rose (2011) and Goodhart (2017) and in plain sight with the Brexit vote, perceptions of reality clearly matter as much as any objective measures. As Tett says 'if there is one thing that the Great Financial Crisis showed, it is that finance and economics are not just about numbers' (Tett, 2015, p. 1). Again, to cite Harari, the rationale for this approach is because 'though the imagined order exists only in our minds, it can be woven into the material reality around us' (Harari, p. 127). Each of us, as individuals, is both responding to and contributing to, through our behaviour, different mythical constructions of contemporary reality. It is the interaction of those constructions with others that both determines objective measurable behaviours and the outcomes that determine future beliefs. Thus models of change are implicit and/or explicit attempts to construct alternative realities (Collins, 2018).

Stories and metaphors provide the social glue that binds people to places, groups and identities. They provide both explanations and catalysts for social behaviour. This is true for places (Whyte, 1943; Tett, 2015) and organisations (Collins, 2018, 2021). Indeed, both Gladwell (2005) and Tett (2015) show, through multiple examples, how numbers focus the mind upon the what but miss out on the breadth of the why that stories convey (Collins, 2018; Easterby-Smith et al., 2018). Whilst their work is designed to provide popular access to relationships between cognition and behaviour, the success of writers such as Gladwell and Tett not only underlines the importance and interest in storytelling, but the power of those who tell them to capture attention. If 'the inter-subjective is something that exists within the communication network linking the subjective consciousness of many individuals' (Harari, p. 132), it is stories that provide a window through which researchers, such as ourselves may view, analyse and interpret it. Mckenzie states that 'we learn to make sense of what sometimes seems senseless through narratives' (McKenzie, 2015). As Tett (2015) says 'these narratives should not be read as fully finished tales of "success" or "failure," but just as snapshots of stories that are still in progress' (Tett, 2015, p. 3). Finally, McKenzie says that 'it is much easier and more interesting to listen to their story from the very beginning and see where it goes' (Mckenzie, 2015).

Any method of collecting data about how and why choices are made by individuals and groups is, at least in part, a study of power with all the difficulties and barriers that it poses. Saunders argues that 'the one technique which appears to offer the best chance for overcoming this difficulty is itself probably the most awkward to use in the analysis of political power, and this is participant-observation' (Saunders, 1979, p. 348). Participant-observation is useful for linking actions to stories and their meanings and can be useful in making the implicit explicit (Nonaka, 1991), but cannot in itself easily explain the values driving behaviour. Anthropologists often overcome this through immersing themselves in communities of study for long periods of time. However, a more commonly used means of triangulating data in social research, to increase validity, are interviews (Arksey & Knight, 1999). Yet, As Clyde-Mitchell has argued:

> using interviews has the disadvantage that the fieldworker becomes aware of the characteristics of the network only from the point of view of his respondent and is, therefore, precluded from checking the actual quality of the relationships ... In many ways, however, the most reliable and adequate information is likely to be obtained through direct observation
>
> (Clyde-Mitchell, 1969)

As all police officers know, there is a difference between what people say about what they do and what they actually do! The difficulty of interviews is that they can lack validity (Burton, Sheather & Roberts, 2003). Hammersley makes this point clearer when stating that to

> rely on what people say about what they believe and do, without also observing what they do, is to neglect the complex relationship between attitudes and behaviour, just as to rely on observation without also talking to people in order to understand their perspectives is to risk misinterpreting their actions
>
> (Hammersley, 1992)

Thus, as noted, we have triangulated data from interviews with data gained from participant-observation.

In order to manage the balance between being true to an interpretivist paradigm (Smith, 1994; Cresswell, 2007, 2014) and the realities of constraints upon the time available to spend researching, we chose to use semi-structured interviews. Thus, enabling us, as researchers, to define the main themes of conversations, but allowing interviewees to frame how those themes are represented, accorded value and described as stories and accounts. In this way, topics were defined, described and attributed value by the subjects to a greater degree than the researcher and it was these definitions and meanings that were as interesting as the descriptions themselves since they signpost the cognitive maps that underlie and drive observable behaviour. This is a tricky balance where we as researchers have tried to ensure that conversation flows as naturally as possible. We have used open questions to pull, rather than push, themes and a mixture of non-specific curiosity and humour to enable interviewees to control how the conversation ebbed and flowed when new issues and information were introduced. We probed for depth, breadth and to check understanding, but tried to avoid imposing our values and meanings.

Each of us has been situated within the case studies as a participant-observer in one way or another. We have observed the actions people have taken compared to the claims that they have made. Claims have been double checked where possible. Whilst we have observed who tends to use more bombastic language and overstate compared to those who prefer to understate. Language constraints have affected our understanding of two of the case studies and with our explicit use of the Rose model (2011), we are not naive enough to think that our cultural preconceptions have not influenced our interpretations either. Nonetheless, the fact that we have been immersed in the cases has provided a level of insight, access and understanding that would otherwise be absent. It is this richness that provides colour and texture to the studies that both provide more compelling stories, but more importantly, capture the perspectives, motivations and capabilities of the subjects under study.

Adam worked closely with Boulevard as they sought to diversify their business model. He also previously was closely connected to the key actors in the Jacksonville case, where he lived and was able to observe and discuss the issues at hand as they emerged. Similarly, Andy has worked as a consultant coordinator of an MBA programme in Cluj for seven years. Our original research cases were to include a newly forming mutual bank in the UK, where a wave of new community-owned banks is planned, as part of a conscious effort to expand the Preston model. However, a combination of the pandemic and the ill health of key actors meant that there simply wasn't the time to do the case justice. Thus, we selected EduCab instead, based initially upon Andy's connection to its founder. This, like much qualitative research (Hammersley, 2006; Collis & Hussey, 2014), clearly makes it quite impossible for us to make any claims to the objectivity of our research. However, on the other hand, the role of participant-observer has allowed us to triangulate data from interviews, such that we can make use of experiential knowledge to compare words with actions and consequently have greater confidence in the validity of subsequent research findings (Whyte, 1943).

We do wish to add at this juncture that, at the time of the writing of this work, there were severe limitations placed upon us and our ability to gather information in a first-hand manner. The impact of restrictions flowing from the COVID-19 pandemic has impacted heavily upon our research. Many interviews were conducted using technology platforms, such as Microsoft Teams, Skype, Google Chat and phone calls, because travel and social-distancing rules often made face-to-face research unrealistic. Although consistently semi-structured in nature and organised around themes to enable interviewees to frame issues, we recognise that Covid restrictions have limited much of this research.

All case studies used a mix of face-to-face and remote interviewing and, despite the impact of Covid, were supported by observations and by the authors familiarity with the case studies prior to the research. So, whilst observational techniques were limited during the pandemic, previous engagement has provided a greater degree of confidence in our analysis than might have otherwise not been the case. Inevitably, this raises questions of bias, but given that the research has been focused upon a course of events that dates back a considerable way prior to the pandemic, this is merely an admission of our previously stated participant-observer role that McKenzie (2015) described as an insider–outsider.

We were both insiders and outsiders, but as McKenzie (2015) notes and we concur:

> I would not have been allowed to collect them [stories and accounts] and represent them here without my relationships with these people and the mutual respect and knowledge that I have built up over many years. Academic researchers have often been accused of being distant, or only speaking to each other - this book is none of those things.
>
> (McKenzie, 2015, p. 4)

We navigated our way through the case studies, usually beginning with purposive sampling (Collis & Hussey, 2014; Sekaran & Bougie, 2016), through persons known to us and then began a process of snowball sampling where one contact point guided us towards others. Clearly, this created issues of potential reliance upon gatekeepers. However, our existing relationships with the case studies and the actors within them mitigated against over-reliance. Furthermore, we have deliberately sought out a multiplicity of people, organisations and opinions in our search for validity. Rather than take a purist view 'A more judicious stance must be to conceptualize community power structures as variable configurations over time and place, amenable to study only through a plurality of methods capable of assessing diverse dimensions of community power' (Knoke, 1990, p. 124).

Whilst we did participate at events, gatherings and online forums our participation was determined by our research interests (Gans, 1969). In our efforts to capture and guide conversations towards our areas of interest, we acknowledge that we have lost some ethnographic purity. However, we hope that the insights revealed sufficiently outweigh the loss of methodological purity for the reader to forgive us. Despite the difficulties flowing from researching during a pandemic, we believe that our research is a valid reflection of the perceptions of those under study.

Having gathered data, we have applied Wolcott's (1994 [italic in original]) timeless method of developing layers of understanding from the empirical to the critical and the abstract:

> *Description* addresses the question, 'What is going on here?' Data consist of observations made by the researcher and/or reported to the researcher by others.
>
> *Analysis* addresses the identification of essential features and the systematic description of inter-relationships among them – in short, how things work ...
>
> *Interpretation* addresses the processual questions of meanings and contexts: 'How does it all mean?' 'What is to be made of it all?'

Ultimately, we have woven the patterns in the data collected into stories which remain valid representations but are also engaging to the reader. As Collins (2018, 2021) notes, whilst storytelling is inherently unreliable, they do provide meaning and purpose to the social world. Thus, whilst we accept that our account of the case studies is just that: an account; this does not make it a work of fiction. Furthermore, given the importance of relationships, networks and community in this study, it will become clear that stories, accounts of activities, ascribed meanings and constructions of reality are central to actors' behaviour and the resilience of the social worlds that they inhabit. As such the methodology described and detailed in this chapter has provided a robust means of describing, analysing and interpreting data thereby enabling us to induct valid insights from the case studies that are worthy of further exploration elsewhere.

The Next Step

The past, as it is often said, is a prologue. The preceding chapters laid out the basis for this new book and the existing literature with respect to models of economic development. This chapter, moving from the theoretical to the substantive, has laid out the basis upon which, and questions relevant to, the four case studies that form the empirical basis of the book. The next step in this journey will detail these four case studies. This deep dive into the substance will be followed by an examination of the patterns and meaning that emerge from these different examples, such that their stories amount to more than the sum of their parts.

References

Arksey, H. & Knight, P., *Interviewing for Social Scientists.* London: Sage, 1999.

Baxter, P. & Jack, S., 'Qualitative Case Study Methodology: Study Design and Implementation for Novice Researchers', *The Qualitative Report* 13(4): 544–559, 2008.

Bloodworth, J., *Hired: Six Months Undercover in Low-Wage Britain.* London: Atlantic Books, 2018.

Burton, S., Sheather, S. & Roberts, J., 'Reality or Perception?', *Journal of Service Research* 5(4): 292–302, 2003.

Clyde-Mitchell, J., *Social Networks in Urban Situations: Analyses of Personal Relationships in Central African Towns.* Manchester: University Press, 1969.

Collins, D., *Stories for Management Success: The Power of Talk in Organizations.* London: Routledge, 2018.

Collins, D., *The Organizational Storytelling Workbook: How to Harness this Powerful Communication and Management Tool.* London: Routledge, 2021.

Collis, J. & Hussey, R., *Business Research*. Basingstoke, Hampshire: Palgrave Macmillan, 2014.

Cresswell, J., *Research Design* (4th ed.). London: Sage, 2014.

Creswell, J., *Qualitative Inquiry & Research Design*. Thousand Oaks, CA: Sage Publications, 2007.

Easterby-Smith, M., Jaspersen, L., Thorpe, R. & Valizade, D., *Management and Business Research*. London: Sage, 2018.

Gans, H., *The Urban Villagers: Group and Class in the Life of Italian-Americans*. London: Free Press, 1969.

Gartell, D. & Gartell, J., 'Positivism in Sociological Practice: 1967–1990', *Canadian Review of Sociology* 33(2), 1996.

Gladwell, M., *Blink: The Power of Thinking Without Thinking*. New York: Back Bay Book, 2005.

Goodhart, D., *The Road to Somewhere*. London: Hurst and Company, 2017.

Gray, D., *Doing Research in the Real World*. London: Sage, 2017.

Hammersley, M., 'Ethnography: Problems and Prospects', *Ethnography and Education* 1(1): 3–14, 1992.

Hammersley, M., *What's Wrong with Ethnography?* London: Routledge, 1992.

Hammersley, M. & Atkinson, P., *Ethnography: Principles in Practice*. London: Routledge, 1983.

Harari, Y. N., *Sapiens: A Brief History of Humankind*. London: Vintage, 2011.

Knoke, D., *Political Networks: The Structural Perspective*. Cambridge: University Press, 1990.

Kvale, S. & Brinkman, S., *Interviews: Learning the Craft of Research Interviewing*. London: Sage, 2009.

Larrain, J., *The Concept of Ideology*. London: Hutchinson, 1979.

McKenzie, L., *Getting By: Estates, Class and Culture in Austerity Britain*. Bristol: Policy Press, 2015.

Newby, H., *Green and Pleasant Land: Social Change in Rural England*. Hounslow, Middlesex: Wildwood, 1985.

Newby, H., *The Countryside in Question*. London: Hutchinson, 1988.

Nonaka, I., 'The Knowledge-Creating Company', *Harvard Business Review*, Nov–Dec, 1991.

Rose, C., *What Makes People Tick: The Hidden World of Settler, Prospectors and Pioneers*. Leicester: Matador, 2011.

Saunders, P., *Urban Politics: A Sociological Interpretation*. London: Penguin, 1979.

Sekaran, U. & Bougie, R., *Research Methods for Business: A Skills Building Approach*. London: Wiley, 2016.

Smith, S., *The Philosophy of Social Science: An Introduction*. Cambridge: University Press, 1994.

Taylor, A. & Bronstone, A., *People, Place and Global Order: Foundations for a Networked Political Economy*. London: Routledge, 2019.

Tett, G., *The Silo Effect: The Peril of Expertise and the Promise of Breaking Down Barriers*. London: Simon & Schuster, 2015.

Whyte, W., *Street Corner Society: The Social Structure of an Italian Slum*. Chicago: University of Chicago Press, 1943.

Wolcott, H., *Transforming Qualitative Data*. London: Sage, 1994.

5

ZOOMING FROM SOMEWHERE TO ANYWHERE

Case Studies

Introduction

The goal of this work is to go beyond the snippets and explore in much greater detail, using case studies, the relationships between people and places that have enabled some to thrive and others not.

The case studies described below include economic development projects for the cities of Cluj (Romania) and Jacksonville (Florida, USA) as well as the community development NGO EduCab (Romania) and the environmental leadership activities at Boulevard Brewing Company in Kansas City (MO). The first section will include the activities in Cluj and Jacksonville with the common thread being that these are case studies of place-based communities where government played and continues to play a substantial role in the processes described in the case study. The second set of case studies is of organisations or 'entities' – Boulevard Brewery and EduCab. One is a for-profit entity and the other is not, but what connects both of these entities is that neither are geographic locations administered by government organisations.

DOI: 10.4324/9781003145295-5

Government-Sponsored Case Studies

In this section, the case studies relating to developments in Cluj (Romania) and North Jacksonville (Florida) are combined. The binding factor between these two examples is that they were and, in the case of Cluj, continue to be, driven in some part with the assistance of the local government.

CASE STUDY 1: The Transformation of Cluj

In the Beginning

Cluj has gone from a large provincial city with problems to a fast-growing engine of growth that is pulling in investment and tourists from around the world. The city dates back to Roman times, but was significantly developed by German merchants during the twelfth century. A part of the Transylvania region, after the fall of the Hapsburg Empire in 1918, it joined Wallachia and Moldavia to form the basis of modern Romania, leaving behind a large Hungarian minority in Transylvania and Cluj.

It is easy to forget that during the late 1990s and early noughties, before Romania joined the EU, Cluj was at the centre of concerns that Romania could collapse into another Yugoslavia due to tensions with its Hungarian minority (Gallagher, 2005). At a wedding party of two Hungarian Romanians in 1997 Cluj, this writer recalls Hungarian students putting lighters on the hair of his Romanian wife. Nothing was more symbolic of such tensions during the 1990s than the infamous nationalist Mayor George Funar adding the word Napoca to the city's name to emphasise its Daco-Roman origins.

Today, the population of Cluj is rising fast and although some reports show only an increase from just under 302,000 in 2010 to just under 308,000 in 2020 (World Population Review, 2021), others estimate it at 429,000 (Primaria Cluj-Napoca, 2019). Most people agree that the actual numbers are far higher. This discrepancy with respect to population is partly because of a large student population which is often registered elsewhere and partly because of the number of people travelling into the city to work from outside. Whatever the actual number, that the city has flourished and grown is not in doubt. Dragan (2018) reported that by 2017 rents in Cluj were 3% higher than the capital city of Bucharest and the number of new company registrations grew by 50% between

2016 and 2017, compared to 23% in Bucharest, whilst the news website *Romania-Insider* (2019) reported that, in 2019, salaries in Cluj were 7% higher than the national average. As Deputy CEO of Banca Transilvania (BT), Tibi Moisa says 'Cluj is growing and increasing its population. It is growing fast from outside, acting as a magnet – an emergent model'. The former Vice Rector (Pro-Vice Chancellor) of the largest university in Cluj and leading university in Romania, Universitatea Babes Bolyai (UBB), Prof. Mihaela Lutas, puts it like this:

> 15 years ago Cluj was less attractive than other cities due to low levels of investment in Cluj. Big companies like Nokia and Emerson, the first generation of the multinationals, transmitted that we can collaborate with the local authority and have skilled labour – 'a trusted place to invest'. Alongside multinational companies were small businesses; call centres, outsourced IT companies, started contacting universities and local authorities and transmitted the idea that everyone can find what they seek here. Small companies in financial services, healthcare and education services were the start.

Professor Lutas goes on to say that there are four factors behind the success of Cluj: economic, political, education and cultural.

The city has become a hub of technology, finance and engineering businesses. The technology and engineering businesses are, especially and to a large extent, providing goods and services to global markets outside Romania and sucking in capital. Capital that BT, headquartered in Cluj and the dominant bank for both business and personal banking, first in the city and now in the country, is recycling into the Romanian economy. In tandem with the growth of entrepreneurial business and inward investment has been the spectacular rise of culture, particularly festival culture as a form of social entrepreneurship. Most cultural events in Cluj have been sponsored by local businesses, the accumulated effect of which has been to nurture an ecosystem that has created mutually reinforcing positive feedback loops. As the business grows, Cluj grows its appeal to educated employees and a positive cycle is set in motion that is now self-sustaining.

That Cluj has developed a successful culture of entrepreneurial enterprise that has transformed the city is not in doubt. The question is how did this come about and what can we learn from the experience? To answer this we shall first dive into the key sectors that have driven this story and then examine the role of entrepreneurs, public authorities, universities and other key actors in moving the city beyond individual and sectoral stories of success to create a wider ecosystem of socio-economic transformation.

Financial Services

Central to the post-communist story of Cluj has to be the rise of BT. Started in three apartments in Cluj by a group of friends in 1993, the bank is now the largest commercial bank in Romania with its headquarters remaining in the city. However, in the early days, it was far from clear that BT would be the success story that it has become. Shortly after BT was formed, two other, pre-existing, private financial institutions from Cluj collapsed under the weight of their own hubris. Dacia Felix Bank floundered on the back of bad debts and Caritas was a classic pyramid-based ponzi scheme. Together, it is estimated that Dacia Felix and Caritas circulated around one-third of Romania's money supply in the first half of the 1990s (Petean, 2006). Caritas collapsed in 1994 and Dacia Felix finally went bankrupt in 1996. Despite the shockwave that such failures sent out and the long shadow that they still cast over bankers, BT felt confident enough to list on the Bucharest stock exchange in 1997.

One of the founders, current Chairman Horia Ciorcila, and Deputy CEO Tibi Moisa both agree that not being in the capital city of Bucharest (where almost all other banks in Romania are based), has been key to their growth. Horia says that coming from Cluj meant that they were 'not contaminated by other bankers', whilst Tibi claims that 'the distance from Bucharest meant it was not eclipsed by it'. A number of smaller firms in insurance, brokerage and advisory have grown out of the activities of former employees of the bank which in turn have provided staff for international investors in what has become a micro-ecosystem of financial services spinning around the knowledge that grew out of BT. To underline the importance of BT and its surrounding ecosystem to the city, the Mayor's office estimated that, in 2019, 45% of the city's workforce was employed in finance and insurance (Primaria Cluj-Napoca, 2019). As Nonaka (1991) puts it 'Tacit knowledge is also deeply rooted in action and in an individual's commitment to a specific context' (p. 98). BT seems to have successfully aligned commitment to the city with commitment to the bank.

Even today, far more than its pro rata share of loans and investments are made in Cluj by BT, relative to its population size, compared to anywhere else in Romania. BT has had an enabling and catalyst role for an entrepreneurial wave. As Tibi says:

> You can measure this quantitatively. The availability of financial services was a big advantage. In the credit committee we all live in Cluj. The biggest community involvement budget is for Cluj. When BT took over the 3rd largest bank in Moldova the assets were less than the value of assets in just their Cluj branch. It is out of proportion, given the size of the city. The former employees of the bank do create a spillover effect. The same at IT companies, like Evozon, formed by employees of earlier IT companies. Positive feedback loops were unintentionally created in both cases.

Even from the outside, the impact of BT on Cluj is understood:

> BT was key to Cluj growth. 'BT asimilat cu Clujul' [BT is associated with Cluj]. They sponsor lots in Transylvania. They are fuelling finance for the city. Sponsorship, as well as loans and have created feedback loops.
>
> (Lutas, 2021)

In addition to its role as a recycler of finance, the bank has used programmes such as its entrepreneurs club to deliberately cultivate entrepreneurialism as a culture. Clearly, and in BT's own self-interest, any discussion with BT managers quickly reveals that this is widely felt to be part of their mission, beyond the bottom line, to contribute to Romania's development.

Information Technology

The IT sector took off during the noughties, but exploded in size, value and importance during the last decade. International companies have invested in Cluj, but, until recently, the sector was dominated by home grown Cluj companies such as iQuest, Softvision, Fortech, Arobs, 3Pillar Global, Brinel, Pitech Plus, Yonder and more recently Evozon, all of which have been joined by companies such as ISDC and Endava, which had headquarters elsewhere but whose operations were driven from Cluj. Some of the early starters, such as Yonder and ISDC, have sold out to larger firms. However, until recently, all were founded upon the idea of outsourcing software development from developed economies to take advantage of lower labour costs in Cluj and arbitrage the difference. So spectacular has their success been that the idea of selling coding hours (as outsourced software development is often called in Cluj) no longer makes economic sense. Demand for software developers is so high that the upward pressure upon wages means that the simple arbitrage model no longer makes sense. As a result, companies have either had to scale rapidly, such as Endava, or sell out to larger groups that have already achieved global scale, such as Softvision, Pitech Plus and Brinel have done. Companies that hold onto their independence, such as Arobs, Fortech and Evozon, are having to find ways to add value or differentiate themselves, such as developing their own software products.

Despite the strategic challenges facing the sector, there is no doubt that the new capital flowing in through acquisitions and the listing of Endava on the US Stock Exchange has only served to fuel the engine of a booming city economy.

It is not only individually competitive businesses that have driven Cluj forward though. The annual Techsylvania event is an example of how IT has become an ecosystem, rather than a business, whose spillover effects have been a catalyst for wider transformation. Originally an event for IT companies to meet and invite guests from outside to showcase their talent, Techsylvania claimed that for their 2020 event they attracted 4,000 participants. Techsylvania is now a major event for both deal-making and start-ups seeking angel investors. Whilst anecdotal evidence from conversations with technology entrepreneurs indicate that they do use the various cultural festivals as platforms to entertain clients from outside Romania, as will be illustrated later, IT companies have supported the cultural life of the city. During the pandemic, for example, Fortech has won plaudits for its support of the healthcare sector in the city (foretch.ro, 2021). Furthermore, as IT companies move up the value chain, they are pioneering new ideas in the city. For example, Pony, an hourly car rental business, controlled with digital technology, was born out of a conversation in an MBA classroom and launched first in Cluj before being rolled out nationally. Furthermore, IT entrepreneurs have collaborated, sometimes explicitly, by way of the formation of clusters. Other times, collaboration has taken place implicitly to support ventures of common interest such as the informal school of IT, to retrain people to work in IT, or in sponsoring employees to undertake the locally delivered British University MBA programme. (See more below.)

Energy and Infrastructure

Less focused upon the production of energy, Cluj entrepreneurs have tended to focus upon designing, producing and providing the systems architecture for energy and communications. Key companies in this sector are Electroglobal, Energobit and Electrogrup (which, in a reflection of the previous sentence, recently changed their name to E-Infra). E-Infra went from putting up the first mobile phone towers to manufacturing electrical power equipment, then branched into constructing and maintaining wind turbines across Europe and more recently launched new businesses in fibre optic cabling and gas distribution. In 2018, the company considered an IPO and appears to have only been dissuaded by underlying market conditions. E-Infra now employs approximately 600 people. Electroglobal streamlines industrial processes through its electrical automation equipment. Started in 2004, the company now employs over 100 people. Energobit manufactures electrical power equipment, such as substations and transformers, for clients across the world now. Bought back from a Polish investment fund by the original owners, the company has refocused upon its core electrical engineering capabilities and employs around 700 people.

With common backgrounds in former state-owned enterprises, the entrepreneurs behind each of these businesses have sought to use their core competencies in electrical engineering and leverage them into higher value, often virgin, marketplaces. A combination of technical expertise and their ability to connect to decision-makers in new economic spaces, therefore, is what has driven their businesses forward. As these companies have entered international markets or sought to partner with multinational enterprises they have acted as connection points between the local and the global.

The arrival of major global engineering enterprises, such as Emerson, Bosch, Nokia and Bombardier have served to both modernise an existing engineering trend and provide professional training to deepen a talent pool that was increasingly globally skilled, but carried lower employment costs. The collapse of Nokia globally led to the closure of their Cluj operation also. However, working with them influenced the founders of companies like Evozon (in IT) and left new competencies in digital engineering. Emerson has grown to over 2,000 employees now, manufacturing machine tools for global markets and providing global shared services centres, whilst Bosch and Bombardier and Emerson have brought in world-class manufacturing systems, such that Cluj managers are being benchmarked to their German, Japanese and US colleagues. To do this, however, they have drawn heavily upon skilled employees, particularly the universities.

Culture

Cluj, with its universities and its status as the largest city in Transylvania, has always had an important role in national and international culture. From the Transylvanian School of Art to theatre and opera, Cluj is blessed with having both Romanian and Hungarian language institutions. The city has 17 museums, eight cinemas, five theatres and five public art galleries (Primaria Cluj-Napoca, 2019). However, in the new millennium Cluj has emerged as a centre of cultural expression, especially with its numerous festivals. Perhaps the first festival to attract significant international attention was the Transylvania International Film Festival (TIFF) which has screenings across the city for a week every summer as film fans pour into the city from all over Europe. Even bigger in recent times have been the Untold and Electric Castle Festivals. Untold is now the largest music festival in Europe, attracting over 330,000 electronic music fans in 2017 (Pop, 2017). Electric Castle is another, more diverse, contemporary music festival that takes place at Banffy Castle (just outside Cluj) that mixes music, art and technology. In 2019, 231,000 people attended the festival (Electric Castle, 2021). The city almost doubles in size for both Untold and Electric Castle and finding accommodation becomes quite impossible. On a smaller scale, there are book festivals, jazz in the park, comedy and Hungarian and German cultural events which cover the squares and streets of the city centre. Through the summer it often seems as if there is a new festival every week.

The success of these events has occurred not because of public subsidy, but instead because of the entrepreneurial spirit of their founders, a pool of both young students and older culturally engaged citizens and, critically, the sponsorship and support of local enterprises, such as BT, which have tied their marketing to the city to create an emergent Cluj identity. That identity is at once cultured, digital, historic and contemporary. There are many university towns around the world but few have experienced the rapid cultural growth of Cluj. The key in Cluj has been the convergence of interests of local entrepreneurs who have supported and sustained cultural emergence. As the British Counsel for Transylvania Shajjad put it:

> BT has a drive to make Cluj feel like home. Cluj has a special spot for them. They sponsored Untold, for example, which brought in 45 million Euro last year. They supported the TIFF and many others.

Equally, Arobs has sponsored the Cluj marathon for many years and NTT Data has sponsored one of the two big Cluj football teams. In time, such entrepreneurs, especially in IT, have come to realise that nurturing the cultural life of the city is important as part of their employer branding. In a tight labour market, the ability to attract skilled talent into the city has become essential.

Beyond cultural events, Cluj has also developed a thriving civic culture around social engagement. Several NGOs have achieved systemic change beyond the city and have become templates for elsewhere. NGOs setting national benchmarks and leading the way forward include the children's cancer charity Little People and the social action NGO Beard Brothers. Little People have pioneered care of children with cancer, providing psycho-social care, postoperative programmes and networks of interaction based upon a mixture of volunteering and sophisticated fundraising from within Romania. Prior to Little People almost all charitable organisations were dependent upon donations, grants and financing from outside Romania. Little People, which is still based in Cluj, set the standard for how to finance a charity from within Romania. Beard Brothers is interesting because it is really no more than a group of young executives who have banded together utilising digital networks to connect and make a difference to the community they live in. From organising community taxis, renovating a floor of a hospital and planting trees, Beard Brothers have demonstrated the value of giving time to others in need. In what Trompenaars and Hampden-Turner (1998) described as the second most individualistic country on earth, this is no small achievement and the organisation has proliferated across Romania. The result in Cluj is an engaged citizenry, especially amongst younger adults, that has a sense of agency which is less true in most other cities in Romania.

Clusters

Lecuta (2016) notes that according to Michael E. Porter 'clusters are geographic concentrations of interconnected companies, often SMEs and research institutions in a particular field' in view to increase the growth and competitiveness within a region, involving also public administration, banks and catalyst institutions'. The formation of associations of businesses, which are often market competitors, to discuss topics of interest and combine resources to address common problems has become a hallmark of Cluj.

Although memories are sketchy, several people suggested that the first cluster was the furniture cluster, bringing together firms utilising the timber resources around Cluj. However, the number of clusters has grown dramatically to include agriculture, food, IT, energy and construction and, most recently, an education cluster. Perhaps the best known are the two IT clusters, which came to public prominence during discussions to create a business park specifically designed and equipped for digital business.

Emila Botezan, the head of the International Affairs & Foreign Investment Department Cluj City Hall, says that clusters are based upon the idea described by 'Calin Hintea [Dean of Political Science] who says if people talk it becomes a strategic thing for a community. This they did with the clusters'. However, if they go beyond talking and co-invest in projects, defined by a common place, the idea of a community of interest starts to assume an architecture of interest. Indeed, Leucuta (2016) argues that 'clusters are an important part of innovation eco-systems'. This has not been limited to formal clusters alone, as the story of Transylvania Executive Education (detailed below) demonstrates.

Both Lecuta (2016) and Emila Botezan described how collaboration between clusters, Universities and public authorities can be transformational. In Cluj, cluster formation has been very much a bottom-up process driven by entrepreneurs who know one another, with the universities and City Hall joining either later or as momentum is developed. Prof. Lutas says that 'people are familiar with the local environment and have a can-do mentality. They created clusters in IT, furniture, agriculture, etc., which became models for the rest of the country'. The success of the clusters in developing local food systems, influencing the growth and content of university computer science teaching, vocational training resources and infrastructure planning has caused the City Hall to proactively drive cluster formation, assuming a central role in the formation of the new education cluster. Further, City Hall has sought to formally connect clusters in Cluj with similar clusters elsewhere in the EU and supported the formation of a cluster of clusters to coordinate common interests and maximise impact, effectively nesting overlapping clusters within the city's socio-economic infrastructure. Dutch Counsel Wouter Reijers claims that 'in Cluj there exists a 'triple helix' [which he explained to mean when government, business and universities work together] cooperation is working well', which is something that Lecuta (2016) notes as central to the functional success of Romanian clusters and people interviewed suggest was learned in Cluj.

City Hall

Moving past the divisive nationalist rhetoric of former Mayor George Funar has been key for Cluj. The arrival of Emil Boc as the mayor released the city from self-imposed isolation. Prof. Lutas describes the change as follows:

> After twelve years of Funar came Boc, as Mayor, and it was a major switch. A turning point for attracting investors. Coke decided to come. The City Hall simply behaved normally (unlike the past), as they should. University, business and city are now developing strategies for the city. The City Hall worked with people like business and Regia de Apa [water company] and banks to develop infrastructure.

Shajjad Rizvi, the British Counsel to Transylvania, also commented that:

> Boc has made the right moves. He is popular locally and with expats. Their international department is key and has existed since Boc started. Amelia Botezan is in charge, with a team of 5. It didn't exist in other cities and was a deliberate effort to brand and market the city. There is a constant flow of international delegations.

Wouter Reijers, the Dutch Counsel for Transylvania, similarly describes the impact of the Mayor's office:

> Mr. Boc, as Mayor, is better at pushing forward cooperation. He has made changes, such as creating an international desk, which is very proactive. The business community is active and the Universities stepped in as they saw there was something to gain. More investment led to more international business clubs, who were all very positive about Cluj, which, of course, led to increased interest in the city.

Even people inside City Hall acknowledge that many of the initiatives that have flourished in Cluj were not their idea. Shajjad notes that 'City Hall is piggybacking upon the networks of older people, like Teo Muresan [*founder of E-Infra*] ... and newer people like Techsylvania'. Rather than see this as a negative, Emilia Botezan, who runs the international relations office at the City Hall, sees these ideas as both reacting to emergent developments and trying to foster overlapping ecosystems.

The international relations office of the City Hall is interesting in itself as it was the first such initiative in Romania. It started off for Emilia Botezan in 2001 as a lowly paid job of writing letters to partner cities around Europe as part of a mass media department. In 2004, when Boc was elected Mayor, Botezan switched to helping companies invest in the city, about which she knew little. As she says 'I needed help, so I reached out to local companies and Universities'. As the global economic crisis hit in 2009, she was asked to take control of both the international relations and media departments. She has used this role to encourage industry cluster initiatives within the city to develop and overlap, to connect into initiatives and developments elsewhere in Europe and within the

EU and to connect entrepreneurial citizens directly to the Mayor and his policymaking team. From 2010, the international relations team tried to understand business and their needs more. Botezan states that 'we took an idea from the Dutch community for Meet the Mayor, a very informal exchange, and it has grown from 15 to 40 and now more leaders of business, education, culture and so on, as a regular event'. The result, Amelia believes, is 'a more outward facing City Hall that mediates relationships between business, public authorities and international programmes'.

In 2015, Emilia's team was instrumental in the formation of an NGO to coordinate the overlap of the various clusters and it has been central to the formation of the latest cluster in education, which is a deliberate effort to connect educational providers to the future needs of the city. This came about following a meeting between Mayor Boc and the Chair of the European Committee of the Regions Marco Marsilo. The meeting was engineered by Marsilo's Chef de Cabinet, who told Emilia Botezan that his boss liked Mayor Boc and would like to talk about doing more together in education.

Emlia's team also organised the EU's Start-Up Europe Summit with 20 other European cities, focused upon new digital businesses, it was one of the more successful events of Romania's Presidency of the EU. Emilia says that 'alongside Valencia, Cluj shone' There is certainly considerable respect for the efforts and achievements of the City Hall amongst business, University and expat community leaders. Wouter Reijers says:

> The city hall has been active on an EU level to access funds directly. It has not waited for the national government, which possibly annoyed the government in Bucharest, but has been effective. Mr. Boc is also an EU Rapporteur. The town hall is not a one man show. In other cities it often is. The mayor has a broad, technocratic and non-political, team, which is unusual.

None of the people interviewed were aware of a specific model of development being followed by City Hall or by other actors and there is certainly no policy to recycle money locally.

Universities

Cluj has 11 universities (five private and six State) and, although numbers vary, the student population of Cluj is somewhere between 80,000

(Primaria Cluj-Napoca, 2019) and 100,000 (Clujbusiness.ro). Emilia Botezan is clear on the importance of the universities to the transformation of Cluj when she states that:

> The Universities were essential, as they have big expertise and provide a young workforce who want to settle in Cluj. The universities always played a key role and the Mayor and my department facilitated common cause.

More succinctly, Prof. Mihaela Lutas said that 'the universities pull talent towards Cluj' Certainly, it is true that, as Prof. Lutas says, 'universities, the State ones, modernised their curricula and created specialisations in foreign languages, so labour was language skilled'. Both senior academics and business leaders acknowledge that early on they both realised the dependence of each upon the other, where the universities serve as a basis for a supply of skilled labour and knowledge and the businesses for sponsorship and graduate employment. At this time (2021), both universities and businesses were hungry for international partnerships to enable growth. The universities formed partnerships to attract EU and other funds which, whilst often successful, sometimes created strange legacies such as a partnership between UBB and Nottingham Trent University to form a business school, as a European TEMPUS project. The Business Faculty still operates (although no longer as a partnership with Nottingham Trent University) in parallel with a pre-existing business school at UBB. As both parties grew and entrepreneurialism, as a culture, accelerated, after the financial crisis, the need to develop higher value competencies necessary to fulfil international ambitions became both clearer and intertwined. As Prof. Mihaela Lutas says:

> There was a search to find partners and get models from the EU. You Andy [co-author] were part of this story. The involvement of business was vital for all universities as it opened us to the labour market.

To exploit the emerging richness of locally established networks, leaders were looking for ways to connect them to bigger, more developed, international networks of knowledge and opportunity. In 2013, during a business meeting between Tibi Mosia, as a rising star within BT (who is now

Deputy CEO), and the co-author of this work, Andrew Taylor, Tibi asked what I thought about the future of business education. I responded that:

> It's rather like airlines. Whilst it is nice to be Tarom (Romanian national carrier), to survive in the real world, they need to line up with a global brand like the Star Alliance, One World, or whatever and code share as the local partner. Business education is the same. It's going global. Even the biggest name business schools cannot afford to build campuses all over the world. They need local partners. As the market for business education becomes global some new brands will emerge that see the opportunity and some existing ones that fail to grasp the moment will decline.

Tibi smiled and said:

> I like what you say, please could you come and meet Vice-Rector Prof. Mihaela Lutas? We want to bring an international MBA to Cluj.

A not-for-profit foundation was formed as a partnership between UBB, BT and Electrogrup (later E-Infra) and in 2014 a contract was signed with the University of Hull to become an agent for their executive MBA. There were considerable doubts about the wisdom and viability of such a move amongst some university staff. However, the personal relationships between academics and business leaders, which were key to building confidence, were strong enough for the push of the business community to be given a chance. The foundation is currently running its seventh class and has over one hundred and forty students that are either studying, or have graduated, with the majority of students sponsored by local employers, mostly from the sectors described here, as they implicitly seek to share the costs of access to bringing global knowledge and skills with a fly-in faculty. Furthermore, the Board of the foundation has now been joined by the Vice-Rector of the Technical University, the General Manager (and alumni of the MBA programme) of Emerson, the Dutch and British Counsels to Transylvania and an alumni representative. Now pioneering executive programmes, the foundation continues to flourish as one of many nodes connecting local entrepreneurialism with wider global networks. This is a prime example of what Wouter Reijers has spoken of when he has asserted that 'Bucharest attracts people, as the capital city, and there are a lot of low-skilled people. Cluj, as a University city, has a higher level of average education. The pace is slower in Cluj and more oriented towards the west'.

Entrepreneurship

The sheer number of start-ups and events geared to encouraging and supporting new ventures is both testimony to the success of existing businesses and underlines a sense of the possibility that pervades conversations on the terraces of the city. Perhaps because, as noted earlier, the city was starved of outside investment for so long, space was created for local enterprises to take advantage of depressed wages for longer. Alternatively, perhaps the influence of the Universities as hubs of youth and creativity provided the fuel for driving change. Under Communism, engineering was a highly regarded field, so aligning that tradition with an emerging internet that enabled immediate access to global markets perhaps indicates that Cluj simply had the right conditions at the right time. Whatever the cause, entrepreneurialism has not only flourished, it has transformed the whole city. Within Cluj, there exists a high level of relational capital (Camagni, 2009). As Wouter Reijers puts it:

> There is a layer of people that are important and know each other well. It is to do with there being very many events and there is always the same group of people. 'This shortens the lines and makes things move faster'. This brings creativity and infrastructure to get idea's off the drawing board.

To explain this empirically and historically Prof. Lutas said that:

> People that changed Cluj were the shareholders of BT, people of her age, with the courage to change things. Prof. Puscas, Mr. Ciorcila, Teo Muresan, etc. Market trust was viable due to better business ethics. The cultural, religious and historical background is different in Transylvania. The influence of Calvinism.

She brought up 'the role of the diaspora. George Roth – the honorary Consul of Romania to Silicon Valley, the German diaspora, etc., all had a key role in bridging networks. International business clubs also provide consulting locally, which helps'. Emilia Botezan pointed to the scale of

Cluj as having a key role in creating and utilising relational capital when she said that 'the city is small enough for people to know each other, which is essential, but big enough to have the potential to grow'. Several people suggested that local entrepreneurialism in Cluj has resulted in higher-value jobs located within the city than if they had relied purely upon outside investment. As Shajjad Rizvi says:

> In Timisoara they developed a manufacturing hub, but the jobs are not well paid. Tech brings more jobs with better pay, leaving more money in the city than global manufacturing. The law on taxes (lower salary taxes on skilled IT roles) helped IT to flourish. The Universities are churning out good programmers, who are working for IT, when elsewhere they are waitresses. Iasi [another city in Romania] is following Cluj.

Without mention of relational or territorial capital, Botezan went on to say:

> People ask how to replicate the Cluj model. In every community there is the power to understand who they are, to think and to work together to go where they want. We have created a series of ecosystems. We didn't dream big; lots of small actions and were brave in a decent way.

There is absolutely no doubt that entrepreneurs in Cluj know each other, meet at events, clubs, restaurants and other locations on a regular basis. Whilst some are what Rose (2011) would describe as Prospectors, they all share at least enlightened self-interest in investing in the city. In the course of this research, all companies examined donated time, money or resources to one cause or another. Whilst their role in clusters, executive education and city planning indicates a level of familiarity that goes beyond cooperation to perhaps be thought of better as active collaboration. This, of course, does not mean that they all collaborate, or even like each other. Pentalnd (2013) says that the emergence of social learning happens when experience is shared as a form of questioning inquiry about existing assumptions:

> Decisions don't happen in a vacuum; the best ones rarely come from deep pondering in isolation. They happen when people learn

> from and draw on the experiences of others. In this process, success depends greatly on the quality of social exploration—and on whether your information and sources of ideas are diverse and independent.
>
> (Pentland, 2013, p. 7)

The collaboration of Cluj entrepreneurs might best be described as a means of providing depth to double-loop learning (Argyris, 1991) to find the sweet spot as a source of competitive advantage. As *de facto* Pioneers (Rose, 2011), they sought to develop sustainable networks around this 'edge' which would, as Tibi Mosia put it when defining the role of TEE, 'ensure Cluj survives as a centre of entrepreneurialism'. In doing so they sought to pool resources into a common space for several reasons. First, to gain access to greater resources than anyone either had or could access individually. The second reason is to share reputational risk. The third reason is to gain the scale to overcome the absence of the State as a central actor. The fourth reason is the belief that each of them would gain more, through the multiplier effect of impacts on employees, partners and customers, than could be gained by acting alone. This was based upon a shared sense of Double Loop learning amongst the private sector actors, that ironically, many senior academics found very difficult to accept. For many in the universities, public sector and beyond, change was to be feared, resisted, or when unavoidable to be evaluated in purely transactional terms – 'what's in for me'.

To avoid this mentality of holding the city's development within the simple box of Cynefin (Snowden, 2007), key private sector actors sought to bring outside actors to them that could use their knowledge/experience to gradually bring seemingly intractable complex problems into the complicated space. This was apparent when the founders of Evozon partnered with the Vienna-based marketing consultant, Iulian Padurariu, to form Pony, or the founders of TEE with Andrew Taylor to launch an executive MBA. This partnership had the dual effect of both making conceptual reach more achievable for local actors, such that global knowledge and standards became more accessible and local executives learned how to embrace double-loop learning to both ensure that the simple space was expanded. Fortunately, sufficient numbers of academics and managers, perhaps afraid of the past and given hope by the emergence of Mayor Boc, threw caution to the wind and supported entrepreneurial leadership. Network reach was gained through either international education, the migration trail of returning entrepreneurs and managers or the desire to expand into international markets. Cluj is remarkable not for any of these, but rather for the early implicit, and later explicit, realisation of the multiplier effects that the overlap of all three offered. There existed sufficient relational and later territorial capital to capture the opportunities based upon the collaboration of interests such that it has led to systemic change in the nature of market competition.

The blurring of the private and public was not purely philanthropic, but neither was it entirely selfish. Undoubtedly, this blurring partly stems from a self-reliance that developed, in the absence of alternatives, during the Funar era. However, the importance of culture and higher education to Cluj seems to have created an almost Calvinist atmosphere, where the business provides a platform for a wider form of leadership.

Whilst the story of Cluj is a story of success, it has not been limited to only the city's elites. Shortages of labour have led to the formation of the informal school of IT to retrain people from other domains to work in IT and to share in its above average salaries. Whilst the impact of festival culture has shone a light upon the city's spectacular architecture and has created a wave of tourism that supports unskilled labour and social engagement in civic life, that impact has assumed positive feedback loops to include more people than most Romanian cities. It is not true to say that there is no poverty or people feeling left behind, but the city has shaken off its reactionary past to engage many more of Rose's (2011) Settlers in the life of the city than might have been expected 20 years ago.

CASE STUDY 2: The *Un-Successful* Development of North Jacksonville

The Preston Model in Jacksonville (Florida)

North Jacksonville is an area of the larger city of Jacksonville that traditionally has been, and continues to be, a community marked by what it does not have, rather than what it has. The community is a food desert, which means that its population lacks easy access to large grocery stores with significant produce sections. It is also a community that also lacks access to capital and, in turn, has a socio-economic status that is lower than the average for the entire city, with related consequences in health, longevity and every other quality of life factor that is impacted by the presence of poverty.

In response to this chronic situation, ICARE, a group of religious organisations from across Jacksonville, gathered together and approached The Democracy Collaborative and the City of Jacksonville with the idea of establishing a community wealth-building project in North Jacksonville as the start of ending a cycle of poverty for the people in that area of the city, given that the majority of the organisations in ICARE are based in that area of the city and the need, as mentioned above, was more than obvious. The goal, for ICARE, was to develop at least one worker-owned cooperative in the community as a starting point to addressing larger economic disparities of the area so that businesses, and people, will not move out of the area once they are successful.

To this end, ICARE researched models of similar success in the US and found the Evergreen Cooperative in Cleveland which was established with the assistance of The Democracy Collaborative. The latter is an organisation whose mission is to:

> help catalyze a moral and political transformation of the US political economy into a next system that is inclusive, just, and ecologically sustainable—in contrast to today's amoral economy of financial extraction. Transforming ownership and redesigning institutions lies at the heart of this work. Critical to catalyzing such a systemic transformation is overcoming the isolation and despair that prevents us from recognizing ourselves as agents of fundamental historical change. Our goal is an American community in which wealth is democratized, ecological resilience is regenerated and the marginalized become the core of concern as the nation reknits the economic fabric of interdependence without which our democracy becomes an empty abstraction.
>
> The Democracy Collaborative turns ideas of systemic design and community wealth building into visions and models that demonstrate new principles of a democratic economy operating within planetary boundaries, while also helping to lay the pathways for systemic transformation. We seek points of maximum leverage that unlock action and inspire on-the-ground change in economic culture, practice, and policy. At the same time, we work to

> stimulate new thinking about how longer term democratic, system-wide change can be achieved. In these ways, we help communities and our nation lay the foundation for a democratic economy built upon liberty, community, and prosperity for all.
>
> (Democracy Collaborative, 2020)

For the above mission to be enacted, The Democracy Collaborative has several guiding principles. These include racial equity and an economy that is democratic through the leveraging of anchor institutions by catalyzing a movement that will build community wealth and through the development of next-generation enterprises that value climate (Ibid.). It is a group that values a program that is inclusive and racially sensitive and is one that believes that the old ways of doing 'business' are not applicable for the needs of communities in despair.

The Collaborative appealed to the ICARE leadership because, in truth, traditional models of and plans for economic development in North Jacksonville had come and gone without much, if any, success. The community was still rife with all of the issues mentioned above, with no end in sight. The success of the Evergreen Cooperative, where worker-owned businesses had been created as 'anchor' institutions in the community, gave hope to the ICARE leadership that similar success could be found in North Jacksonville.

The Preston Influence

The community wealth-building approach ofThe Democracy Collaboration that ICARE found appealing can be traced back to the 'Preston Model' of economic development that was highlighted in the second chapter of this book. This model, based upon work done in Preston (UK), has as its goal the creation of a 'collective and inclusive economy kept in the hands of the city's inhabitants' (Jones, 2020). There is no need to repeat the many facets of this model since that was already accomplished in the earlier chapter. However, there are a few highlights that appear to be important as a contextualisation of the Jacksonville experiment.

The key pillars of a community wealth-building model such as that of Preston are:

- Plural ownership of the economy.
- Making financial power work for local places.

- Fair employment and just labour markets.
- Progressive procurement of goods and services.
- Socially productive use of land and property.

Further, the model offers an attempt to keep more procurement money circulating within a local economy; to encourage and enable cooperative and more democratic participation in the local economy; and to consciously try to connect and overlap such local ecosystems.

After the telling of the Jacksonville story, we will revisit the pillars of the model to see where the successes and failures occurred and to see how close Jacksonville came to replicating the Preston experience.

A Confluence of Interests

In 2011, a strange thing took place in Jacksonville, Florida. For the first time, an African-American became the mayor of the city. In and of itself, the electoral victory of Alvin Brown was historic, but even more so because of how it happened. Brown was running as a Democrat in a city where it was presumed that the person running as a Republican candidate would emerge victorious for no other reason than the 'money' was in favour of this person. However, after a meeting between the Republican candidate with several large and influential Republican-leaning businessmen, the latter openly switched and supported Alvin Brown with their votes, influences and donations. The rationale for the switching of support was that the Republican did not have a vision of and for the city, but rather saw himself as a 'manager'. In comparison, Alvin, given his background, did have a plan for the city. For Brown, this vision was about 'uniting the city, bringing the city together, so that we can improve the quality of life for everyone that lives in Jacksonville' (Gibbons, 2011). Brown further stated that the city has to be a place where 'people can come, work, live and raise a family. That they would see Jacksonville is open for business and that this city believes in opportunity for all' (Ibid).

It was that vision that won Alvin Brown cross-over political support and the mayoral race. It also convinced ICARE leadership that it had an ally in the city who would be interested in its community wealth-building project. That Brown was African-American, and the majority of the people living in North Jacksonville were of the same race and most likely also voted for him, made the possibility of this project more likely than ever.

It was more than enough to persuade the ICARE leadership to approach him about this project.

The ICARE leadership also knew that Alvin Brown being mayor was only one piece of a puzzle, albeit an important one, that needed to be in place to make this project successful. This model, even with the above principles, was about individuals – many, many individuals – who were positioned in the right places, be it in government, business, anchor organisations, the nonprofit world or community leaders – and leaders not only from 'the establishment', but also from North Jacksonville. The after-report written by city staff emphasises the inclusion of this last group of people. The report asserts that because Community Wealth Building focuses on the community, it is 'important to include individual resident leaders who are the "voices" for the areas' (Ibid.). This need for as many voices as possible is critical because these different individuals would need to be able to network with each other in order to find common ground to work together on this project (see Appendix 5.1 for the full list of invitees).

Considering the need to bring a diverse group of people together, The City of Jacksonville, along with ICARE and the Democracy Collaborative, interviewed a range of leaders with respect to developing a better understanding of the project which was to create a

> systemic inclusive economic development strategy that focuses on the development of community-owned enterprises—usually small, for-profit businesses owned by the employees living in the area—that can generate living wage jobs and business ownership for residents of low-income communities ... through the development of... community-owned businesses, or cooperatives
>
> (Barth, 7)

These conversations aimed to create a set of partners in the community that to date did not exist. The conversations also made it obvious for City staff to identify those who would be invited to the first-ever community wealth building roundtable forum with the goal of using the event to launch the wealth-building project itself.

At the forum itself, invitees were broken up into three sub-groups dealing with issues pertaining to the role of three specific types of organisations in the future development of this initiative. The three groups were (1) the City of Jacksonville, (2) community-wide non-profits and philanthropic institutions and (3) anchor institutions and large employers. The results of each sub-group are detailed and to be found in the final report (City of Jacksonville, 2014). In brief, the recommendations of the subgroups are as follows.

City of Jacksonville Subgroup

- Adopt a responsible banking ordinance
- Establish a city land bank
- Leverage Northwest Jacksonville Economic Development Trust Fund for Community Wealth Building

Nonprofits and Philanthropies Subgroup

- Build on LISC Jacksonville's EPIC Communities in Northwest Jacksonville through the support of the Jaguars Foundation, the Jessie Ball duPont Fund and The Community Foundation for Northeast Florida (LISC Jacksonville started its work in 1999). In particular, LISC Jacksonville's EPIC Communities aims 'to utilize LISC Jacksonville's investment to improve the quality of life' in Jacksonville's Eastside and Northwest Jacksonville. Residents have been integrally involved in the approach by helping to prioritise local concerns through 'Quality of Life Plans'. We reviewed these reports as background for this project.
- Support a feasibility study to advance a Community Wealth Building Initiative.
- Create a community engagement strategy that includes a small grants program.

Anchors Institutions and Large Employers Subgroup

- Identify a senior executive to serve as a chief liaison to the Community Wealth Building team.
- Commit to engaging in supply chain analysis to help identify local procurement opportunities.
- Support business mentoring programs and inclusive targeted hiring policies.

After the Roundtable

The community wealth-building project in Jacksonville started with much excitement and energy. The roundtable was graced with the presence of community leaders from not only North Jacksonville, but large corporations, academic institutions and foundations. However, a confluence of events did not bode well for the long-term future of this project. Alvin Brown, the then mayor of Jacksonville, was elected with a razor-thin majority and, within four years, lost his re-election bid by an equally slim majority. The new mayor, a Republican, appeared to be not as interested in the project as Brown had been. One indicator of this 'not as equal' sense of enthusiasm was that the people, albeit political appointees, who were spearheading the project, were no longer in the same position and were not replaced. A second development was that, try as they might, there was a lack of interest by 'anchor' institutions to come into the community and assist in the development of local wealth through the establishment of a co-op venture. In the instance of Jacksonville, the initial idea was a locally owned and run dry cleaning business that would service one of the large area hospitals.

In response to the evolving situation, the project shifted from being under the guidance of the city to the Northwest Jacksonville Community Development Corporation (NWJCDC), run by Paul Tutwiler. Established in 2001, the NWJCDC was founded 'out of a concern for community decline and blight' (NWJCDC, 2020). The current mission of the organisation is to

> transform Northwest Jacksonville neighborhoods by creating opportunities that lead to economic recovery and empower residents to create a better life for the community. NWJCDC works throughout the City of Jacksonville but focuses on bringing resources for the betterment of Northwest Jacksonville
>
> (Ibid.)

What is notable for this work, the second last point of the mission, is that the CDC works 'through' the City of Jacksonville. This is so because, with a change in political leadership and because of a lack of an interested 'anchor', the leadership of the CDC, now charged with carrying on with this project, changed its focus from establishing local co-ops to addressing the food desert issue that marks Northwest Jacksonville. While this is a worthy and very important issue, one of the additional rationales behind the change was that the new city leadership did not buy into the wealth-building project in the way that the former mayor did. Others involved in the initial phase of the wealth-building project will also contend that the lack of equal interest in this project by the new mayor made it easier for others to not engage in a substantial manner.

The last point is key because in other communities that have been successful, such as Rochester, New York, with its 'Own Rochester' program, continued political and economic leadership engagement on a daily basis that was cited as a key element to the continuation of that city's project. In the instance of Rochester, Own Rochester is a quasi-independent organisation, but it still relies on the political interest of the mayor (who has been in office since the outset of the project) to make it easier for others in the community to be actively committed to the mission of the organisation. Having said that, and even with this support, Own Rochester staff do concede that success is based on a tremendous amount of day-by-day work, with the hand-holding of all involved so that the networks of relationships that have been established over time can be both maintained and successful. The reasoning for this need of constant care of these networks is that these networks, be they in Rochester or Jacksonville, were and continue to not be organic. Simply put, there continues to exist a divide between the people who need the wealth-building project and those who have the wealth. The people in these two circles tend to not be found in the same networks of associations, and thus new networks had to be created, nurtured and maintained with hard work on the part of the staff of organisations such as Own Rochester, and, over a long period of time, by people who are heavily committed to the overall goals of the program. The fact that the mayor of Rochester who helped user in this project is still in office, as compared to Alvin Brown in Jacksonville, would appear to be a significant benefit to those in Rochester (and Cleveland and Preston) who care about this project, given the need for sustained interest at the highest levels. That interest makes it possible for long-term funding to be available and drives the interest of others in the community who may otherwise commit their time to other worthy projects.

If We Could Have Had a 'Do Over'...

These lessons from Rochester are not lost on the people who were at the forefront of the Jacksonville project. Kristin Powell, a central ICARE figure in the championing of this project, contends that the project never amounted to what was hoped for. She based her opinion on observing what took place in Cleveland with the Evergreen Project and on recognising the initially limited goal of the establishment of a co-op grocery store for North Jacksonville. From her perspective, Powell contends that several factors were at play that led to the lack of success for this project. These factors include a continued lack of interest from the Mayor's Office after Alvin Brown left office, as well as an equal lack of interest from the private sector in general, noting the absence of a 'champion', a person or company or foundation who would have led the project and who would have been able to attract the necessary financing. These factors, coupled with the fact that no foundation of note was interested in being one of these champions, helped stall the project (Personal Interview, 2020).

Chris Hand of the Mayor's Office echoed at least one of these sentiments. Hand asserts that the project was, looking back, too much that of the Mayor's Office. The structure for the project was established by executive order and not through a city council vote which would have given the project the possibility of more long-term stability. The council, which suffers from less turnover than the Mayor's Office, would have felt a sense of ownership instead of the project being seen as a 'pet project' of Alvin Brown. The second issue that Hand notes, which goes directly to the issue of networking and partnerships, is that the project should have had an appointed board of directors from across the spectrum of the community. For Hand, either, or both, of these developments would have, from his inside perspective, lowered the

> risk that a Community Wealth Building initiative ends with the administration that launched it. If multiple arms of the local government have approved and funded the structure and process, they will have more of a vested interest in sustaining the mission over time
>
> (Ibid., p. 44)

In the end, and as mentioned above, the NJCDC took over the project and has had to re-assess over time goals of the project for the reasons also mentioned above.

Long-Term Impact

The North Jacksonville exercise has been considered by those on the 'inside' both a failure and a success. The project, as originally conceived, did not achieve its stated goals. The establishment of an employee-owned grocery store did not take place. It would have marked the end of this community being a food desert as well as fostering the creation of other local businesses that could serve as long-term anchors for other establishments to be built around. Kristin Powell has commented that this project was 'quite' complicated and the authors of this work may make the assumption that because it required so many moving parts, it was destined not to be successful.

However, and with the above in mind, in the report about the roundtable forum, Michelle Barth, one of Mayor Brown's key staff on this project, contends at the end that while the wealth-building project was not as successful as it was hoped for, many positive outcomes have taken place because of the process itself. For Barth, these positive outcomes include:

- The CWB 'language' is now embedded in multiple local discussions about how to improve the lives of those living in distressed communities.
- Discussions have inspired promising partnerships. A relatively new group of nonprofits engaged in food, nutrition and health-related efforts in Jacksonville reviewed a Technical Assistance Grant opportunity with the US Department of Agriculture in August 2015. They agreed it would be best for two to apply jointly for a grant to fund plans for a proposed retail grocery store connected to a retail-modeled food bank with a community kitchen and training opportunities in the northwest quadrant of Jacksonville, a food desert and the focus area of the original CWB effort. When discussing the idea, more than one member of the group (most of whom attended our conference) referenced the Community Wealth Building model and suggested that the retail grocery be employee-owned so that it would generate more benefits for the community at large. While the exact implementation of the Community Wealth Building model in Jacksonville remains to be seen, it is promising that over a year after the conference stakeholders continue to discuss its potential for transforming communities.
- The process reaffirms that for this area, expanding the event so that it includes a broader segment of community partners was exactly the

> right thing to do. Indeed, it was this inclusive approach that has given the model the best chance for success by extending 'ownership' of the concept beyond City Hall.

Barth will contend that, at the end of her report, the 'seed [*with respect to the importance of community wealth building, and the need to be as inclusive as possible in these types of projects*] ... is planted, and many hands are now nurturing the growth of this transformative model for our community' (Ibid., p. 47).

Back to Preston

It might be that Ms. Barth was, at the end of an unsuccessful attempt of community wealth building, trying to make something out of nothing (or better said, trying to find a silver lining where it would appear that one does not exist), given that the goal to build local wealth in a specific area of the city failed. The truth might be that the experiment failed not because local forces were not interested in building their own wealth, but because one of the key pillars of the Preston model was not able to be accessed. That key pillar is the ability to make financial power work for local places, and in this instance the people of North Jacksonville.

The Preston Model is such that the attempt to build networks of people who can create a resilient community where wealth can be built upon wealth requires not one, two or even a majority of the basic pillars to exist, but that all the pillars need to be in place for them to feed off each other. With respect to the pillars, there were people in the community who were interested in this project (and remain so to this day), along with a desire to use land and property for the benefit of the local community and to develop ownership that was locally rooted. What was not local was the financial power to make all the other pieces be able to come together. In Jacksonville, like many communities, financial power is either local to the overall community but not local to the specific area under redevelopment or not local to the community at all. More often than not it is held by a few immensely large foundations, private and public, that are run by well-meaning people who are not tied to the community that is in need. Had there already been capital local to North Jacksonville the community may not have needed additional assistance in the building of a locally owned economy? But because it did not have such capital, non-local (not local to the specific area) was necessary, was asked for by people such as

Ms. Barth and the then mayor of the city, and was denied. It was denied by those who had the necessary capital but who were not 'local' to that community in more ways than one, geographical location and also by ethnic/racial background.

The above was and continues to be an instance where a community was working towards being able to simultaneously stay in its place so as to be able to maintain its identity and achieve prosperity. However, the community was unable to access such desired success because the people who were necessary for the project to be successful were not rooted to or in this locality and therefore not interested in the development of resilience through a network of locally owned enterprises. It could be said that the model did not 'fail', since it was never able to get off the ground because of a classic divide between those who have and those who have not and by the lack of desire by the former to share with the latter.

Non-Government Stories

The third and fourth case studies, unlike the first two, are linked through the fact that both are 'entities' that are not government-related. EduCab is a not-for-profit and Boulevard Brewing Company is a for-profit organisation. Thus providing insight into the extent to which the hidden hand of the market affects outcomes.

CASE STUDY 3: The Story of a Local Company Ahead of Its Time – Kansas City's Boulevard Brewing Company

Introduction

Being a 'green' company and setting up internal practices that would encourage sustainable thinking was not high on the agenda of most companies at the turn of the late 1990s and into the early 2000s. Corporations, and especially smaller ones with a much narrower profit margin and fewer employees and the organisations that served these companies, were commonly found to be not on the forefront of environmental policy. It is within this context that the story of a small albeit locally well-known brewery in the heart of Kansas City, MO, aided and abetted by a Chamber of Commerce and a pro-business environmental organisation, makes for one of our case studies of how leadership from the top, rooted in 'simple' principles of stewardship, may tell us a larger tale about the future of business.

The Greening of Boulevard

In 2001, Boulevard Brewing Company, a business local to the Greater Kansas City market and a recent winner of 'Best Small Business' by the Greater Kansas City Chamber of Commerce, announced that, because of sales, it was going to embark on an expansion of its manufacturing facility. At the same time, The Chamber's Environment Committee had begun to commit itself and the organisation (and hopefully its member-companies) to be more environmentally aware of its practices. In coordination with the regional planning organisation, the committee published a 'green handbook' for businesses and developed a building-wide recycling program. The committee had also begun to develop a substantial relationship with a business-friendly environmental organisation, Bridging the Gap (BTG). BTG, according to its founder and executive director, Robert Mann, is not a traditional environmental organisation. BTG, for Mann,

> cannot look at environmental problems or social or economic problems separately, we must see that they are all related. Our survival as a species depends upon our ability to find sustainable social and economic solutions that do not destroy the air, water and soil that are critical to our daily life

To this end, some of the programs of the organisation included, at that time, six community recycling centres in the Kansas City area, sponsorship of the city's Earth Day festival and a partnership with AmeriCorps' Volunteers In Service to America (VISTA) program to help low-income homeowners lower utility bills while making their homes environmentally sound. Through these programs, BTG, assisted by a representative of the State of Missouri Department of Natural Resources, helped 'to bring together people and businesses that at first glance, seem so different it's hard to imagine much common ground' (Berry, 2002).

It made sense then that Bob Mann, who was a regular participant in The Chamber's Environment Committee, and who had heard that Boulevard was seeking to expand its manufacturing processes, asked the professional staff of the Chamber to introduce him to John McDonald. The goal of this meeting was to convince the leadership of Boulevard that it would be able to expand and reconfigure its manufacturing processes in a way that not only saved money but also, because of the 'lean' nature of these changes, would reduce the waste produced by the company. Boulevard would not only save money and add to its profit, but also become more environmentally friendly. In return, BTG would, as it had done with other companies, promote Boulevard as a pro-environment business.

The Boulevard Mission

The meeting was a success. It was from this engagement that a relationship between Boulevard and BTG was formed and a change in the direction of the company took place which has continued to this day. Boulevard became, and continues to be today, a company that is committed to sustainability. The sub-mission of the organisation is that

> embedded deep in our DNA is a profound sense of responsibility for protecting the environment and promoting sustainable business practices. We're always looking for new ways to reduce our environmental impact, while working to ensure a positive future for our local and global communities
>
> (Boulevard, 2021)

To illustrate the company's commitment there are several programs that are listed on the corporate website indicative of the desire of the company to enact its mission. These programs include:

- A 2010 process where Boulevard was committed to becoming a zero-landfill company. The brewer now (2019) recycles or composts almost all its 'waste'. The fraction of waste that cannot be recycled is incinerated with re-usable energy as the by-product of that process.
- For energy, the company installed an 18kw array in 2011 on the roof of Brewhouse Two, and in 2019 added a larger 200kw system on its

24,000 square foot Canning Hall. In addition to reducing the company's dependence on fossil fuels, employees (and visitors) who drive e-vehicles are able to use, for free, electric car charging stations.

All the packaging used by the company for its products are green-friendly. All the cartons are recyclable and the materials used are at least 70% post-consumer recycled in origin. Through the use of these recycled materials, the environmental audit of the company notes that over 18,000 trees have been saved, along with 4.7 million tons of carbon dioxide, as but a few of the examples of the benefit of this decision.

- The company installed a green roof for the brewhouse and packaging buildings. This roof reduced heating and conditioning loads by increasing the insulation value of the roof. In turn, this state of affairs lowers the overall consumption of energy of these buildings. Further, the surface of the roof absorbs rainwater, which reduces runoff, and sustains a variety of plant life. These plants lower the overall thermal footprint of the building, absorb carbon dioxide and produce oxygen.
- Boulevard, over time, implemented new HVAC systems which were and continue to be designed to deliver 'comfort' and to be as efficient as possible. The implication of the efficiency of these new systems is that heating and cooling adjustments are made in real-time, thus reducing waste in this area of plant management and the environmental waste of energy.
- The new packaging facility was designed to utilise and maximise natural sunlight, and all exterior lighting is controlled through photocells. The benefit of this design is the prevention of the waste of energy. In 2011, solar panels were added to the brewhouse roof. These panels produce enough electricity to power three homes.
- Hosted the 2017 BTG Annual Fall Social.

The Ripple Effect

The above are all examples of how, from one meeting, Boulevard Brewing Company did become a local champion of lean manufacturing processes that were aimed to save the company money and also make its processes as environmentally friendly as possible. However, this is not the end of the story.

In an audit of waste conducted in 2009, it was calculated that 150 pounds of glass were being thrown away in the Greater Kansas City region, including 10 million empty bottles of Boulevard beer. For a company committed to sustainability, this was considered to be unacceptable. The challenge, at the time, was that there was not a local facility to process this glass because there was also almost no local recycling taking place.

The leadership of Boulevard decided that they were 'tired of being part of the problem'. The solution was, rather than ignoring the issue, to establish a separate non-profit organisation whose mission was to take in, process and recycle all this wasted glass. Ripple Glass was born.

The organisational leadership constructed a 'state-of-the-art' processing plant dedicated to the recycling of glass-based containers, with a metro-wide reach. With the assistance of a local customer who turns recycled glass into fiberglass insulation, and another business in Tulsa that turns amber glass (often used for beer bottles) back into bottles, the waste of all of this glass was significantly reduced.

Over time, the purple bins of Ripple Glass have spread to cities such as Branson (MO), as well as Omaha (Nebraska) and Sioux City (Iowa). There are 80 communities that are working with Ripple Glass. For the leadership of this organisation, this work is 'a great way to close the loop, protect the environment, support area businesses and even make homes more energy efficient' (Ripple Glass, 2020).

The Question Is Still ... 'Why?'

There are many obvious reasons why John McDonald said yes to working with Bob Mann and BTG. To begin, as an active and prominent member-company of The Chamber and an organisation with much influence in the economic life of Greater Kansas City, it would have been a challenge for McDonald to not take this meeting, one arranged by The Chamber. Second, Bob Mann approached McDonald, as he has with other companies, not from a 'do good for the environment' position but rather an economic one – the company, in its move to expand its manufacturing processes, would be able to save money thereby increasing its overall profit. The benefit of being mentioned and promoted as an environmentally friendly business was secondary, *not* the lead rationale for making such a decision. Third, Boulevard, as a well-known local company with a very positive perception in the community, may have seen the downside to not doing this as something that may have damaged the goodwill that the company enjoyed in the eyes of the public. All of the above are now, and most likely then, very valid reasons for why McDonald not only agreed to have the meeting, but moved his company to a place that even this author, who was at the meeting, could not have imagined.

There may have been, at the time of the first meeting with BTG and at present, one more reason behind McDonald's decision to agree to work with BTG. John McDonald, it would appear, always let the people who worked with and for him at Boulevard answer why these environmental steps were taken. It was – and continues to be very simple – the right thing to do. Several senior managers and employees at Boulevard were interviewed with the first question being why did the company go down this road given that in 2001 being a pro-environmental company was not the promotional item that it is in 2020. Individually and on separate occasions, each and every person spoken to came back with the very same answer – that it was economically a smart thing to do because there would be a reduction in expenses and, therefore, hopefully an increase in profits, but, moreover, it was simply the right thing to do. McDonald, to all these people, came across as a person who understood that it was critical to be a good steward of the environment. In fact, that very phrase – steward – was echoed by more than one person and always in conversations that were held separately. As a person who grew up on the land, McDonald understands that there is a relationship between the land and human beings and the need to be mindful of that relationship. For these Boulevard employees, from top to bottom, that message of stewardship was conveyed over and over again, so much so that it was clear that profit was an important motivation for the company, but also that the company had to be about more than just profit – there had to be a social justice component, to use a phrase, to the ethic of the organisation.

The Benefit of Saying Yes

A result of these principles of stewardship and social justice, a voluntary team that still exists today was established inside the company whose remit was to bring environmentally related ideas to senior management. This team was filled by members of the company from all areas with the purpose of having a cross-team understanding of the organisation about which ideas would work not only in one area, but throughout the company, be it in engineering or in guest services. The goal was to bring bottom-up ideas to the top, which is exactly what has taken place over time even if these ideas required funding. For example, a waste audit was recommended to develop a baseline understanding of where Boulevard was and senior management agreed with the need for such an expense. From this audit, several programs, as mentioned above, came to fruition, including the establishment of Ripple Glass. This process was, and continues to be, informal by nature. McDonald and the current leadership of the company maintain an 'open-door' policy where no formal feedback processes are in place – employees, be it from this team or not, are encouraged to share upwards ideas on any issue that they believe can be beneficial to the company's mission. Jeff Krum, who has taken over as CEO of the firm from McDonald upon the latter's retirement, has maintained the same policy with respect to employee feedback and initiatives and the environment group that was established some 20 years ago still exists. Further, as evidence of a desire to showcase the environmental work of Boulevard, Krum was open in letting members of the environment team speak about the company, its record on sustainability and its processes.

In 2013, Duvel Moortgat, a Belgian-based brewery, bought Boulevard. Often, one hears stories that when a company the size of Duvel acquires a smaller company such as Boulevard, the internal processes and principles of the acquired firm tend to be 'swallowed up', and the latter ceases to look and feel like what it used to be, when it was locally owned. Duvel, when speaking to senior corporate management, is a company that is highly selective of what it purchases and is not one to acquire simply and become larger for the sake of its corporate bottom line. The Boulevard acquisition was only the second one of its kind for Duvel, and as brewers and operators, the company was not interested in stripping Boulevard for parts and selling to the highest bidder. From this vantage point, Duvel was interested in Boulevard for many reasons, one of which was its bottom-line performance, and another, the synergy in market share that Boulevard could bring to Duvel in the American market. Another, asserted Mr. Moortgat, is that 'we [*at Duvel*] realized that we are both family businesses and share the same values [*and*] believe that people and quality of beers are important' (Furnari, 2013). Even so, McDonald conceded that he understood the realities of this deal and assumed that 'henceforth, things will be a little different' (Ibid.).

In conversation with Boulevard employees and Duvel senior management, some things may be different at Boulevard today in comparison to the day before it was purchased including that the company was no longer locally owned and that final decisions could be made elsewhere. With respect to the desire to continue to be a company that has an 'open door' feedback process, it strives to be as environmentally conscious as possible, willing to spend money on processes such as next phase environmental audits. It is interested in maintaining the environment group that McDonald established. All of these internal activities have continued regardless of the change in ownership. More than just the details, Duvel management asserted that when Mr. Moortgat spoke of 'same values', the commitment of Boulevard to be more than just a profit-driven company was one of those key values that the two companies share as a commitment to more than profit motivation. This 'more', in addition to all the other business-related reasons for an acquisition, was asserted as being an important benchmark in the Duvel decisions regarding with which companies to engage in some type of partnership. In fact, McDonald, in his quest to maintain Boulevard past his retirement, was speaking with several companies, not only Duvel. The choice to go with the latter was, in part, because the company was held in high regard both for its product and its values. This was apparent after the acquisition when McDonald is quoted as saying that being bought out by Duvel was the 'right path' for Boulevard, which also included a maintaining of the corporate commitment to sustainability. For this reason, in an open letter to Boulevard drinkers, amongst everything else that he said, McDonald asserted that 'although Boulevard is combining with Duvel Moortgat [*Boulevard's*] commitment to sustainability initiatives will continue, as will Boulevard's support of Ripple Glass, the glass recycling company' (Beeradvocate, 2013). The rationale for this statement about sustainability from a beer-making company was to highlight the commitment to these values by Boulevard and that Duvel not only shares these same values, but will continue in this vision of a company dedicated to sustainability and a 'light' footprint.

Back to John Cadbury

In our first book, *People, Place and Global Order*, our starting paradigms were the callousness of the editorial board of *The Economist* when it referred to people asking for government assistance as 'scroungers', and then the social justice ethos of John Cadbury, who was adamant, based on his Quaker principles, that a company cannot be just for profit; that there must be a social justice component to the work of the company or else the company stands for little. The policies enacted by Cadbury – an employee-management council, the introduction of a full-time on-duty nurse and the building of low-cost housing for his employees – all stand the test of time with respect to the lived understanding of his principles especially since all of this took place in the 1800s when the spending of money on such 'things' was not done. (I would dare say that even today many of the policies put into place by Cadbury at that time are still often done grudgingly by corporate executives.)

We are of the belief that in order for inequity in society to be eased, if not eradicated over time, there must be a more than profit understanding (a real one, and not just a 'let's give our employees a few days of the year so that they can do some volunteering, and while they do so, they should be wearing shirts with our corporate logo on them) to the mission and vision of a company, so that Settlers are able to take part in this world that is more networked and hyper-linked than ever before; a world where those at the bottom feel left out, both economically and culturally, and have expressed this rage through decisions such as Brexit and a turn towards Donald Trump and Bernie Sanders (showing that this is not a right or left issue, but one of those who have, and those who do not have and feel that they will never have). In this first work, we pointed, in a small manner, to several organisations and activities that sought and continue to seek ways by which this gap can be closed; such as through more inclusive policies and business practices and by listening to those who have felt and continue to feel marginalised. (At the time of the writing of this work, and even in the midst of the worst pandemic since the Spanish Flu of 1918, Donald Trump is still able to count on at least 30% of the electorate, no matter what he says, in large part because of this feeling of being left out and shut out.) The goal of this work is to look at fewer case studies, but in greater depth, so as to illustrate that companies with sound business practices that also have a strong and continuing social justice motivation do exist, that they are able to generate profit and that they can exist within the realm of the market-driven worlds of the US and the UK. These businesses demonstrate that a true and substantial commitment to principles that are beyond just profit are not incompatible with a free-market economy. Comments were made that the buy-out of Cadbury by Kraft indicated that the days of a company being able to have a 'higher purpose' beyond profit were dead, with Cadbury as the poster child of such a company that, in the fast-paced global economy, was simply not able to survive unless the company was willing to modify its principles (Ramsey, 2012; see also Cadbury, 2010; Moeller, 2021).

The sale of Boulevard to Duvel may, to some, be more of the same – that a small company with high-minded principles cannot survive on its own if it wishes to grow, unless the company changes its mission and vision. However, it would appear that what enticed Duvel leadership about Boulevard was not only the quality of its beer, but also the quality of the company itself. One could assert that Boulevard makes very good beer because of the very commitment to a 'more than profit' philosophy and that the beer it makes is an outgrowth of this commitment and not an aside to these principles. The beer and the mission, in the case of Boulevard, like that of Cadbury many years earlier, are one and the same, not separate from each other. Duvel's leadership knew that it was so and wanted to buy both, for this very reason.

CASE STUDY 4: EduCab: Networking Villages of the Mind

Introduction

EduCab was born out of conversations between Mihai, the manager of a programme to bring digital technology to Romanian libraries called Biblionet, financed by the Bill and Melinda Gates Foundation and the Dimbovita county manager of libraries, Vladut. As the funding from Biblionet was coming to an end, Mihai saw an opportunity to support newly connected libraries as points of social resilience at a time when there was an exodus of working-age people from the Romanian countryside to work in richer EU countries, such as Spain, Italy and the UK. Vladut connected Mihai to the more active librarians in his county and Mihai brought in volunteers from the multinational company where he was employed.

Connecting Elephants and Fleas

Education capacity building is the idea behind EduCab. Founded in 2015 by Mihai Lupu in Romania, it is a model that has now been adopted in 12 countries. Mihai describes it as follows:

> EduCab was conceived as a sustainable way to enter small towns and villages to make a bridge between their communities and groups of professionals from companies, NGO's, non-profits and other government institutions.
>
> At this moment there is no connection between bigger and smaller communities in most countries. Usually people seek to escape small places in search of more resources and opportunities. They leave behind an older frustrated community where civic, cultural, economic and other development is a desert, left behind. If not exposed to good quality culture, education, etc they don't bring anything when they move to larger places. It's a lose-lose situation.
>
> The central institution in small places is the bar. It is not a Parisian cafe boosting civic movements! Second, is the church, but it is not always open and the church is very dogmatic. Small places consume the worst media as it is bombastic and populist. The Mayor's office is next, but is often perceived to be corrupt and anyway embodies a level of power distance from many people.

Mihai chose the library because anyone can go in and there is no curriculum or agenda. The trouble is, Mihai argues, that in many small places 'once people leave school there is no further access to knowledge available in small places'.

EduCab is, therefore, about connecting large places with left behind small places. EduCab is doing this by connecting people with an interest and the time, often working for large organisations, in creating practical actions in small communities. When Rose's Model of Motivation was explained, Mihai agreed that EduCab seeks to connect Pioneers with

Settlers – the former being people who seek to connect their ability to prospect and think commercially with their desire to do it in the service of a cause that matters beyond the bottom line. One could frame such activity as economic centres reaching out to their respective peripheries. However, the pioneers that have worked on EduCab projects, that the authors of this work have spoken to, emphasise the importance of developing resilience of place and people, rather than reducing them to a cog in an efficient and robust socio-economic machine. One such person stated that 'innovation flows from knowledge and resilience, not compliance and efficiency'.

In the places where EduCab operates, the opportunities for travel and reach beyond subsistence are limited by a mixture of economic circumstance, culture, poor infrastructure and limited knowledge. In Romania, for example, most villages are based upon a peasant lifestyle, often supplemented by low-wage jobs in nearby factories, shops and warehouses. Yet whilst poverty is endemic in much of the countryside, many of Romania's cities are booming and this state of affairs has created a widening gap of wealth and experience which only serves to reinforce Settlers' views that the world is rigged against them and their values, rooted in this place.

EduCab has developed three streams of activity using libraries which:

1. Can be the organiser/curator of things – playgroups, computer training, etc.
2. Can be a facilitator of knowledge, such as how to write a CV. EduCab brings people from cities to small towns and villages to do this.
3. Can be a host – a provider of space for the above two.

To do this effectively, EduCab trains the librarian to become a community organiser rather than simply a curator of books. Where EduCab has been most effective, the librarian has typically assumed the role of a social entrepreneur utilising the reach of connections to bring a richness of experience that would not otherwise be available. Mihai argues that democracy is about participation in society and not just ballot boxes. For example, Mihai says 'if an old woman cannot print her plane ticket, sent by her daughter in Italy, how can she be connected to wider society?'.

What the pioneers from the cities do is provide a stream of resources and activities that engage residents and position the library and the role of the librarian centrally in civic participation? At a simple level, therefore, people can donate books. Beyond that, individuals from cities can run courses in a variety of areas, including, but not limited to, interview skills, English language, crafts and the mentoring of small business people to name a few. EduCab also brings the employees of corporations (as individuals and groups) to improve the infrastructure of libraries which are often neglected. In Nepal, libraries have been constructed by a local partner with EduCab connecting them to people who can donate books that they collect and bring to the library. Typically, such work is supervised by experienced local craftspeople, a process that deliberately turns typical power relations around. Programmes are designed to encourage independence, personal and community pride and to build connections between people at a personal level that transcends geography.

Claudia is in her late thirties, an HR manager with a background in large multinational companies and an EduCab volunteer. She described how working with a theatre company that performed in village barns brought village people together across generations. Many of the people dressed up smartly and several had not seen a play performed by professional actors for years and some never before. Claudia has commented that 'when you see 200 people laughing (most shows are comedies) together and connecting with the actors after as the drama quickly becomes a village party you see people's horizons stretching'. Crina, in Valcea, echoed these sentiments when 350 people showed up for a theatre performance in someone's yard. She said, 'I never imagined that so many country people would come to a theatre show'. One of the most widely copied programmes developed has been the short film breaks festivals. Bringing culture into smaller places, the festivals are simultaneously run inside large corporations, thus engaging companies in their hinterland, whilst also offering a purposeful form of employer branding. As Claudia put it:

> we transfer capabilities to expand a circular economy. For example when we [Mihai and Claudia] worked at Ipsos we used the resources of an on-line business to show libraries how to use social media and digital technology to connect and promote people and place.

For Mihai, EduCab is about engaging people in democracy at a civic level, beyond political parties and ballot boxes, such that socio-economic resilience can provide greater resilience economically and politically. In countries like Romania, politics is often perceived to be corrupt and leaves people shrugging their shoulders helplessly. The role of libraries as a catalyst in overcoming inertia, power distancing and nourishing the idea of democracy as an engaged citizenry is central to the EduCab model.

Pillars of Engagement

More recently work has been undertaken to define four pillars of EduCab:

1. To renew book collections.
2. To improve the physical infrastructure, furniture, IT, etc.
3. Programmes – to connect relationships between urban executives and rural communities that enable them to develop and enable things to happen beyond Mihai or EduCab.
4. Social Entrepreneurship – to start a few pilots.

The last pillar is particularly interesting as it is about overlapping social resilience into economic resilience in a more direct and concrete way. Examples of this resilience building include helping local craftspeople/artisans form a legal structure to work together. EduCab can help them find clients sometimes, too. One example of this is in a village called Mircea Voda (near the city of Braila in SE Romania) where Cornelia (the librarian) noticed that there were women in the village who had previously been seamstresses in clothing factories which had, like many other industrial enterprises in the region, closed. These women had now returned to family-based subsistence agriculture and occasional cash work that used their sewing skills. With EduCab's network of city business people, Cornelia helped four of them to form an association whilst Mihai connected them to the owner of a factory in the capital city of Bucharest that produced beanbags. This act of connecting people worked well, with the factory owner pleased with the quality of work and not needing to have them as a regular cost on the payroll. At the same time, they maintained their independence and captured more of the value than had they been employed.

Once the new association started invoicing, it became clear to Cornelia that EduCab needed to help the women to manage the money, to learn basic accounting skills and to enable them to take part in the taxable economy. In exchange, the women donate a percentage of profits to their local library to ensure sustainability and reduce dependence upon EduCab. This is important in developing self-sustaining resilience in libraries. In Romania, for example, in one county, Dimbovita, 70% of libraries received zero budget for books or refurbishment in 2020. In the midst of a global pandemic that has hit rural Romania's hand-to-mouth economy hard, EduCab offers motivation, competence and resources to grow resilience and adaptability.

In an effort to both expand the entrepreneurial dimension of EduCab and hold onto its community focus and mutuality in Mircea Voda, they have adopted an ecosystem approach. EduCab has learnt from communities in Transylvania supported by the Eminescu trust and thus is promoting active rural tourism. Visitors come to take part in local activities, such as grape picking, pressing or for seasonal festivals and become immersed in the local community. Attached to this has been the creation of a brand called facut cu drag in Mircea Voda (made with love in Mircea Voda). It is a label that can be applied to many products from crafts to food, but which emphasises the centrality of the place and the community at the heart of value creation. It is early days, but both have attracted outside interest and are being watched closely by other communities.

Structure

What one can see through the above instances is that EduCab is acting as a networked catalyst for the application of entrepreneurial ideas and capabilities that transcend place. Rather like Wikipedia, it is reliant upon individuals and companies choosing to collaborate in a community of practice (Wenger & Snyder, 2000), rather than any formal structures, which, as we will see below, it eschews. There are often multiple projects at various stages of development simultaneously within the network as a whole. Often overlapping, they rely upon the adaptability of participants over the efficiency of any processes or structures thereby providing resilience at the deliberate exclusion of developing a robust system.

The entire model is rooted in a profound sense of stewardship that connects people to place through a community of practice. Mihai was most influenced, when working at the United Nations Development Programme (UNDP), by his dislike of the World Bank and big non-governmental organisations (NGOs) like the Red Cross and World Vision. These organisations appeared to be more interested in salaries and ticking boxes than changing things. Mihai believes that if you want development to be sustainable you cannot do it through project-based approaches. EduCab began by Mihai wondering 'can we use fractions of resources: people who have jobs already to give some time, for example'. Mihai and Claudia agreed that they are 'nurturing an ecosystem of knowledge'. Yet, it also lacks formal structure and in management speak would be, imperfectly, but best described as an adhocracy (Mintzberg, 1989). Claudia describes it as having 'no structure and free flowing', mission driven, based upon international teams who configure according to needs. Indeed Mintzberg claims that:

> the adhocracy provides sophisticated innovation. That comes at the price of a good deal of disruption, if not chaos, and wasted resources ... [it] achieves its effectiveness by being inefficient ... The innovative organisation may be necessary, but it is not conventional.
> (Mintzberg, 1989, p. 196)

The aim of this project is to harness voluntary effort into nurturing a community, not to develop bureaucratic skills and hierarchical structures or to worry about salaries. It is an informal network, not a formal NGO in itself. Mihai wants to spend as little time as possible on public relations and does not want to invest in image and, as he puts it 'be beholden to corporate PR'. When asked about how EduCab grows, Mihai said 'we use the worm network – friends and friends of friends'. People come to them now, after eight years. At the end of the year he says that 'we try to measure, not the number of books donated, but the quality of friendships developed'.

Aurora, the librarian in Valea Mare, described how she took a group of children, who had made simple craft products, to a Christmas fair at Mihai's company. From that encounter, volunteers from the company Mihai worked at combined some corporate donations and money from the local Mayors office and, along with local labour, renovated the library building in Valea Mare. From this and similar experiences, Mihai was able to persuade corporations that were updating furniture to start donating the old furniture. Mayors were then prevailed upon to provide the transport and local communities and EduCab volunteers provided labour.

Building Resilience

Roxana was one of Mihai's early partners and she took charge of launching EduCab in Valcea county. She describes working with the county head of libraries to find active librarians to start with a success in a community that would be open to try. She says:

> I was more practical and tried to get things done in a few small places, but Mihai had a vision. He probably always thought of a national network.

Roxana has supported people like Crina in connecting the traditional to the digital in a search for resilience. Crina now runs a programming club for children as well as literature, film and craft workshops. Whilst Anca in Albesti is sharing her pottery workshops using WhatsApp and trying to learn to use Telegram.

In many libraries, children, who work in groups, now take part in Christmas craft fairs in Bucharest with a small percentage of the income generated going back to the library. In this way, people with limited resources are developing a sense of pride and investing in their own communities. Some communities have taken this further with craft workshops explicitly designed to connect older people who teach children traditional crafts such as traditional shirtmaking, knitting, weaving, etc. Steliana, who has worked as a librarian in Gura Ocnitei for 31 years, told me how this is helping to create a sense of resilience and pride in a place that has, in many ways, been hollowed out by migration abroad.

Connecting generations and Pioneers with the children of Settlers has been central to the 'Dare to Care' programme aimed at talking to teenagers about issues such as drugs, sex and people trafficking, which, in a traditional society, are often not spoken about at home. Yet they present real challenges to young people keen to widen their horizons and experience the world. The programme has not only proved popular in many villages it has also transformed the perception of libraries and librarians. In Gura Ocnita, the newly found status of the librarian enabled her to organise a programme with the mayor, shopkeepers, the doctor and the priest, to collect and donate presents for poorer children at Christmas.

Violeta, librarian in Ocnita since 1990, described how her relationship with EduCab began with book donations and blossomed into providing vocational training and skills such as writing CVs, business plans and so forth. The village hairdresser was in fact trained this way! Displaying a clear pride and determination to help her community, despite struggles with political leaders that have gone all the way to the European Court of Human Rights, the library (containing an incredible number of books in the available space) also offers access to the internet, training courses and hobby groups. The walls are dripping with traditional local handmade clothing, craft objects that speak of pride in this place and this community. Embodying Mihai's vision of a library as a mixture of resource, community and citizens advice centre, the contrast between a traditional decor and digital tools is a visual demonstration of what we might call rooted potential.

Crina, in Valcea, described how in her community many parents are working abroad and have left children with grandparents. So when EduCab organised a touring writers festival with authors reading to the children, it both brought generations together and created aspiration.

Violeta (Gura Ocnitei), Crina (Valcea) and Flore, the librarian in Ciocanesti, agreed that the most valuable contribution that EduCab brings is ideas, followed by people with skills that they don't have in their communities. With only the exception of Aurora in Valea Mare, these librarians would all be classified by Rose (2011) as Settlers. Deeply attached to a sense of place, local people, traditions and lacking agency, they looked to people like Mihai and Vladut to provide the platform structure, examples and inspiration required to mobilise their own resources and find the self-belief and motivation to organise. As Flore, in Ciocanesti, put it, EduCab 'no longer brings donations, but brings ideas and things to do and improve'.

Networked Mutuality

Interestingly, Aurora said that as librarians have experienced success in developing programmes, they are now comfortable using Google

Docs, WhatsApp and other digital tools 'to share needs and ideas'. Whilst Flore proudly described how librarians share activities using their Facebook and YouTube channels, Anca told of how critical EduCab has been in helping her use technology during the pandemic to connect her community to the outside world. This remarkable step in connecting people and places, based upon reciprocity, not only creates a network that is less reliant upon individual pioneers, such as Mihai and Vladut, EduCab, also, in the words of Vladut, 'cuts out political processes and hierarchies of bureaucracies'. For Vladut, creating a connected community of librarians, encouraged by the provision of outside Pioneers' sense of agency, is providing the fuel to adapt socially which, if it could be translated into the economic sphere, would be transformational.

The bottom-up nature of EduCab and the explicit interlinkages at different scales of governance does imply an effort to develop overlapping private, commons and not-for-profit enterprise that the many in EduCab would clearly like to become an emergent form of polycentrism. However, one of the key challenges facing EduCab is the dominance of key individuals as providers of energy, drive and vision, most notably with Mihai Lupu. EduCab has sought to address this by using local coordinators such as Roxana In Valcea. However, it is true to say that Mihai remains a towering figure of inspiration across the network. Conscious of this, Mihai himself says that encouraging individual librarians to step forward with initiatives takes time, but that gradually it is happening and increasingly he is being informed of new happenings, rather than being asked for advice or ideas. Certainly, conversations with volunteers and anecdotal evidence of networked development and sharing of projects, using digital collaboration tools, indicate that his role is shifting from director to facilitator. The pace of this change will be driven by both the extent to which librarians grow as social entrepreneurs and the success of their enterprise pillar. Both of which will have a significant impact upon the sustainability and scaling of the network going forward.

Think Global and Act Local

The EduCab network now exists in 12 countries – Bangladesh, Guatemala, Indonesia, Kenya, Malaysia, Nepal, Papua New Guinea, Romania, Senegal,

Somalia, Tanzania and Uganda. This growth came about initially through community activists and organisations hearing about the work in Romania and seeking to learn from it. Increasingly the 'worm network' is connecting across the EduCab network, rather than to a central hub. Volunteers that have travelled to countries such as Indonesia and Nepal say that there is an ongoing and endless dialogue within and between local, national and the international network, about how to do things and priorities. However, volunteers and librarians alike, all seemed to agree upon a shared set of values, which centred upon the value of time over money, a desire to collaborate and a search for a sense of community, which having found, they wanted to share.

In most countries, EduCab has worked with existing local NGOs and libraries. However, in Nepal they really only existed in schools and, over time, EduCab's properly furnished school libraries became too small for the demand. Local partners, therefore, have built new public libraries and the international network furnished them with books and other resources.

Going Forward

The real challenge to developing sustainable resilience in the communities that EduCab works with is to translate their success in the social and cultural fields into the economic field. Without this step, talk of polycentrism (see Chapter 2) will remain an idea because both the EduCab network and the communities themselves will remain dependent upon others' financial resources. Tentative steps have been made with some craft-based enterprises, the nurturing of an emergent local brand in their *Facut cu drag in Mircea Voda* label and rural tourism in the same location. However, to become a compelling template such steps need to have a wider reach within Mircea Voda, to generate income for more people and to reach into other communities, also, without losing the mutuality and reciprocity of their core idea.

EduCab is now exploring crowdfunding as an opportunity to connect urban wealth with rural needs. To this end, Mihai has been connected to the founder of the micro-enterprise division of BT who appears in more detail in the Cluj case study and who was very influenced by the Triodos bank model (See Taylor & Bronstone, 2019). Triodos has seen spectacular growth by nurturing community enterprise through preparing bond and equity offerings which they brand with their badge and offer to small investors all over the world, effectively facilitating a network of knowledge to innovate the development of new business and markets. We cannot know where this journey will end, but it is interesting how both BT and EduCab have seen the logic of crowdfunding as a digitally networked means to deliver transformational economic change for small enterprises and communities.

What EduCab has achieved in a short time is impressive and a great story. Relying upon goodwill, reciprocity and nurturing a form of mutuality that provides templates and examples of how small places can thrive. It exists without the support of governments (local or national), or a big sponsor and the network itself spends almost nothing on salaries and almost nothing on other resources. Very much a bottom-up model of development, it does show that the engagement of Rose's (2011) Pioneers with Settlers can enable Settlers to engage with wider networks and flourish without having to abandon their attachment to place. In the context of a mass migration of working-age people out of the Romanian countryside to work abroad, this provides hope for the future and an urgency to efforts to develop the entrepreneurial pillar of the EduCab model.

The Next Step

The case studies here reveal that there do exist purposeful and powerful relationships between entrepreneurialism, oikophilia and a pooling of relational capital. As Nonaka (1991) noted about corporations many years ago 'The essence of innovation is to re-create the world according to a particular vision or ideal' (Nonaka, 1991, p. 97). Chapter 6 will connect the dots between Chapters 2 and 3 and the case studies described above in a search for patterns of causation, networks of feedback loops and processes of socio-economic change.

Appendix 5.1

Participants Community Wealth Building Roundtable Attendees (March 27–28, 2014)

Anchor Institutions (Hospitals and Universities)

- Marion Anderson, Executive Director, Community Health, Brooks Rehab Hospital
- Robin Bass, Vice President, Director of Planning, UF Health (Shands)
- Irvin PeDro Cohen, Director of New Town Success Zone,
- Edward Waters College Janice Donaldson, Regional Director, Small Business Development Center, University of North Florida
- Mark Falbo, Director, Center for Community Based Learning, University of North Florida Greg Flowers, Process Owner for Strategic Partnership with Community Organizations, Florida Blue
- David Jaffee, Professor, Department of Sociology, Anthropology & Social Work, University of North Florida Chris Johnson, Chair, Department of Economics & Geography, University of North Florida

- Michelle Leak, Administrator for Community Engagement and Longitudinal Care, Mayo Clinic
- Tracie Loftis, System Director, Mission Operations, St. Vincent's Healthcare
- Bill McConnell, General Manager, SMG Jacksonville
- Peter Moberg, Assistant Vice President of Marketing, Memorial Hospital
- Audrey Moran, Senior Vice President, Social Responsibility and Community Advocacy Baptist Health
- Lynn Sherman, Director, Social Responsibility and Community Health, Baptist Health James E. Sylvester, Director, Office of Facility Resources, Nemours Children's Clinic
- Penny Thompson, Vice President, Government Affairs, UF Health at Jacksonville (Shands) Business Community Alex Alston, Director of Marketing, SMG Jacksonville
- Martha Barrett, Senior Vice President, Corporate Social Responsibility, Bank of America Sandy Bartow, Vice President, Entrepreneurial Growth, JAX Chamber, and President, Chamber Foundation
- James Breaker, Vice President of Board of Directors, Moncrief Myrtle Avenue Business Association
- Niki Brunson, Founder, Celebs Corner Kitchen
- Anthony Butler, Founder and Executive Director, E3 Business Group
- Lara Diettrich, Principal, Diettrich Planning, LLC
- Jeff Edwards, Chief Financial Officer, Beaver Street Fisheries
- Ignacio Esteban, Executive Director, Florida Community Loan Fund
- Michael Fleming, Managing Director, Head of DB Jacksonville, Deutsche Bank
- Janet Hamer, Community Development Manager, TD Bank
- Valerie Hendriex Jenkins, Vice President, Senior Community Development Officer, Wells Fargo, Social Responsibility Group Lane
- Jeer Manis, Former Executive Director, AIA Jacksonville
- Iris Jones, Vice President of Community Development, BB&T Inez Long, Executive Director, Black Business Investment Fund Florida
- Ruth Owen, Senior Vice President, EverBank Missy Peters, Community Affairs Manager, Community First Credit Union
- Ann Reinert, Global Philanthropy, JPMorgan Chase Bank
- Connie Smith, Senior Vice President Community Affairs Manager, Wells Fargo

- Greg Tison, General Manager, Jacksonville Farmers Market Judy Walz, Senior Vice President Marketing, VyStar Credit Union
- Ysryl, CEO, President, Jacksonville Black Chamber of Commerce
- Faith-based Organizations & Community Members
- Pastor Bill Bailey, Member, ICARE/Ebenezer UMC Ross Beckworth, Executive Director, Lazarus project Corporation, Mount Vernon Baptist Church
- Stephon Boggs, Jacksonville Masjid Al-Islam
- Pastor Reginald L. Bryant, Pastor/Director of Outreach, Shiloh Metro Baptist Church
- Father Hugh Chapman, Member, ICARE/St. Phillip's Episcopal
- Rosa Carter, Chair for Economic Development, Southern Christian Leadership Conference
- Rev. Torin T. Dailey, Pastor, First Baptist Church of Oakland
- Rev. Kent Dorsey, Founder, Chairman and Chief Executive Officer, ICARE/Riverside Ave. Christian Church
- Pastor Darryl Edwards, Member in NW Jacksonville, ICARE/Greater Bethany Baptist
- Rev. Aaron T. Flagg, Jr., Reverend, Emanuel Missionary Baptist Church
- Pastor Mark Griffin, Pastor, Wayman Chapel AME/ Wayman CDC
- Rev. Marquise Hardrick, Pastor, ICARE/Central Metropolitan CME
- Church Elder Lee Harris, Mt. Olive Primitive Baptist Church Robert Lee, CEO, Fresh Ministries Shelly Marino, Director, External Relations, Fresh Ministries
- Bishop Rudolph McKissick, Jr., Senior Pastor, Bethel Baptist Institutional Church
- Rev. Tan Moss, Pastor, ICARE/Greater Great Memorial AME
- Powell, Lead Organizer, ICARE
- Khaliah Shakir, Jacksonville Masjid Al-Islam
- Rev. James Wiggins, Co-President, ICARE/St. Paul's Lutheran Church Philanthropy
- Katie Ensign, Senior Program Officer,
- Jessie Ball DuPont Fund Doreen Flippin, Vice President for Administration, The Arthur Vining Davis Foundations
- Ashley Smith Juarez, Northeast Florida Regional Director, Clinton Health Matters Initiative Nina Waters, President, The Community Foundation for Northeast Florida Nonprofit Sector Alfred Arzuaga,

Director of Community & Economic Development, Habitat for Humanity Jacksonville (HabiJax)
- Michelle Braun, Chief Operating Officer, United Way of Northeast Florida
- Terry Chelikowsky, Executive Director, Florida Alliance of Community Development Corporations
- Charles Dabney, Jr., Senior Program Officer, LISC Jacksonville
- Richard Danford, Jr., President and CEO, Jacksonville Urban League
- Carrie Davis, President, Wealth Watchers, Inc.
- Alison DeBelder, Director of Advocacy, Jacksonville Area Legal Aid
- Erick Dittus, Senior Advisor to the CEO, Strategic Communications and Sustainability, Jacksonville Urban League
- The Hon. Reggie Fullwood, Executive Director, Metro North Community Development Corporation
- Cindy Funkhouser, President and CEO, SulzbacherSulzbecher Center
- James Kowalski, Executive Director, Jacksonville Area Legal Aid
- Karen Landry, Director, War on Poverty
- Dawn Lockhart, President and CEO, Family Foundations
- Berneitha McNair, Executive Director, North East Florida Community Action Agency Margo Moehring, Managing Director of Policy & Planning, North East Florida Regional Council
- Mary Kay O'Rourke, President and CEO, HabiJax
- Janet Owens, Executive Director, LISC Jacksonville
- Robert Ownby, Housing Development Manager, Operation New Hope
- Ju'Coby Pittman, President and CEO,
- Clara White Mission Sonia Roberts, Economic Development Director, Grace and Truth Community Development Corporation
- Paul Tutwiler, Executive Director, Northwest Jacksonville Community Development Corporation
- Ben Warner, President and CEO, Jacksonville Community Council Inc.
- Eric Williams, Executive Director, YMCA of Florida's First Coast
- Sirretta Williams, Director, Breaking the Silence
- Jeff Winkler, Director, Real$ense, United Way of Northeast Florida the democracy collaborative 24 Public Sector April Atkins, Community Affairs Specialist, FDIC
- Michelle Barth, Deputy Chief of Staff, City of Jacksonville
- The Hon. Alvin Brown, Mayor, City of Jacksonville

- Ted Carter, Executive Director, Office of Economic Development, City of Jacksonville Paul Crawford, Deputy Director, Office of Economic Development, City of Jacksonville The Hon. Kim Daniels, At-Large, Group 1, Jacksonville City Council
- Teresa Eichner, Policy Director, City of Jacksonville
- Earnie Franklin, Director, Office of Public-Private Partnerships, City of Jacksonville, Office of Economic Development
- The Hon. Dr. Johnny Gaffney, Council District 7, Jacksonville City Council
- Todd Greene, Vice President of Community & Economic Development, Federal Reserve Bank of Atlanta
- The Hon. Bill Gulliford, District 13, Council President, Jacksonville City Council
- Chris Hand, Chief of Staff, City of Jacksonville
- Tony Hill, Federal Policy Director, City of Jacksonville
- Laureen Husband, Director, Healthy Jacksonville, Florida Department of Health in Duval County
- The Hon. Mia Jones, Mayor's Office, Boards & Commissions, City of Jacksonville
- The Hon. Warren A. Jones, District 9, Jacksonville City Council
- Wendy Kahan, Grants Project & Asset Coordinator, Jacksonville Transportation Authority David Kaufman, Senior Director, Planning & Commercial Development, JaxPort
- Joanne Kazmierski, Manager of Community Outreach & Environmental Advocacy, JaxPort
- Margo Klosterman, City Council Liaison, City of Jacksonville
- The Hon. Jim Love, District 14, Jacksonville City Council
- Katryne Lukens Bull, Coordinator, Florida Department of Public Health in Duval County Fred McKinnies, President, Jacksonville Housing Authority
- Capt. Joseph G. McQuade, MD, Director, Public Health, Naval Hospital, Jacksonville
- Mike Miller, Manager of Business Relations, Jacksonville Transportation Authority
- Louis Naranjo, Director of Procurement Services, JAXPort P.G.
- (Bud) Para, Chief Public Affairs Officer, JEA
- Grace Pettus, Staff Assistant/Support, City of Jacksonville

- Dave Roman, Senior Policy Advisor, City of Jacksonville
- Larry Roziers, Executive Director, Special Programs, Duval County Public Schools
- Jennifer Schrader, Division of Community Development, Florida Department of Economic Opportunity
- Taurean Sinclair, Jacksonville Journey Coordinator, City of Jacksonville
- Elaine Spencer, Chief of Housing & Community Development, City of Jacksonville, Housing and Community Development
- Matthew Stewart, Management Analyst, Housing and Urban Development
- Thomas Waters, Grant Administrator, City of Jacksonville
- Joseph Whitaker, Business Development Project Manager, Office of Economic Development, City of Jacksonville
- Wayne Young, Director of Governmental Affairs and Economic Development, JEA Invited Guests and Democracy Collaborative Staff
- Steve Dubb, Research Director, The Democracy Collaborative
- Bill Generett, CEO, Urban Innovation21
- John Hamilton, President, City First Enterprises
- Ted Howard, Executive Director, The Democracy Collaborative
- Angela Lust, Senior Vice President, Amarillo Area Foundation
- Alicia Philipp, President, The Community Foundation for Greater Atlanta India
- Pierce Lee, Program Director for Neighborhoods, Housing & Community Development, The Cleveland Foundation
- Jason Washington, Senior Vice President, City First Enterprises
- David Zuckerman, Research Associate, The Democracy Collaborative

CEO Breakfast Attendees (March 28, 2014)

- Douglas Baer, CEO, Brooks Rehabilitation
- Martha Barrett, Senior Vice President, Corporate Social Responsibility, Bank of America Michelle Barth, Deputy Chief of Staff, City of Jacksonville
- Michelle Braun, COO, United Way of Northeast Florida
- The Hon. Alvin Brown, Mayor, City of Jacksonville
- Janet Burnside, Director of Finance & Funding Development, Jaguars Foundation

- Steve Dubb, Research Director, Democracy Collaborative
- Michael Fleming, Managing Director, Head of DB Jacksonville, Deutsche Bank Doreen Flippin, Vice President for Administration, The Arthur Vining Davis Foundations
- Greg Flowers, Process Owner for Strategic Partnership with Community Organizations, Florida Blue, Branded Marketing Team Nathaniel Ford, CEO, Jacksonville Transit Authority Marvin Grant, Vice President of Academic Affairs,
- Edward Waters College Ted Howard, Executive Director, Democracy Collaborative The Hon. Mia Jones, Special Assistant to Mayor/Boards & Commissions, City of Jacksonville Dave Kaufman, Senior Director, Planning & Commercial Development, JAXPort
- Michelle Leak, Administrator, Longitudinal Care & Community Engagement, Mayo Clinic Robert Lee, Chairman & CEO, Fresh Ministries Bill McConnell, General Manager, SMG
- Paul McElroy, CEO, JEA
- Audrey Moran, Senior VP, Social Responsibility and Community Advocacy, Baptist Health Louis Naranjo, Procurement Director, JAXPort
- Ruth Owen, Senior Vice President, EverBank
- Janet Owens, Executive Director, LISC Jacksonville
- Ju'Coby Pittman, President and CEO, Clara White Mission
- Peter Racine, President, Jaguars Foundation
- Devin Reed, Director of Procurement, Jacksonville Aviation Authority
- Ann Reinert, Vice President, Community Relations and Global Philanthropy, JPMorgan Chase Bank, N.A.
- Kathleen Shaw, Vice President of Programs, The Community Foundation for Northeast Florida
- Susan Towler, Vice President, Community Affairs, Blue Foundation
- Nikolai P. Vitti, Superintendent, Duval County Public Schools
- Nina Waters, President, The Community Foundation for Northeast Florida
- Terry West, CEO, VyStar Credit Union

References

Argyris, C., 'Teaching Smart People to Learn', *Harvard Business Review*, May–June 1991.

Barth, M., *Community Wealthy Building Report*, 2014.

Beeradvocate, 'Duvel Moortgat Buys Boulevard Brewing Company', Oct 2013.
Berry, BTG Works with Missouri Department of Natural Resources', 2002.
Boulevard Brewering Company, boulevard.com, 2021.
Cadbury, D., *Chocolate Wars, Public Affairs*, New York, Douglas & Mcintyre, 2010.
Camagni, R., 'Territorial Capital & Regional Development', in Capello & Nijkamp (Eds), *Handbook of Regional Growth and Development Theories*. Cheltenham: Edward Elger, 2009.
City of Jacksonville, *Community Wealth Building Project*, 2014.
CLUJ Business, https://clujbusiness.ro/business-support/education/universities/#:~:text=One%20of%20the%20most%20important,219%20students%2F1.000%20resident%20population.
Democracy Collaborative, 2020, https://democracycollaborative.org/.
Dragan, A., 'Bucharest vs. Cluj-Napoca: The Transylvanian City Tops the Capital in the Main Economic, Social and Demographic Indicators', *The Business Review*, Dec 10, 2018.
Electric Castle, https://electriccastle.ro/about, viewed Mar 12, 2021.
Fortech, Mar 17, 2021, https://www.fortech.ro/fortech-wins-internal-csr-campaign-of-the-year-award/.
Furnari, C., 'Duval USA CEO on Reinventing Beer as an "Acceptable Luxury"', May 2013, brewbound.com.
Gallagher, T., *Theft of a Nation: Romania Since Communism*. London: Hurst, 2005.
Jones, P., 'Look to Preston for an Answer to Labour's – and Britain's – Woes', *The Guardian*, Jan 13, 2020.
Leucuta, C., 'Clusters as Innovative Partnerships for Economic Growth and new Jobs in Romania', The 2nd International Scientific Conference SAMRO 2016 Romania, Oct 2016.
Lutas, Prof. Mihaela, Personal Interview, 2021.
McDonald, J., Personal Interview, 2021.
Moeller, S., Personal Interview, 2021.
Nonaka, I., 'The Knowledge-Creating Company', *Harvard Business Review*, Nov–Dec 1991.
NWJCDC (Northwest Jacksonville Community Development Corporation), https://www.nwjaxcdc.com/, 2020.
Pentland, A., 'Beyond the Echo Chamber', *Harvard Business Review*, Nov 2013.
Petean, M., 'Banca Dacia Felix a vrut un CNN de Cluj', www.hotnews.ro, Sept 25, 2006.

Pop, F., 'Untold 2017 în cifrele oficiale: peste 330.000 de petrecăreţi, mai mult decât populaţia oraşului Cluj-Napoca', Adevaral, Aug 7, 2017.

'Povestea Untold 2017 continuă cu 10 milioane de euro. La Cluj vor veni cei mai buni DJ şi cele mai bune voci ale momentului', Adevărul (in Romanian), June 22, 2017.

Powell, Kristin, Personal Interview, 2020.

Primaria Cluj-Napoca, https://issuu.com/primariamunicipiuluiclujnapoca/docs/brosura_web

Ramsey, D., 'Philadelphia with Cadbury: Death of a Brand?', *Chocablog*, Jan 2012.

Ripple Glass, https://www.rippleglass.com/, 2020.

Romania-Insider, 'Wages in Cluj-Napoca Supass those in Bucharest', *Romania-Insider*, Sept 26, 2019.

Rose, C., *What Makes People Tick: The Hidden World of Settler, Prospectors and Pioneers*. Leicester: Matador, 2011.

Snowden, D. & Boone, M. E., 'A Leader's Framework for Decision Making', *Harvard Business Review*, Nov 2007.

Techsylvania, https://techsylvania.com/, Mar 13, 2021.

Trompenaars, F. & Hampden-Turner, C., *Riding the Waves of Culture* (2nd ed.). New York: McGraw Hill, 1998.

World Population Review, https://worldpopulationreview.com/world-cities/cluj-napoca-population, Mar 13, 2021.

6

PIONEERING STEWARDSHIP

Thriving in a Networked World

Introduction

The pandemic has only served to underline and inject urgency into thinking about a widening of societal complexity in its relationship with technology and globalisation. The goal of this chapter is to identify and explore the key characteristics that have emerged from the case studies as factors that have enabled some people and places to flourish and others not. We shall seek to examine the value of the patterns and models outlined in Chapters 2 and 3 through the lens of empirical experience in order to determine which concepts, models and combinations of them may be useful in development at the level of the firm, city and region in an increasingly global network economy. We do not seek to make claims about the universal applicability of our findings, but we will examine commonalities, so that patterns can be established for further investigation, by others, to establish their wider utility.

In this chapter, we will first examine the role of stewardship and attachment to place that Scruton (2013) calls oikophilia in our case studies.

DOI: 10.4324/9781003145295-6

This will lead into a discussion of how oikophilia has engaged with network scale and complexity to provide socio-economic resilience. Having examined the role of business and entrepreneurs as key actors in notions of stewardship and network panarchy, the next section will seek to examine the role of government and NGOs in our case studies. Finally, we will examine the contribution of contemporary models of development to make sense of our case studies before outlining a model of our own. We will put forward a model of development grounded in an entrepreneurial and networked form of stewardship, led by Pioneers, that positions the connections between people and place at its core.

Transformational Oikophilia

Stewardship and Attachment to Place

Scruton (2013) describes oikophilia as the cherishing of a place as a home. This combines the classic tensions inherent within idea's of stewardship to both conserve and to grow. A tension that is visible in all of our case studies, but one which when implicitly understood and expressed through shared norms, has proven to offer a key transformational ingredient.

When speaking with employees and corporate leadership at Boulevard, the word stewardship is one that came up time and again. It is also a concept that appeared in the press release upon the sale of the company to a larger conglomerate, where Boulevard leaders wanted to make it clear that the company was and would maintain a commitment to being a steward of the environment. However, Boulevard took their interest in sustainability beyond purely instrumental utilitarianism. Central to their business strategy was a sense of purpose that in caring for the environment, employees and customers were caring for their home, such that the business and its brand became deeply embedded in a sense of place. This belief in stewardship found in current employees comes directly from the founder of the company, John McDonald. For McDonald, stewardship – a concern for the environment and tying this concept to a specific place – is very much rooted in his background where waste was not a positive. For this reason, McDonald, like the Cadbury family before (Taylor & Bronstone, 2019), sees no struggle between making a profit and being good stewards of the earth and, in specific, of the place where Boulevard was founded. McDonald, for these reasons, has worked hard to stress the importance of these themes throughout the company so that they are present long after his direct involvement. For Boulevard, place as a source of identity and shared norms has acquired 'an economic value whenever they can be transformed into marketable products' (Camagni, 2009, p. 120).

It is less clear that 'stewardship' would be a word that the faith groups of North Jacksonville would use, but they certainly were of the belief that their religious principles were guiding them to help the people of the community be as successful in all ways possible, and not just financially. However, the work of the ICARE representatives could be seen in the same light given the assertion that these people brought 'a system of cultural elements and values which attribute sense and meaning to local practices and structures and define local identities' (Camagni, 2009, p. 120). Having said this, while one group of people had a sense of meaning that related to local practices and wanted to lift up a community through the development of communal wealth-building and resilience, these same values were not wholly shared by those not rooted in North Jacksonville either by their locality or their sense of identification. In short, there was, at the end of the day, no common sense of purpose or values.

Unlike Jacksonville, stewardship has been central to the explosion of entrepreneurial activity that has transformed Cluj. The sharing of relational capital, development of shared norms and the open nurturing attitude of the city hall have created multiplier effects that have delivered both improvements in the wealth and sense of pride in place that has created almost a sense of obligation to contribute to the city's social enrichment amongst business leaders. For example, having developed undergraduate programmes in computer science to support the emerging IT sector, IT entrepreneurs have supported a wide range of higher education projects. Recognising the value of a thriving cultural life to encourage young graduates to stay in the city, businesses of all types have supported a wide variety of festivals. Businesses have sponsored public infrastructure projects, whilst the city hall has actively sought to provide infrastructure to nurture enterprise. TEE was created as a partnership of businesses and universities to bring global executive education to ensure that the city is able to thrive as a centre of entrepreneurialism. The idea behind this activity was to enable Cluj businesses to compete in global markets more effectively. Furthermore, as seen in the section on feedback loops, mechanisms of social nudging exist to ensure that rights to extract profit are conditional upon duties when pooling relational capital and also as an implicit obligation of leadership, that is felt as reputational pressure, within the city. Thus in Cluj stewardship, as a code of virtue that ties people to place, has, as we shall see, emerged as the territorial capital, arising from positive feedback loops flowing from the pooling of relational capital.

Despite the failure of government and governance in Romania, the weaknesses of the legal system and a self-serving political class (Gallagher, 2005), Cluj has assumed responsibility for its own future as a shared socio-economic venture. The significance of such a highly developed code of stewardship should not be underestimated in a country where property rights were in living memory highly contested (Verdery, 2003). Under communism, the property was owned by everyone and something that was owned by everyone was, for all practical purposes, owned by nobody. This shorthand explanation for the cause of systemic externalities has remarkably been replaced not just with a functioning system of private property, driving entrepreneurs. It has successfully been pooled as a source of identity and norms that channel behaviour. Overcoming that historic baggage to construct a social system that is a model that many places in Western Europe would aspire to is a very considerable achievement.

In the cases of both Boulevard and Cluj, investment in people and 'place' that does not have immediate utilitarianism value is about recognising ends before means and legitimising your role as a steward of that place and an implicit acknowledgement that rights are conditional upon duties if you wish to develop more than simply transactional short-term business.

EduCab really exists to connect through networks, in order to promote and enhance stewardship, as a means to cherish attachments to a place. Celebrating an identity of place has been recognised as key to providing sufficient security for settlers to find enough agency to change both their social and economic circumstances. The fact that librarians are themselves rooted in a sense of place has provided a renewed sense of pride in both the librarians themselves and in Mayors and citizens. Furthermore, the physical and cultural proximity of the librarians that we met to their own communities gave them a legitimacy, which through a networked form of shared agency, provided the means to nurture sufficient agency to deliver worthwhile projects. Work as a means to celebrate and contribute to the flourishing of a place that they call home has a powerful appeal to settlers. In a country where aspiration has historically been to leave and move in search of a better life, defining rural life in positive and optimistic terms is unusual. Defining social entrepreneurialism as an expression of a place-based identity has proved highly effective in reducing the precariousness of social systems and overcoming resistance to change. Librarians sharing emergent success is creating positive feedback loops that increase panarchy and expand systemic latitude. We cannot be sure that the same will be true in the economic space, but early signs with place-based brands and emerging conversations about community energy have left us feeling optimistic.

Our case studies indicate that the power of stewardship is, through its ability for those with the agency to show respect for their sense of place, leveraging that heritage as a shared set of norms and values that can bind a common determination to flourish in the present and the future. It is the physical and social investment in an agreed identity of place that appears to provide the security for success to be more widely shared and scaled.

Relational and Territorial Capital

There is evidence in Cluj of Myrdal's (1957) clustering around increasing returns to scale in sectors like IT, to the extent that an argument could be made for it as a growth pole (Perrouz, 1950; Darwent, 1969). However, noting this and that resulting shortages of labour create spillover effects (Myrdal, 1957) is to miss the point. Nobody we met believed that the emergence of Cluj can be explained by economic factors alone since they miss the cognitive and behavioural aspects that link entrepreneurship to shared values, norms and enterprises, which have been key. It is clear that none of our case studies can be fitted comfortably into traditional models of economic development. We find that Capello and Nijkamps (2009) argument, that increasing returns flow from innovation arising from a mixture of geographic proximity, relational capital and institutional proximity does appear to be benefiting Cluj. The arguments of Powell (1990) and Cooke and Morgan (1993) that shared resources, clustering and the drawing of expertise from outside of industry and personal networks have been essential to channelling emergent pooled opportunities, such as TEE, have been shown to be insightful. Whilst aspirational participation in global networks of business and culture push leadership further into Snowden and Boones (2007) complex space. Similarly, in the Boulevard and EduCab examples, partnering and pooling resources, based upon a shared sense of purpose and values, have been central to their success. It is the interplay of feedback loops between these features that Camagni (2009) described as territorial capital. Camagni's observation that competitive advantage, arising from shared values, practices and proximity is, therefore, something that can be pooled to drive externalities that have local multiplier effects is seen to be evident in Boulevard, Cluj and EduCab, whilst the absence of shared values, vision and norms has clearly been a hindrance in Jacksonville. Yet, we are less clear that production and design networks' claimed need for proximity (Chesanais, 1988; Johanson, 1991; Cooke & Morgan, 1993) is the best explanation for a city or region's growth. It is less utilitarian than that. The clustering that we have seen has been designed to widen network panarchy and latitude and is better explained as a mixture of relational capital and transformational entrepreneurship, rooted in a sense of place and expressed through pooled relational capital, as asserted by Maas, when stating that 'in order to address transformational entrepreneurship, a supportive entrepreneurship ecosystem should exist' (Maas, Jones & Lockyer, 2019, p. 8).

Pioneering Leadership

Agency has been a central theme in all our case studies. This was true of both Cluj and EduCab. The same can be said of Boulevard, where individuals such as John McDonald played an outsized role in making the green stewardship project happen, and it happened with an agreed-upon set of shared values, beginning with that of stewardship and also of the critical role that employees should play within the context of leading a company. In many ways, EduCab is a counterpoint to Cluj insofar as it is short on relational capital with a sense of agency, but grounded in a clear sense of place. Both Boulevard and EduCab are examples of Pioneers using their entrepreneurial ability to drive change in search of something more transformational than just profit. Boulevard has developed this capability at the level of a firm and EduCab continues to develop more systemic social architecture. Yet in both cases, the organisations have been inspired by the vision of key individuals, who have provided both the vision and the drive. This is not to ignore the contribution of others, but the projects flowing from both organisations would not have taken off without such individuals. Cluj, on the other hand, has relied less on one or two key individuals and perhaps shows that the development of territorial capital is conditional upon the development of numerous Pioneers able to actively pool resources. In other words, relational capital is, to be transformational, a sharing of pioneer values that are partnered with the pooled agency. It is not about leadership as an individual acts alone.

Certainly, EduCab, in its drive to develop both regional coordinators and librarians themselves, implicitly recognise that leadership requires a systemic view. Rooting shared values and a sense of agency in a sense of place to create a sufficient sense of security for Settlers to be able to engage is the core strategy of EduCab. Given their success to date in the social sphere, there are grounds for believing this to have merit. Furthermore, the dependence of the faith leaders of North Jacksonville upon an individual model of leadership, tied to a top-down template and failure to develop a specifically local (modular) pattern of the systemic model of leadership, was key to the project failure.

In all cases, there has been much discussion about the nature of change and how it might be driven, but a key question for our research has been the extent to which Settlers can be engaged. What we have found in both Boulevard and Cluj is that securing innovation in ways that reinforce attachment to people and place is key. Furthermore, removing barriers to access, through pooling resources to reduce costs such as undergraduate degrees, retraining to learn to become a programmer or moving production skills into a recycling business, that enable people to take pride in their place and provide security for their families by participating in global networks creates positive feedback loops. When this is reinforced by festivals and cultural events that use pride in a place as a platform to celebrate not only is system latitude expanded, but resistance to widened panarchy is reduced. As feedback loops develop the overall system precariousness is reduced as growing numbers of people enjoy benefits and a systemic flourishing of people and place emerges. Put simply, the ability of Pioneers to pool agency and risk-taking to sustain people and place includes, but this ability stretches beyond their own enterprises and provides the security for Settlers to participate. Work, in such an environment, increasingly comes to be representative of an investment in Settlers' own communities.

This is most clearly visible in Boulevard, where they have pioneered a circular ecosystem that crosses economic and social spaces and where they have enjoyed profitable success, employee engagement and community participation. This innovative ecosystem is very much a product of its founder, John McDonald. For McDonald grew up with a family member who he referred to as a 'millionaire socialist' and he has always understood that 'saving money and being more ecologically sound are not mutually exclusive' (McDonald, 2021). This was the rationale for Boulevard going 'green' in its manufacturing processes and has continued to do so with the desire to make less waste of its glass products through the innovative creation of Ripple Glass. When speaking to Boulevard employees, what is striking is how they feel that the company truly does model what it says it values – stewardship and the desire to engage its employees in a feedback loop where good ideas – be it about the product itself or a heightened degree of sustainability – are welcomed, valued and more often than not adopted as standard business practice. One employee commented that it is because of this engagement that he does not feel that there is a struggle between the company being profitable on one hand and being socially conscious on the other. In fact, the same employee stated that since the takeover of the company by a larger corporate entity, albeit still in the drinks industry (unlike an investment fund for example), the feedback loops have become better and the drive to become more sustainable has gone unabated. Whilst ongoing efforts to nourish technical colleges, apprenticeships and retraining programmes, supported by local and international enterprises, indicate the implicit support for such a model in Cluj. Although there is no deliberate effort to engage Settlers, as such, in Boulevard or Cluj, the flourishing of both does indicate that EduCab's efforts to bridge relational capital in the social sphere can be translated into the economic sphere also.

The case studies here indicate that for leadership to engage Settlers it needs to be smaller, to embody a stewardship of place and to be pooled if it is to deliver the systemic impact required to engage Settlers in transformational change. Both Cluj and Boulevard indicate that Settlers are not afraid of innovation, but they need to see a purpose to it that positively affects their community and a systemic pattern of activities to have sufficient confidence to engage with it.

Innovation and Overlap

Both Boulevard and Cluj do seem to be examples of the second-order innovation (Knickel et al., 2009) as the basis of effective transformational entrepreneurship. EduCab has demonstrated its capability to use the agency of Pioneers to deliver first order innovation (Knickel et al., 2009) to enable social transformation. EduCab has yet to demonstrate that it can enable systemic economic transformation or connect the two, as Cluj has so effectively. Indeed, the desire to do so indicates an implicit recognition by leaders of EduCab that the second-order innovation is key to converting relational capital into territorial capital and making it sustainable. In Jacksonville, the faith-based groups may have shared a common goal, but they lacked the entrepreneurial individuals or networks capable of either capitalising or activating positive feedback loops to sustain their model.

The owners of Boulevard were not intending to be innovative in their approach to the expansion and redesign of their business and their business model. John McDonald did not and most likely was not going to go out of his way to call the staff from Bridging the Gap, nor was he looking to a corporate model of environmental leadership. However, when presented with the idea and opportunity, McDonald, and the company even since his departure, has embraced an innovative spirit with respect to stewardship beyond that of its traditional business model, not only in spirit but also in its operation and the ability of its employees to be able to bring ideas forward to corporate leaders from the ground up. The creation of Ripple Glass is only one example of this innovative spirit that, while also profitable, would not have been on the radar of the company had the leadership not been open to being innovative in more ways than just 'selling beer'. This is also evident in the company's ever-present commitment to be energy efficient and the final decision to sell to Duvel. The latter decision was made because John McDonald felt that Duvel was the best fit with the company given the Boulevard's commitment to stewardship, innovation and commitment to place. Boulevard's owners have had several offers over time, with all but the one from Duvel being rejected because of the lack of a feeling of this 'fit'. The inclusion of sustainability as the new third leg of the Duvel mission statement, recently announced in 2021, gives innovators committed to stewardship like McDonald hope that the fit between the two companies will continue and evolve over time.

This spirit of innovation may not have been exactly the same in North Jacksonville, since the economic development of less-developed areas of communities is nothing new. However, the faith-based community, in their desire to revitalise this area of the city, did not seek out a model that was 'tried and true'. Instead, the leaders of this project sought out an idea that is not universally well-known, even though its track record is one of great accomplishments. Working to implement a version of the Preston/ Cleveland model in Jacksonville was an innovative approach to an old idea, in a part of the community where economic development had been tried over time, again and again, without much success. This perhaps suggests that it is less the model of development that is problematic and more the shortage of territorial and relational capital, specific to the context.

Cluj has been and continues to be driven by city-wide innovative thinking and practice. From the formation of BT, energy companies and development of embattled relational capital during the Funar years, innovation was less a choice than a necessary tool of survival. The combination of firm-level innovation with relational capital has widened to newer industries, such as IT, continues to transform education and given rise to growing territorial capital. Central to innovation in Cluj has been an implicit acceptance early on by entrepreneurs and leaders of civil society of the need to develop experiments as a way to overcome and manage the unusual levels of complexity imposed by local political circumstances. This was a big part of the drive to reach out to wider networks in search of resources, ideas and opportunities. We see this with the move from putting up mobile phone towers into electrical substations, to the erection and maintenance of renewables platforms across Europe by Electrogrup, outreach to foreign universities by UBB and early festivals, such as the TIFF. Relational capital was, in part, developed to overcome a shortage of individual resources and local systemic barriers to pool risk so that experiments to address more complex challenges, such as the launch of a global MBA programme, could become safe to fail. Failure would involve reputational damage, which acted as a push to succeed, but would not be catastrophic for any individual party or actor. That model of experimentation and coupling it with pooled resources has continued as newer industries, such as IT, have emerged, forming the informal school of IT to retrain low-paid workers into programmers and testers, for example. The importance of both innovation and pooling resources has been formally acknowledged through the formation of clusters, that the City Hall is currently seeking to join together as a means of widening network latitude and expanding panarchy.

EduCab is, by design, an innovative model of connecting small-world networks with larger networks, making interaction enriching and enabling, rather than prescriptive or domineering. The model supports and encourages individual librarians to both conduct their own safe-to-fail experiments, such as the *facut cu drag in Mircea Voda* brand, and enables the amplification of emergent practice through the network. In so-doing EduCab is strengthening the internal resilience of small places and securing those gains within a community of shared practice to expand panarchy. EduCab coordinators would likely be described by Rose (2011) as pioneers, but as librarians gain confidence and experience they are beginning to assume levels of agency that position themselves and the library itself as points of community transformation. In short, EduCab is proving to be an effective vehicle for engaging Rose's (2011) settlers in the wider (and increasingly digital) world, based upon enhancing their sense of place, rather than undermining it.

Network Scale, Complexity and Resilience

Resilience

Cluj is a clear example of a type 2 'evolutionary or transformative response' (Wahl, 2020, p. 25) to the disruption of the immediate post-Communist transition, which was unusually complex due to the nationalist politics of the city. Amidst the complexities of such a transition society (Gallgher, 2005) the absence of even legal certainties (Jolly & Kettaneh, 1999) made the idea of robustness absurd and developing resilience a survival strategy. In order to overcome local systemic resistance (Walker et al., 2004), entrepreneurs, academics and cultural leaders have sought to develop more punctuated (Merali & Snowden, 2019) feedback loops, which in time allow for greater permeability (Merali & Snowden, 2019), panarchy (Walker et al., 2004) and social resilience (Cuthill et al., 2008). It is this punctuated context that has provided the foundation for the development of relational and subsequently territorial capital. In the face of values and systemic limitations, those with the agency have, out of necessity, pooled resources to access and develop networks of support and opportunity, both within and beyond the city. To put it simply, those with the desire to change and grow, without leaving, have developed an embattled capability to adapt, transform, and become stronger (Cuthill et al., 2008) that is the foundation of what has become a complex adaptive system (Maclean, Cuthill and

Ross, 2014), rooted in self organisation and what Argyris (1991) would call double-loop learning capacity. Although not a conscious effort to increase resilience at the outset, the role of the City Hall in widening the panarchy and reducing resistance (Walker et al., 2004) (built upon the underlying resilience, developed during the Funar years) has unleashed the potential to transform. With projects such as the TEE MBA foundation, the development of BT's microenterprise business, their recent entry into environmental finance, the development of businesses such as Pony and software products (rather than simply outsourcing), we see the emergence of consciously structured safe-to-fail experiments (Snowden & Boone, 2007), that seek to embrace complexity, as an opportunity, based upon sharing risk and expertise within pooled local resilience.

EduCab is effectively running a series of safe-to-fail experiments in every community that it operates. Their efforts to develop local social resilience are explicitly about developing local agencies sufficient to expand system latitude, use greater panarchy to apply pressure upon resistance to reduce the precariousness of the social system (Walker et al., 2004) and thus allow emergence to take place. It is not true to say that they have created systemic social resilience in the same way that Cluj has. However, we can see evidence of emergent resilience in some locations that is being consciously used to bridge across networks and to expand the adaptive and learning capacity (Maclean, Cuthill and Ross, 2014) of more communities. Most of their librarians initially work with EduCab as a means to grow type 1 resilience. However, EduCab organisers seek to log roll type 1 success into support and agency for reaching toward type 2 resilience (Wahl, 2020). The attempt to develop the fourth pillar of social entrepreneurship is based upon the implicit belief that sufficient type 1 resilience has been developed within the network to reach for type 2.

In contrast to Cluj, the failure of Jacksonville to build sufficient relational capital amongst stakeholders at the outset significantly undermined capacity to construct social resilience. The project was dependent upon one key individual and participants underestimated systemic passive resistance, creating a systemic precariousness (Walker et al., 2004), which ultimately proved fatal. Essentially, project participants hadn't considered, or remained in the dark about, the 'dark' (Merali & Snowden, 2019) aspects of the project. Although there was an openness to the Evergreen network, this was less panarchy (Walker et al., 2004) and more an attempt to drag and drop a template without contextual punctuation (Merali & Snowden, 2019). Without either relational capital, or a powerful individual to sustain momentum, resilience remained no more than an idea.

Boulevard, initially dependent upon the drive and vision of two key individuals, Bob Mann and John McDonald, succeeded in developing a culture of double-loop learning that positioned environmental issues directly into employees' and customers' immediate experiences. As the owner of Boulevard, McDonald was able to brush resistance aside, whilst Mann brought community stakeholders to widen panarchy and inject vision (see below). With Mann's vision and McDonald's drive, Boulevard was able to conduct safe-to-fail experiments that converted negative feedback loops into positive social feedback loops (as with glass waste) and internalised externalities at zero or negative cost. Spinning Ripple Glass off as a separate not-for-profit enterprise has both widened relational capital with other customers, new partner businesses and embedded the company into the territorial capital of the Kansas City region. It is very much the depth of brand capital that flows from Boulevard's position within its community and partner relationships that Duval saw as driving financial value. Boulevard has demonstrated that being 'rooted' (Burlingham, 2016) combined with adaptive learning capacity can provide both dynamic and transformational social resilience. However, whilst discussions with Senior Managers at Duvel revealed a strong, commercially grounded, desire to allow different breweries to differentiate themselves, there was little evidence of interest in leveraging environmental or community engagement projects across the business. This reinforces the idea, stated above, that for territorial capital to develop a pooling of pioneering entrepreneurs is required that is unlikely to emerge from one company alone.

Networks

All of our case studies raise questions of appropriate scale. None of our cases can be described as constituting a scale-free network. However, the network structure of each case study and the extent to which it is connected to other networks has a significant impact upon its resilience and sustainability.

Boulevard, as a market structured network (Boisot, 1995) from the start and run as a for-profit enterprise, led by an entrepreneur, was always the most open network of the four studied here. The challenge for this organisation was to enable a blurring of the boundaries of the firm, so that communities of practice, including partner firms, the chamber of commerce and community institutions could develop experiments to internalise the firm's externalities. In so-doing they both strengthened the sense of community, by injecting it with a financially self-sustaining purpose and positioned Boulevard as a key node within the community.

In complete contrast, the communities that EduCab works with would most often be best described as fief or clan-type networks, which tend to be self-referential and largely closed. This is made worse by high levels of outward migration, which both reinforce a sense of difference from more successful places and reinforce the turning inwards, as a defence mechanism. What EduCab seeks to do is use the combination of supporting local agencies through their volunteers, within a context of a community of practice (Wenger & Snyder, 2000) to widen both internal network latitude and widen its panarchy. Network intersection is occurring through librarians developing more horizontal network-level agency between themselves. The evidence suggests that positive feedback loops are being developed as local success, shared, breeds confidence in the power of local agency to transform.

During the Funar years, in Cluj, local entrepreneurs developed clan-like networks and sought to punctuate the limitations of the city by opening business networks beyond. The combination of the election of Mayor Boc and then joining the EU widened latitude, reduced policy resistance and allowed relational capital to be deployed as a pooled resource to expand network panarchy. As noted previously, a modular approach to networks works best, as Cross put it, 'where components of a problem and solution are known but the combination or sequence of those components is not yet known' (Cross, Liedtka & Weiss, 2005, p. 125). Both the Techsylvania festival and the formation of TEE are examples of modular approaches to networks that were built upon relational capital seeking to reach beyond a self-referencing clan. Equally, Cluj has not been subsumed into larger, or scale-free networks. Those interviewed take pride in the social as well as the economic aspects of territorial capital. Whilst they wish to bring in knowledge from wider networks and access larger markets, ultimately there is a confidence that they possess the collective relational agency to not only take from network bridging, but also contribute. This suggests a high level of agency that exists as a constant psychological and sociological feedback loop connecting what has been achieved and what can be achieved.

Jacksonville is a case where network effects have not really been unlocked. Assumed levels of systemic resistance to change were underestimated and the application of a template as a form of best practice was to misread a complex space as a complicated one that would be responsive to expertise (Snowden & Boone, 2007). Instead of channelling context-specific emergence, the use of an external template encouraged the idea that this was a problem responsive to expert analysis. The election of Mayor Alvin Brown seems to have created a sense that the problem of implementation was now a question of applying best practices. This illusion caused the project to fall over the cliff from Snowden and Boone's (2007) simple space into the chaotic space and, of course, ultimately fail. Simply put, reliance upon the election of a key individual to be able to assume sufficient authority to copy-paste ignored the limited systemic latitude for change, shortage of punctuation and offered limited network bridging, to provide support. Frankly, the failure of Jacksonville demonstrates the problems that Pentland (2013) describes as getting trapped within an echo chamber:

> Decision makers need to tap diverse social networks. If your circle is too tight and the members of it are too similar, you risk being trapped in an echo chamber where the same ideas keep circulating, limiting the payoff of social learning.

EduCab is about taking places from the fief network structure, to become more diffuse and gradually enabling people to take part in more codified networks, as they begin to overlap similar to Iansati & Lakhani's Uber model. To escape routine responses and develop more modular capabilities. Cluj is a story of trying to escape formal networks of bureaucracy (Boisot) and informal clan relationships that characterised 1990s Romania and develop more market networks that seek to construct links to scale-free networks. EduCab is also about making connections in their network and using tech to widen the reach of small places. Relational and location capital from Cluj is what is making entrepreneurship transformational.

The Mattress Effect

It is clear that a central problem for Jacksonville was in trying to apply an integrated top-down model, since failure occurred both at project and systemic level. The bitter experience of experimentation at survival in Cluj (during the Funar years) led directly to an implicit understanding that complex systems are best understood through the evolutionary interplay of systemic and actor level interactions (Von Bertalanffy, 2010; Merali, 2006) and practice of an ongoing culture of safe-to-fail experiments, which if successful could be amplified and if not dampened. Failure of experiments may cause a disturbance, but not systemic failure, whilst success could and was quickly amplified, with network effects quickly kicking in to drive multiplier effects. A simple example of this is the development of an MBA partnership between Cluj universities, business leaders and a British university. What was for the British university a standard template of a local agent recruiting for a fly-in faculty, that had been tried and tested over years around the world, quickly led to overlapping research, consulting, writing, academic and undergraduate exchange programmes. Success with what had traditionally been a fairly transactional model very quickly became a model for wider transformation that was used to widen panarchy and latitude, to the point where senior academics at the British university became frustrated at the constant push to do more from Cluj.

We can see in both EduCab and Boulevard how new projects and locations were designed on the safe-to-fail principle, so as to protect the wider organisational mattress from systemic failure. Doing so continues to enable both to minimise risk as they explore how to channel emergent opportunities, whilst maintaining the opportunity to amplify success systemically.

Scale is the problem with the application of models like the Cleveland model in places like Jacksonville for people like Mihai. His experience working at UNDP has led him to believe that whilst socio-economic development requires vision and entrepreneurial agency, the channelling of emergence from the bottom is far more sustainable and likely to succeed, beyond a project level, systemically than trying to apply top-down models. Our research indicates that Merali (2022) is correct in her observation that 'multiple place-based clusters embodying the requisite heterogeneity' provide space for contextual specifics. In other words, one size does not fit all and whilst the spirit of the Preston model is something we find laudable the application may be better when applied flexibly to existing emergent patterns of community wealth building. Furthermore, development is rarely an even path and channelling emergence also allows for 'local repair adjustments to local perturbations [which] may be fast paced and instantaneous' (Merali, 2022).

Tight Feedback Loops

We have seen how in Cluj there exists systemic peer pressure upon leaders to invest in their community. It is subtle pressure that is about establishing and maintaining legitimacy as a leader based upon demonstration of commitment to this place. Nurtured by a political leadership which both encourages such behaviour has created features of civil society, such as volunteering and public–private sector collaboration, that is unusual in Romania. Feedback loops flowing from successful entrepreneurial activity (pooled and private) are powerful motivators in a community where such news travels fast and the actors all know one another. A mixture of jealous rivalry and shared pride have proved a heady mixture for feedback loops to prove transformational.

EduCab, on the other hand, is all about widening panarchy to reduce precariousness, widen latitude, reduce resistance and expand agency in places where entrepreneurial activity is mostly absent. These relationships flow from nurturing positive social feedback loops. Organisers are less interested in specific activities than their systemic impact upon both the confidence and subsequent agency of librarians and their ability to provide examples that can be used, through the network, to create systemic multiplier effects. The extent to which they can be expanded into economic spaces remains to be seen, but as noted previously, we have grounds to be cautiously optimistic.

Boulevard may have begun by developing a new business venture, but, over time, managers have learned from repeated experience. This is a business where social and ecological systems have been intermeshed, by exploring how liabilities can be reconceptualised as opportunities. Such activity is essentially about identifying negative feedback loops and exploring how partnerships with other actors can extract value by internalising such externalities, thereby reducing impact and creating value. Thus management at Boulevard is based upon double-loop learning and looking for feedback loops, rather than simply trying to reduce costs and escape liabilities.

The failure to appreciate the important role of feedback loops appears to have been critical in Jacksonville, such that the project teams application of defined best practice were unable to channel emergence and underestimated parallel feedback loops working against them across the political divide.

Systemic Complexity

As we have seen in all of our case studies, relationships between people and 'place' are systemic in nature and key components cannot be meaningfully understood in isolation, as Hitchens asserts 'behaviours emerge both from the elements and their interactions' (Hitchens, 2003). Thus, looking for patterns of cause and effect is less useful than looking for patterns of emergence. The presence of multiple and interconnected feedback loops is what gives rise to complexity in a system and makes it difficult to predict (Maani & Cavani, 2000). Furthermore, whilst patterns of causation do exist they are not visible without the benefit of hindsight (Snowden & Boone, 2007). It is, therefore, because a system cannot be explained, or boundaries identified, that defines its complexity (Waldrop, 1993).

Merali (2022 [italics in original]) has cogently argued that socio-economic systems are Complex Adaptive Systems, embodying a network form of organisation with 'an integrated *network of networks*'. Such an approach builds 'multiple place-based clusters embodying the requisite heterogeneity' (Merali, 2022) and 'providing the requisite connectivity between clusters ... to achieve a synergistic, place-based enhancement of well-being' (Merali, 2022). Merali goes on to argue that the three key factors for community sustainability are generative capacity and evolutionary mechanisms, retention of microdiversity, which need to be supported by larger networks seeding the requisite diversity and capability, support for a local agency and harnessing local expertise (Merali, 2022). Merali's case supports our argument that the role of pioneers in developing a sense of purpose-based agency to widen panarchy is key in engaging settlers and reducing network precariousness. Something that has been borne out in our case studies, perhaps most explicitly in the EduCab case, but it is also evident in both Boulevard and Cluj.

Merali (2022) notes that both her model and that of Ostrom (2009) are about the ability of place-based community mechanisms to develop congruence between the members' collective understanding of the wider ecosystem and the impact of their actions. A critical factor is 'their identification with the need to invest themselves in ensuring the sustainability of that resource' (Merali, 2022). Underlining the role of pioneers in combining the ethical dimensions of stewardship with the agency to deliver practical action, such that settlers have something tangible to engage with locally. The 'distributed network form of organising overcomes the deficiency of centrally-determined "one size fits all" policies' (Merali, 2022). Reliance upon top-down policies and leadership we have seen were an issue in Jacksonville and the success of the other case studies has, to varying degrees, been based upon more distributed networked forms of organisation.

In the cases of Cluj, EduCab and Boulevard, there are clear feedback loops driving patterns of emergence, which suggests that what makes transformational entrepreneurship transformational is the ability to utilise relational capital to channel and facilitate patterns of emergence around a defined place. The resulting territorial capital appears to hinge upon positive peer pressure, as feedback loops, to acknowledge the importance of place in entrepreneurial success through investing rewards into multiplier effects that further enhance place and attachment to it.

Institutional Leadership

Non-Governmental Organisations as Agents of Change (Financial, Educational)

In all four case studies, non-governmental organisations play a significant role, if not a lead role in the development of each of these initiatives. In Jacksonville, faith-based groups led the process by which the government was encouraged to become involved in the redevelopment project, whereas libraries are at the heart of the EduCab model, which is itself an NGO. In Kansas City, while Boulevard is a for-profit company, the partnership between the Chamber of Commerce and the environmental organisation Bridging the Gap that led to the decision by the company to move in this direction was critical. In fact, the Chamber of Commerce was, in the late 1990s, a community leader in promoting an agenda of environmentalism that belies a traditional notion of what a chamber of commerce's environment committee would be focused on. At that moment in time, the leadership of the committee was committed to having the Chamber be a role model by way of committing itself to an internal recycling program and working with organisations like Bridging the Gap to encourage local 'champion' companies like Boulevard to become more sustainable in their thinking and processes. Finally, in Cluj, institutions such as the university have not really led as such, but they have been willing to adapt to support, legitimise and encourage relational and territorial capital. In all cases, they have been central to pooling relational capital and have played an entrepreneurial role in transforming the places where they operate. Contrary to the popular perception we find from the case studies here that NGOs are not only central to the development of territorial capital, but are the source of a considerable degree of entrepreneurialism. As the centrepoint of pooled relational capital, they are often the linkage to other networks and have a key role in widening panarchy, reducing resistance to change and developing network resilience. As the centrepoint of entrepreneurial collaboration, rather than competition, they blur the boundary between means and ends, such that norms are increasingly shared and become more substantive. A simple example is when a board member of TEE became angry that one of his employees had left it late to complete registration for the MBA, the board member demanded that an exception be made and his employee admitted. Other board members took him aside and reminded him why TEE mattered because 'we don't do things this way'. It was a nudge that resulted in an apology as he recognised that whilst he wanted to get his way he was risking the purpose and meaning of TEE and, in so-doing, undermining his own reputation as 'one of us', who shares the values and norms. Inside his own firm, without an NGO to pool relational capital, a quite different outcome is most likely.

Equally, EduCab is able to gain access to communities precisely because it is not a capitalist or political organisation. The organisation threatens no one by its presence and the absence of salaries for its volunteers removes the question of what's in it for me. Their support for libraries represents potential political capital for the Mayor if he (and it mostly is a he) is able to confer legitimacy on their activities, thus beginning a cycle of positive feedback loops that widen panarchy, latitude and reduce precariousness. In a low trust country like Romania (Gallagher, 2005; Trompenaars &

Hampden-Turner, 2012), this would simply not be possible if any of the actors perceived self-interest, visible or otherwise.

Government

This is another checklist item where 'government', at one level or another, and in both positive and negative ways, has as an entity played a role in most of the projects described in the case studies. Local mayors have been at times helpful to the growth of the EduCab process, albeit a limited one at times because of the lack of funds available to them. In Cluj, the Mayor, City Hall and their international relations team have been both a catalyst and hub to support and legitimise the accumulation of territorial capital. They are now actively seeking to nurture and develop positive feedback loops between relational and territorial capital, through clustering and an explicit search for overlap between the economic and the social spaces, with festivals, educational opportunities providing arenas for such emergence. The mayor's office in Jacksonville has played both positive and negative roles in the North Jacksonville redevelopment project. Alvin Brown's office was fully supportive and then when he was not re-elected, the new mayor, from a different party, acted in a manner that inhibited the project. Finally, in Kansas City, the local government did not play a role in the decision of the company to move forward with its green industrial plans but did not inhibit these plans.

The importance of the role of government in driving development in the cases presented here depends upon the existing levels of relational capital and local agency. Where it has been incomplete or not based upon a shared vision such as in Jacksonville the role of government assumed a centrality that was critical to project failure. Whilst recognising that relationships with local Mayors have been central to the success of the EduCab model, perhaps what is more interesting is that pooled relational capital appears, from the cases here, to precede any role for government. The role of government, as noted, was quite limited in most of our case studies, but where it was present; in Cluj, assuming the role of facilitator of territorial capital, through expanding both system latitude and panarchy to reduce resistance and precariousness, was key. The city hall in Cluj followed the flow of relational capital, sought to facilitate it, legitimise and embed it through clusters and widen its impact. In short, the key appears to be about connecting Rose's (2011) pioneers to settlers to provide sufficient agency to develop increased systemic sustainability in attachment to place.

Reflections Upon Models of Development

Transition Towns and Foundational Economy Models

The recognition of innovation as having a value beyond the economic alone (Morgan, 2019) resonates in many aspects of the case studies presented here. However, there is little evidence of the emergence of what could be reasonably described as a foundational economy (Morgan, 2020). EduCab, with its bottom-up focus and success with social development, has potential to develop the foundational model. Yet, at the time of writing, nobody in the organisation was familiar with the model.

An aspiration towards some aspects of the Transition towns movement can be seen in Boulevard, EduCab and Cluj, but maybe better described as the beginning of a conscious, if incomplete, effort to develop transformational entrepreneurship, with entrepreneurship defined 'as the creation of an innovative virtue-based organization for the purpose of shifting resources out of an area of lower and into an area of higher purpose and greater value under conditions requiring a holistic perspective' (Maas, Jones & Lockyer, 2019, p. 6) is, to varying degrees, an accurate description of the development of Boulevard, Cluj and EduCab. Furthermore, the model's emphasis upon adaptive thinking, which we would describe as double-loop learning (Argyris, 1991), is a useful description of the drivers behind Boulevard, Cluj and EduCab.

Transformational Entrepreneurship

If entrepreneurship is rooted in an activated sense of agency, we can say that all of our case studies demonstrated efforts to use it. However, the extent to which that was successful varied. All except Jacksonville understood entrepreneurship to have a systemic component, where entrepreneurs individually or collectively, sought to use social networks to leverage positive feedback loops. Beyond that, they all actively sought to connect local networks to wider networks beyond their own immediate ones. Jacksonville was not able to develop a systemic approach to entrepreneurship and this undoubtedly contributed to the ultimate failure of the initiative there.

What has driven the success of Boulevard, EduCab and Cluj is the intersection of transformational entrepreneurship and relational capital, which together have formed the basis of a sustainable Territorial capital. It is not only the connections of familiarity, but the shared belief that enterprise is not only an end in itself that has been key in Cluj and Boulevard. The role of entrepreneurs as Pioneers (Rose, 2011), willing to pool resources for common and collective goals (Powell, 1990; Cooke & Morgan, 1993) has created positive feedback loops both for the entrepreneurs and their communities.

There is little doubt that both Cluj and Boulevard combined 'the individual and other subsystems (such as society and institutions) interacting and collaborating to create a positive framework in which opportunities can be exploited beyond the local level' (Maas, Jones & Lockyer, 2019, p. 1). Furthermore, proponents of transformational entrepreneurship claim that 'leaders need to create compelling narratives in terms of entrepreneurship' (Maas, Jones & Lockyer, 2019, p. 9) is demonstrably accurate in the case of Boulevard as a central component to their brand value and in Cluj through the example of Banca Transilvania (BT). Having grown dramatically in recent years the bank's strategy had to change to accommodate new regulatory and market challenges. Rather than hire consultants to develop employee engagement programmes, as might be expected, they reached through the TEE network to a British professor to develop a project to capture the stories of BT. He then briefed the Board and, subsequent to the pandemic, workshops have been planned to help managers learn how to use this bank of stories to maintain engagement and commitment. This is but one example of a bank of stories, which consistently construct a narrative that emphasises the difference between Cluj and a perceived national culture. Cluj stories emphasise more of a protestant work ethic (which implicitly speaks to their German heritage), less individualistic, more cultured and ultimately not like the capital city of Bucharest. As someone told us 'The EU saved us from their [Bucharest's] sunflower seed society' – a reference to the habit of eating sunflower seeds and spitting the shells onto the floor in the South of Romania, where Bucharest is located.

Whilst there is no formal effort at storytelling within EduCab, every interviewee used stories to describe the purpose of the network and the actors within it. Given the socio-cultural nature of their projects undertaken, that narratives should be central to bridging conversations should, perhaps, not be a surprise. There is no one overarching story that EduCab is trying to communicate. As noted, it is a bottom-up approach, where the narrative runs more like the infamous line from the film *Jerry McGuire*: 'help me help you'. That said the success of EduCab is heavily reliant upon using its network to spread stories of success to both widen panarchy, encourage agency and develop resilience.

Cluj is interesting because it indicates that universities could have a central role in enabling transformational entrepreneurship. In Cluj, their role was mostly that of following the needs of employers. Nonetheless, they were flexible and often provided a common personal experience that supported the development of shared norms, which we have witnessed as being key to the development of entrepreneurial partnerships. They were often central to pooling relational capital, such as the TEE MBA, that both delivered immediate benefits, but also created spillover effects that widened and deepened entrepreneurial potential. Furthermore, the universities in Cluj have played a central role in providing a platform for capturing and distributing such benefits. There is some evidence that the use of courses of teaching, as seen in TEE, for example, can be a catalytic accelerator of relational capital. Certainly, the formation of TEE was about providing world-class executive education so that Cluj may thrive as a centre of entrepreneurialism. However, in Cluj, this happened organically, led by entrepreneurs and not in the planned way by universities, described in the literature (Maas & Jones, 2017). Certainly, the Universities have provided an arena to pool relational capital and been supportive of it, but to define them as architects of planned systemic change is to overstate their role.

The Preston Model

The Preston model also allocates a central role for universities as anchor institutions and recyclers of local capital. This model was of great interest to us at the outset as it appeared to offer both a template and a track record of success. The universities in Cluj have played a central role, if not in driving the development of territorial capital, then in providing a platform for capturing and distributing such benefits. Certainly, the international relations office in Cluj is openly defining local cooperation, mutualities and clustering as going beyond individual organisational strategies to become central to a successful development strategy for the city. However, whilst the universities are clearly central to city life there was no attempt to recycle money locally, or use university spending to nurture specifically local, or community owned, businesses in any sort of strategic manner as per the Preston model.

BT would also fit many of the characteristics of the financial pillar of the Preston model and is certainly an anchor institution in the city. However, whilst it is true that BT does contribute a disproportionate amount of financial and social investment in Cluj and has been transformational in lots of ways to the city's development. The bank is not a mutual society of any kind and their impact has not been part of any effort to implement a unified or strategic model of community wealth building. Quite the reverse in fact, it has been very much a bottom-up effort, with initiatives emerging from the commitment and interest of individuals within the organisation, with coordination being brought later to amplify success only. BT remains a capitalist institution.

The city hall in Cluj has won plaudits for its far-sighted approach to the city's development. Certainly, the international relations office in Cluj is openly defining local cooperation, mutualities and clustering as going beyond individual organisational strategies to become central to a development strategy for the city. However, they have, until recently, defined their role as a key channeller and amplifier of emergence, rather than architect of a predefined design. As they develop structure around clusters to embed a form of what Ostrom (2015) might call nested social systems, the role of the facilitator is increasingly becoming that of coordinator.

It is not the case that Cluj is an example of community wealth building, but it has achieved many of the notable features that model aspires to deliver. Furthermore, given the disposition of many of the key actors, the willingness of anchor institutions (such as BT, the universities and City Hall) to pool relational capital, increasingly nested and overlapping nature of feedback loops that have been developed, we are left wondering what might be achieved in Cluj if an agreement to apply the Preston model was reached.

Boulevard, as an important employer carrying a place-based brand, would certainly fit many of the characteristics of an anchor institution in Kansas City. However, whilst the company has certainly adopted a systemic approach to connecting the business to the community and the ecology that support both, there has been no conscious attempt to challenge the capitalist framework through which they have structured their engagement. There is some evidence of the development of ecosystem services that have reached beyond the firm and had some systemic impact. Nonetheless, we see Boulevard as an example of an entrepreneurial catalyst that has the potential to grow into systemic change, but is not, in itself, an example of systemic change just yet. Whilst the disposition and track record of key actors like McDonald indicates that community wealth building could be of interest, there is little evidence from our research that there is, as yet, sufficient territorial capital beyond Boulevard to avoid the problems of Jacksonville.

If Jacksonville is the failure of the Preston model, with its reliance upon the alignment of policy between public and private sectors, then EduCab is striving towards, bottom up, polycentricity (Ostrom, 2009, 2015), without the need to partner with political or bureaucratic authority. EduCab operates in places where governance is weak or absent. In the absence of political leadership, EduCab leaders are leveraging a networked form of entrepreneurship that is socially dynamic and assuming an emergent economic nature. EduCab is a deliberate effort to develop a network based upon connecting Pioneers to Librarians that are central to local Settler (Rose, 2011) networks so that relational capital, rooted in emerging proximity of contact and repeated demonstrations of ethical agency, in order to develop territorial capital, where previously there existed mostly migration. Such an approach implicitly recognises that development is contingent upon a sense of agency that is best nurtured within a network and unlikely to emerge from traditional linear models of development and governance.

Polycentricity

Ostrom (2009, 2015) and more recently Merali (2022) note how top-down universal prescriptions fail because of the gap between central norms and rules and local practices, which is also the basis of the emphasis upon modularity from the Preston model (Lewis, 2017). Ostrom (2015) describes overlapping commons and community governance regimes, which ripple out and provide a kind of 'nesting' that she refers to as polycentricity. Heikkila says 'polycentric governance involves multiple overlapping centres of decision-making, which interact within an overarching set of rules' (Heikkila, Villamayor-Tomas & Garrick, 2018, p. 207). Whilst Ostrom identifies a series of conditions as the requisite for self-governing nested regimes that she calls polycentric. Merali (2022) identifies five as linked to her model of *Cognitive Congruence Framework*, which also resonates with our experience from this research: collective agency and autonomy, norms and social capital, local leadership and knowledge of socio-ecological systems. However, we venture to go further and suggest that there is evidence from our case studies that the conditions exist for the emergence of Ostrom's (1990, 2015) polycentricity. Whilst polycentricity is traditionally associated with common property regimes, and this is certainly central to the overlap with the Preston model, Ostrom (2012) is clear that polycentricity is broader than purely commons regimes and may extend to include capitalist organisations that are willing to share the norms and values that define the common purpose and operation of the regime.

Tarko argues that 'polycentricity differs from anarchy in that the interactions between the decision centres are governed by well-established rules' (Tarko, 2012, p. 61). Tarko goes on to say that polycentricity creates 'at a local level, a structure of incentives favourable to building trust'. In short, developing local systems of commons, rather than individual standalone enterprises is more likely to lead to what Snowden and Merali (2019) might well describe as a complex-adaptive system and produce enhanced adaptive capacity (Carlisle & Gruby, 2018; Biddle & Baehler, 2018). Indeed, our research indicates that, contrary to the findings of Biddle and Baehler (2019), polycentricity can be an effective response to problems and cultures of 'blame avoidance over problem solving, persistent power imbalances, large wealth inequalities, and deficits of social capital and leadership' (Biddle & Baehler, 2019, p. 344). To be clear, we are not trying to claim that the case studies represented here are perfect examples of polycentrism in action. However, we do see evidence of many of the features of Ostrom's model arising from nested and overlapping socio-economic ecosystems that appear to indicate the emergence of complex adaptive systems that cannot be ignored.

Taking Ostrom's conditions one at a time, it is tricky to speak of group boundaries in terms of geographic limitations in the cases we have studied here, despite the importance of place as a source of identity. This is largely because that place is defined as much in sociological as geographic terms.

Thus group boundaries seem to be defined more by norms, values, shared experience and proximity than lines in the sand. Group boundaries are, therefore, defined by Ostrom's second and third condition of shared participatory rules, which is, as we have seen, essential to pooling relational capital and the nesting of networks. Whilst often not explicitly defined, nudging to conform with rules and norms has been shown to take place. Furthermore, the development of clusters is, at least in part, about developing more formally accepted patterns of governance. The fourth and fifth points concerning empowering and monitoring the rule-making authority of network participants underline the facilitative role that the city hall has assumed in Cluj and EduCab and provides to their networks. Whilst a system of peer pressure and reputational risk has been shown, in Cluj to create the feedback loops to apply graduated sanctions to violators of the norms. Interestingly, it has often been both university academics and civil servants, with their absence of interest in capitalist gain, that have provided informal low cost means for resolving disputes in Cluj, whilst in EduCab the librarians definition of themselves as local facilitators enables them to be both catalysts and legitimate arbiters of disputes in their localities. As we have seen, it is the combination of these factors acting together and injected with entrepreneurial agency that forms the basis of nested tiers of territorial capital that we see in Cluj and EduCab aspire towards.

The Pioneering Stewardship Model

Although they may be helpful, it is not geography, resources, central policies, proximity to markets or any of the traditional factors considered important to city and regional development that are key to success in the digital age. The case studies from this research indicate that it is the combination of pooled relational capital with entrepreneurship, driven by Pioneers, grounded in a sense of place, that creates nested and overlapping social ecosystems that produce positive feedback loops which lie at the heart of territorial capital (Camagni, 2009). Figure 6.1 shows how, together, they reduce precariousness, expand latitude and panarchy and in so-doing reduce resistance to further change, thereby creating a positive cycle. This creates a high level of social resilience that maintains system function in the face of change (Maclean, Cuthill and Ross, 2014) and provides the resilience, and adaptive capacity (Jackson, 2003) to drive second

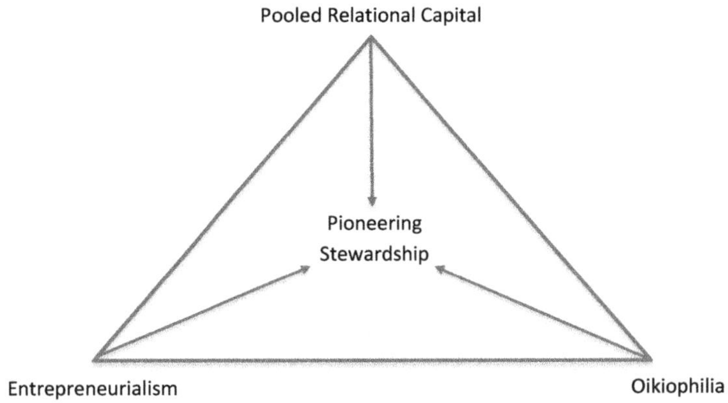

Figure 6.1 Pioneering Stewardship

order innovation (Knickel et al., 2009). In turn, this creates a mattress effect (Kohr, 1957) that limits the typical business-led search for robust efficiencies of scale.

Whilst Cooke and Morgan (1993) correctly identified the importance of networks of pooled relational capital, a better understanding of the systemic nature of network characteristics enables us to see that it is the entrepreneurial ability to engage with complexity that is central to creating value. Combining that capability with a sense of purpose that is grounded in an identity of place is a powerful force in itself, but when positioned within networks of sufficiently shared norms and values to be able to pool resources to expand network panarchy creates multiplier effects. Those multiplier effects emerge from exponentially positive feedback loops that access to global knowledge in MBAs, tech fairs, exposure to new ways of thinking, alternative models and the like provide. Most importantly, the expansion of network panarchy seems to have a profound multiplier effect upon agency when actors are able to demonstrate that they can use expanded connections to deliver benefits that go beyond themselves. Thus the pooling of relational capital has a double benefit. First, it shares risk, distributes rewards more widely and increases the range of what is possible. Second, it embeds agency within an identification of values and norms that become associated with this place.

Combining the insights of Rose's model (2011) with elements of transformational entrepreneurship (Maas, Jones & Lockyer, 2019), the Preston model (Peck, 2019), territorial capital model (Camagni, 2009), insights from complexity thinkers such as Merali, Boisot and Snowden and grounding them in a sense of Oikophilia (Scruton, 2013) is the foundation of a model that provides placed based agency, based upon pooled relational capital. Pooling relational capital allows Pioneers (Rose, 2011) to conduct safe-to-fail experiments (Snoden & Boone, 2007), that are as much networked double-loop learning (Argyris, 1991) as they are entrepreneurialism, as they seek to engage with higher levels of complexity. This process is illustrated in Figure 6.2.

As such, socio-economic networks start to overlap and they become nested (Ostrom, 2009, 2015), creating tiers of depth and increase the scope and range of pooled resources that create positive feedback loops at a systemic level. Furthermore in Cluj, we have observed clear evidence of informal methods of actors nudging other actors to conform to shared norms of behaviour as increasingly formalised as processes of nesting grow. For example, when one entrepreneur tried to gain an advantage for his employee in a shared project that put at risk the underlying values of the project itself, other stakeholders took him aside and in his apology the shared norms and values gained further strength. EduCab is actively trying to encourage librarians to develop similar self-governing feedback loops. Although nested networks intersect, they do not become scale free,

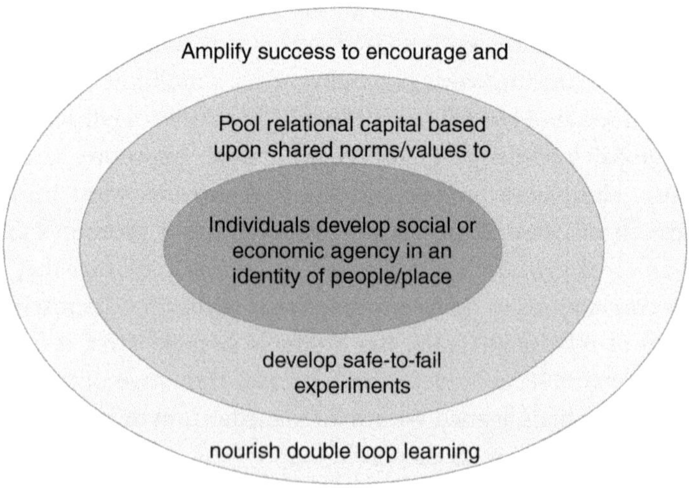

Figure 6.2 Developing Pioneering Stewardship

but rather become overlapping clusters. Embedding this culture in patterns of governance is something that the Mayor's office in Cluj has actively encouraged. In turn, this grows resilience through the development of the mattress effect (Kohr, 1957), both within the city and also within wider networks. This process also creates greater potential for polycentric forms of governance to emerge. From these studies, we see some evidence in Cluj of emergent aspects of polycentrism.

We do see multiple projects, organisations and clusters with overlapping actors, centres of decision-making and regimes of governance. They do form a mosaic of local regimes able to increase adaptive capacity (Biddle & Baehler, 2018; Carlisle & Gruby, 2018). Furthermore they are increasingly being structured 'within an overarching set of rules' (Heikkila, Villamayor-Tomas & Garrick, 2018, p. 207). We are seeing signs of a complex adaptive system emerging, with wider network panarchy, diffusion and codification all emerging from pooled relational capital.

Although the pioneering stewardship model does not require common ownership, the pooling of resources, values and norms of behaviour that we have seen in Cluj and to a lesser degree in EduCab and Boulevard, has enabled the development of many of the characteristics, described by Ostrom (1990, 2015), of commons regimes. Attachment to place and the practice of pooling relational capital has clearly enabled the definition of group boundaries in Cluj, to some degree in EduCab and Boulevard. Rules governing activities flowing from pooled relational capital are specific to local needs and conditions and have emerged from them in Cluj and Boulevard. They are perhaps emergent in EduCab. The above-described case of the common good in TEE (Cluj) is but one illustration that those affected by the rules can participate in modifying the rules. This case is especially interesting since participants who had less economic power and less capital invested were not less able to exert influence. In EduCab, Mihai is explicitly encouraging wider participation in the development of locally specific patterns of governance. The formation of clusters, partnerships with powerful local institutions and the Mayor's office, in Cluj, have all been used to ensure that outside bureaucratic authorities, even if they do not respect at least, don't harm the rule-making rights of community members, whilst EduCab works in partnership with local librarians and their county-level coordinators to pressure village mayors to honour their financial obligations to support libraries, which otherwise many do not.

The formation of clusters in Cluj is in part about developing a peer-based system for monitoring members' behaviour that starting with social nudging is (as we have seen) able to apply graduated sanctions for rule violators. Clusters such as the IT clusters have provided accessible, low-cost means for dispute resolution about issues such as the development of technology parks, city infrastructure and broader planning, whilst the Mayor's office in Cluj is clearly building responsibility for governing through clusters in nested tiers from the lowest level up to the entire interconnected system. The EduCab network is developing a framework for governance and using its mentoring network as an arena for resolving disputes and governance.

Although the adoption of many of the habits of the transformational mindset of Boulevard by its new owner indicates that a scaling of relational capital is possible, we have no evidence to suggest that they have radically shifted the pre-existing culture of the acquiring organisation. Nonetheless the culture of looking for local innovations, reaching out for partners to internalise social and environmental costs and create new opportunities goes on in Kansas. Thus, it is fair to describe Boulevard as an example of a contributor to the development of pioneering stewardship in Kansas City. Yet although there is overlap between projects and businesses that they have founded in their search for greater stewardship responsibility, we do not see new bottom-up patterns of governance emerging. We cannot see evidence of polycentricity. Of course, rather like Cluj, other actors may engage more widely to develop projects less directly linked to their business, but we are not there yet.

It is the combination of networks of entrepreneurial agencies that are grounded in a sense of place that provides both the anchor and the vision to join the local to the global in a more inclusive way that is the source of transformation. Such processes do not happen overnight, and our research indicates that whilst they can be nurtured (as EduCab is having some success doing), they seem more likely to flourish if they emerge from the bottom than are imposed (no matter with what good intentions) from the top. If nothing else, this research shows that simply trying to roll out large-scale transformational models of development, such as the Preston model, without intermediate steps to create a receptive climate that has already experienced success in transforming from within, is likely to fail.

Based upon the findings of our research here, we have developed a staged model of how to go about designing and delivering pioneering stewardship in practice.

Staged model:

- Develop relational capital around shared norms, experiences and values to open discussion of how social and business entrepreneurs can enable their home to flourish, using attachment to place as a system boundary and double loop learning (Argyris, 1991) as the mode of inquiry.
- Identify the scope for pooling relational capital that would deliver positive multiplier effects. Ensure that such pooling has a social dimension and, if not already present, gradually develops an economic dimension, with actors taking real financial and/or reputational risk.
- Emphasise that innovative pooling actions are about invigorating the identity of a place and developing opportunities to cherish that identity, such that those who take part may flourish securely within it.
- Involve partners, especially Universities in supporting and sustaining the pooling process.
- Actively seek to overlap network subsystems, to activate patterns of nesting.

We realise that our model requires further research and analysis to establish the extent of its wider applicability, but we do believe that the combination of our central tenets offers a way forward that enables people and places that have often been left behind to flourish within an emerging network economy.

What's Next

What is next is the conclusion of this work, where we will return to the research questions outlined at the start of this book, to draw together the theoretical and empirical learnings from our research. Finally, we will offer a roadmap to guide future research to further explore the development of the pioneering stewardship model.

References

Argyris, C., 'Teaching Smart People to Learn', *Harvard Business Review*, May–June 1991.

Biddle, J. & Baehler, K., 'Breaking Bad: When Does Polycentricity Lead to Maladaptation Rather Than Adaptation?' *Environmental Policy & Governance* 29(5): 344–359, 2019.

Burlingham, B., *Small Giants: Companies that Choose to be Great Instead of Big* (10th ed.), New York: Portfolio, 2016.

Camagni, R., 'Territorial Capital & Regional Development', in Capello, R. & Nijkamp, P. (Eds), *Handbook of Regional Growth and Development Theories*. Cheltenham: Edward Elger, 2009.

Capello, R. & Nijkamp, P., *Handbook of Regional Growth and Development Theories*. Cheltenham: Edward Elger, 2009.

Carlisle, K. & Gruby, R., 'Why the Path to Polycentricity Matters: Evidence from Fisheries Governance in Palau', *Environmental Policy & Governance* 28(4): 223–235, 2018.

Chesanais, F., 'Technical Cooperation Agreements between Firms', *STI Review*, 4: 52–115, 1988. Paris: OECD.

CLUJ Business, https://clujbusiness.ro/business-support/education/universities/#:~:text=One%20of%20the%20most%20important, 219%20students%2F1.000%20resident%20population.

Cooke, P. & Morgan, K., 'The Network Paradigm: New Departures in Corporate and Regional Development', *Environment and Planning D: Society & Space* 11: 543–564, 1993.

Cross, R., Liedtka, J. & Weiss, L., 'A Practical Guide to Social Networks', *Harvard Business Review*, Mar 2005.

Cuthill, M., Ross, H., Maclean, K., Owens, K. & Witt, B., 'Reporting Social Outcomes of Development: An Analysis of Diverse Approaches', *The International Journal of Interdisciplinary Social Science* 3: 145–158, 2008.

Gallagher, T., *Theft of a Nation: Romania since Communism*. London: Hurst, 2005.

Heikkila, Y, Villamayor-Tomas, S. & Garrick, D., 'Bringing Polycentric Systems into Focus for Environmental Governance', Environ*mental Policy & Political Networks: The Structural Perspective Governance* 28(4): 2017–2211, 2018.

Hitchens, D., *Advanced Systems Thinking, Engineering, and Management*. Boston, MA: Artech House, 2013.

Jackson, M., *Systems Thinking: Creative Holism for Managers*. Chicehster: Wiley, 2003.

Johanson, J., 'Interfirm Networks in Swedish Industry'. A Paper presented to the European Commission conference Europerspective II: Visions and Actions, Namur, Apr 1991.

Jolly, A. & Kettaneh, N., *Doing Business in Romania*. London: Kogan Page, 1999.

Knickel, K., Brunori, G., Rand, S. & Proost, M., 'Towards a Better Conceptual Framework for Innovation Processes in Agriculture and Rural Development: From Linear Models to Systemic Approaches', *The Journal of Agricultural Education and Extension* 15(2): 131–146, 2009.

Kohr, L. *The Breakdown of Nations*. Croydon: Green Books, 2001. Originally published by Routledge & Kegan Paul, 1957.

Lewis, M., 2017, https://thenextsystem.org/sites/default/files/2017-08/MichaelLewis.pdf.

Maani, K. & Cavani, R., *Systems Thinking and Modelling: Understanding Change and Complexity*. London: Prentice Hall, 2000.

Maas, G. & Jones, P. (Eds), *Entrepreneurship Centres: Global Perspectives on Their Contributions to Higher Education Institutions*. Switzerland: Palgrave Macmillan, 2017.

Maas, G., Jones, P. & Lockyer, J., *The Journey to Transformational Entrepreneurship*. New York: Springer, 2019.

Maclean, K., Cuthill, M. & Ross, H., 'Six Attributes of Social Resilience', *Journal of Environmental Planning and Management* 57(1): 144–156, 2014.

Merali, Y., 'Complexity and Information Systems: The Emergent Domain'. *Journal of Information Technology* 21(4): 216–228, 2006.

Merali, Y., 'Complexity & Systems', in Taylor, A. (Ed.), *Rethinking Leadership for a Green World*. London: Routledge, 2022.

Merali, Y. & Snowden, D., 'Mastering Complexity in the Networked World: Strategy & Leadership', Cluj, Romania, 2019.

Morgan, K., June 12, 2020, https://www.cardiff.ac.uk/people/view/35240-morgan-kevin.

Myrdal, G., *Economic Theory and Underdeveloped Regions*. London: Duckworth, 1957.

Ostrom, E., 'A General Framework for Analyzing Sustainability of Social-Ecological Systems', *Science* 325: 419–422, 2009.

Ostrom, E., *Governing the Commons: The Evolution of Institutions for Collective Action*, Cambridge: Cambridge University Press, 2015.

Peck, J., 'Putting Banking Back in the Hands of the People – RSA', www.thersa.org. Royal Society of Arts, July 15, 2019.

Pentland, A., 'Beyond the Echo Chamber', *Harvard Business Review*, Nov 2013.

Rose, C., *What Makes People Tick: The Hidden World of Settler, Prospectors and Pioneers*, Leicester: Matador, 2011.

Scruton, R., *Green Philosophy: How to Think Seriously About the Planet*. London: Atlantic Books, 2012.

Snowden, D. & Boone, M. E., 'A Leader's Framework for Decision Making', *Harvard Business Review*, Nov 2007.

Tarko, V., 'Elinor Ostrom's Life and Work', in Ostrom, E. (Ed.), *The Future of The Commons: Beyond Market Failure and Government Regulation*. London: IEA, 2012.

Taylor, A. & Bronstone, A., *People, Place & Global Order: Foundations for a Networked Political Economy*. London: Routledge, 2019.

Verdery, K., *The Vanishing Hectare: Property and Value in Postsocialist Transylvania*. Ithaca, NY: Cornell University Press, 2003.

Von Bertalanffy, L., *The Science of Synthesis: Exploring the Social Implications of General Systems Theory*. General Systems Theory, Issue 103, 2010.

Wahl, D., 'Building A New Normal'. Resurgence & Ecologist. Issue 321, July/Aug 2020.

Waldrop, M., *Complexity: The Emerging Science at the Edge of Order and Chaos*, London: Simon and Schuster, 1993.

Walker, B., Holling, C. S., Carpenter, S. R. & Kinzig, A., 'Resilience, Adaptability and Transformability in Social–Ecological Systems', *Ecology and Society* 9(2): 5, 2004.

7

CONCLUSION

Introduction

This work was based upon a high level of interest in our previous book (Taylor & Bronstone, 2019) and a desire to take a more empirically grounded, bottom-up approach to understand models of development compared to the reality of engaging with a digitally networked world that is leaving many people behind. Through our four case studies we sought to explore the following questions:

1. What are the key characteristics that underpin the success of small places and organisations to thrive within complex global networks?
   a) What role can entrepreneurialism play in the development of networked forms of stewardship?
   b) What role do shared values and experiences have in both constructing identity and economic development?
2. How do models of development inform our understanding of local flourishing?

DOI: 10.4324/9781003145295-7

3. Is there a new model of development that we can identify from our research?
4. Is there any evidence of polycentric modes of development and governance and, if so, how far do they reach?

In this chapter, we shall seek to develop answers to these questions and draw out the key practical lessons and theoretical implications that flow from our research. As noted in Chapter 4, the qualitative nature of our research limits any claims that we may make about the universality of our findings. Nonetheless, we have identified a number of trends that are worthy of further research, to establish their wider validity. Ultimately, we have developed a model of development that draws upon both existing models and the empirical data presented here that we hope can be tested and potentially used to enable more people and places to flourish within the network economy.

Lessons Learned

Empirical Lessons – Practical Applications

The empirical findings of our research have enabled us to induce the following 'lessons' about the key characteristics that underpin the success of small places and organisations that allow both to thrive within complex global networks.

Lesson 1: There is a role for shared values and experiences in both constructing identity and economic development: Shared values, norms and an identity of people and place, with institutions capable of leveraging and leaders able and willing to inject identity with agency.

Lesson 2: Technology is enabling those norms to be extended through overlapping networks that recognise common interest and purpose whilst still acknowledging cultural differences.

Lesson 3: Entrepreneurialism plays a critical role in the development of networked forms of stewardship. Numerous places have developed strong collaborative ties within and between social spaces. The difficulty is that, without an economic dimension, such networks have a financial dependence and cannot be truly sustainable. Connecting entrepreneurs, therefore, around shared values, norms and an identity of place, injects a sense of duty into the former and an aspiration into the latter.

Lesson 4: Innovative pooling actions are defined as about invigorating the identity of a place and developing opportunities to cherish that identity, such that those who take part may flourish securely within it.

Lesson 5: Pioneers using attachment to place as a system boundary and double-loop learning (Argyris, 1991) as the mode of inquiry provide the agency to conduct safe-to-fail experiments that breathe life into the oikophilia of small-world networks. In turn, this engages Settlers, reduces network precariousness and expands adaptive capacity.

Lesson 6: The role of universities is critical, both as an arena to source and share norms and in creating the potential to join up anchor institutions in a later application of the Preston model.

Lesson 7: Clustering (informal and formal) has been shown to be a useful process where pioneers actively seek to overlap network subsystems in order to activate structural patterns of social nesting.

Lesson 8: There is a role for 'city hall' in facilitating and structuring (or in the instance of Jacksonville of inhibiting) nesting at a systemic level.

Lesson 9: There is emergent evidence of polycentric modes of development and governance, especially in Cluj, with deliberate efforts to nurture it in EduCab. The challenge to theorists is that what we see in Cluj is mostly driven by private sector entrepreneurs and not community commons.

Lesson 10: Models of development do inform our understanding of local flourishing. Aspects of transformational entrepreneurialism, the Preston model and especially the territorial capital model have been identified in this research. However, none of them describes the complete picture.

What Have We Learned – Theoretical Developments

Lesson 1: The importance of pooled relational capital as a means of managing risk, developing resilience and investing in the development of oikophilia, such that a positive cycle of agency is developed. Closely linked to indications of emerging polycentrism (Ostrom, 2015), the pioneering stewardship model provides a means for private interest to be harnessed for public gain without a significant role for formal commons regimes.

Driven by pooled relational capital of entrepreneurs, Cluj has developed a series of increasingly overlapping and nested clusters. These clusters are being consciously integrated into common governance regimes by the city hall. In Cluj, there is little doubt that a mosaic of local regimes has produced enhanced adaptive capacity (Carlisle & Gruby, 2018) and there is evidence that it is showing signs of emerging polycentricity. Informal understandings have increasingly been structured within organisations such as TEE, which acts as a semi-commons-based arena to pool relational capital, clusters of regimes of governance and the clustering of clusters. Where actors previously informally cooperated, they are now being more formally integrated and more central to public development policies.

Clearly, EduCab is designed to have polycentric potential and the process of overlapping nesting within and between networks is central to how they are trying to create systemic momentum. Given that they are only beginning to move forward with an economic dimension to their model we cannot know the extent to which the polycentric potential that they have facilitated to date can be self-sustaining. Nonetheless, the underlying values of attachment to place as the root and shared norms that provide the security to reach out and develop agency that has driven their success to date indicate both a common pattern with Cluj.

Attachment to place and the practice of pooling relational capital have clearly enabled the definition of group boundaries in Cluj and to some degree in EduCab and Boulevard. Rules governing activities flowing from pooled relational capital are specific to local needs and conditions and have emerged from them in Cluj and Boulevard. They are perhaps emergent in EduCab. The above-described case of the common good in TEE (Cluj) is but one illustration that those affected by the rules can participate in modifying the rules. This case is especially interesting since participants who had less economic power and less capital invested were not less able to exert influence. In EduCab, Mihai is explicitly encouraging wider participation in the development of locally specific patterns of governance. The formation of clusters, partnerships with powerful local institutions and the Mayor's office in Cluj have all been used to ensure that outside bureaucratic authorities, even if they do not respect at least do not harm, the rule-making rights of community members. Whilst EduCab works in partnership with local librarians and their county-level coordinators to pressure village mayors to honour their financial obligations to support libraries which, otherwise, many don't. The formation of clusters in Cluj is in part about developing a peer-based system for monitoring members' behaviour that, starting with social nudging, is (as we have seen) able to apply graduated sanctions for rule violators. Clusters such as the IT clusters have provided accessible, low-cost means for dispute resolution about issues such as the development of technology parks, city infrastructure and broader planning, whilst the mayor's office in Cluj is clearly building responsibility for governing through clusters in nested tiers from the lowest level up to the entire interconnected system. The EduCab network is developing a framework for governance and using its mentoring network as an arena for resolving disputes and governance.

Although the adoption of many of the habits of the transformational mindset of Boulevard by its new owner indicates that a scaling of relational capital is possible, we have no evidence to suggest that they have radically shifted the pre-existing culture of the acquiring organisation. Nonetheless, the culture of looking for local innovations, reaching out for partners to internalise social and environmental costs and create new opportunities goes on in Kansas City. Thus, it is fair to describe Boulevard as an example of a contributor to the development of pioneering stewardship in Kansas City. Yet, although there is overlap between projects and businesses that they have founded in their search for greater stewardship responsibility, we do not yet see new bottom-up patterns of governance emerging at the global level. We cannot see evidence of polycentricity. Of course, rather like Cluj, other actors may engage more widely to develop projects less directly linked to their business, but we are not there yet.

The challenge that we find that exists with polycentrism is, in the context of this research, first, that, although Ostrom (2015) suggests that there is space for private enterprise, it primarily describes commons regimes. Yet our research indicates the importance of entrepreneurialism as a capitalist venture, which may be pooled for stakeholder and community gain, but is not specifically about the commons. Second, it is far from obvious how polycentrism can be networked without a formal sharing of regime governance. However, it is clear from organisations like Triodos (described in Taylor & Bronstone, 2019), examples such as Preston and networks like EduCab, that digital technology is enabling emergent signs of oikophilia to be more effectively networked through communities of practice (Crippen & Cortes, 2022).

The Cluj model is explicitly designed to link up small world networks from the start. Furthermore, whilst Cluj has gone a considerable way towards overcoming power and wealth imbalances, shortages of social capital and so forth, that Biddle and Baehler (2019) describe as limiting polycentric potential, we are mindful that for places to thrive within a networked world, rather than be consumed by it, they need to go beyond their system boundaries to secure resources, markets and realise potential. There are limits to the transformative potential of local networks, without reference to a broader systemic view that joins polycentric hubs together.

Lesson 2: The case studies from this work illustrate that the convergence of technology and globalisation is enabling networks of shared values and norms to spillover and connect beyond the territorial lines that were drawn on maps when the modern state system began, long ago in 1648 with the breakup of the Holy Roman Empire. The modern-state system is one where the principle of sovereignty – that which takes place within certain defined borders of a political entity – is not the purview of anyone else. Traditional theories of International Relations – Realism, Neorealism and Complex Interdependence theory – all of which spring from the same root – somewhat live and die on the foundation of this principle of sovereignty and the international system that was established where states were the primary units of interest (Morgenthau, 1985). Given how the world has changed since 1648, considerable debate has arisen amongst scholars about the extent to which the domestic influences the international and vice-versa – the inside/outside debate captured in the work of Walker (1992). There are 'mainstream' models of international relations such as Complex Interdependence that do take some account of the interplay between domestic and international forces, a lack of a hierarchy of issues and accounts for the importance of political-economic forces (Keohane & Nye, 1977). However, we believe that this approach is still fundamentally a top-down approach to politics, insofar as Keohane and Nye speak of an interest in relationships that exist at the level of governmental and non-governmental elites, transnational organisations such as banks and corporations and interstate relationships (Keohane & Nye, 1977, p. 21). Non-elites actors, such as the various groups of people that we speak of in this new world, the people that *The Economist* spoke of as 'scroungers', are as much left out of this equation as they are when Realists speak of international politics. The move away from Complex Interdependence may be a shift away from Realist thought, but not nearly the shift necessary for this discussion because what we have seen in our research, and has been reported elsewhere (Hammer, 1990; Wenger & Snyder, 2000; Mason, 2015; Iansati & Lakhani, 2017), however, is that the convergence of technology and globalisation is driving an emergent bottom-up world of relationships, and therefore the need for a different approach that is driven by those at the bottom and not just by those at the top is important.

A Future Research Agenda: The Pioneering Stewardship Model

Our contention is that polycentrism, as summarised in this work in Chapter 2, captures a significant amount of depth of the empirical activity that we have discovered. However, its foundation in geographically bounded commons regimes limits its applicability to the pooling of entrepreneurial activity increasingly using digital networks to widen adaptive capacity beyond political and geographic boundaries Our research indicates that a new model is needed that acknowledges and draws upon existing models, but addresses the emergent opportunities being created to use network technologies to not only combine pooled relational capital with entrepreneurialism and oikophilia, but to also bridge success beyond traditional boundaries.

We do see multiple projects, organisations and clusters with overlapping actors, centres of decision-making and regimes of governance. They do form a mosaic of local regimes able to increase adaptive capacity (Biddle & Baehler, 2018; Carlisle & Gruby, 2018). Furthermore, they are increasingly being structured 'within an overarching set of rules' (Heikkila, Villamayor-Tomas & Garrick, 2018, p. 207). We are seeing signs of a complex adaptive system emerging, with wider network panarchy, diffusion and codification all emerging from pooled relational capital. However, this research suggests that Boisot's (1995) case that networks require a higher level of codification to be resilient as they grow is less true than perhaps previously thought. Clearly, there is a limit to the significance of personal relationships, but our research indicates that shared norms and values are more important than levels of codification.

It is the combination of networks of entrepreneurial agencies that are grounded in a sense of place that provides both the anchor and the vision to join the local to the global in a more inclusive way that is the source of transformation. However, such processes do not happen overnight, and our research indicates that whilst they can be nurtured (as EduCab is having some success doing), they seem more likely to flourish if they emerge from the bottom than are imposed (no matter with what good intentions) from the top.

A bottom-up, networked, model of organisation, based upon shared values, norms and pooled relational capital that is driven by pioneering entrepreneurs raises the intriguing question of whether emergent signs of relational and territorial capital spilling over might cross geopolitical boundaries. Evidence of such spillover would present a significant challenge to existing models of international relations. As noted previously, traditional models are rooted in the sanctity of sovereignty, the primacy of the international system and states and actors that flow from these states (Morgenthau, 1985). Although the complex interdependence model (Keohane & Nye, 1977) acknowledges that the formation of economic and political blocs, such as the EU, indicate a close relationship between the domestic and international spaces, the model defines such a relationship as top-down, driven by global elites, including corporations and states. Yet, what we are seeing is the emergence of bottom-up networks blurring the boundaries of the inside and outside in a way that traditional theories of international relations have not, and are not, able to account for in their attempt to explain or understand the world.[1]

A Road Map ... and Final Thoughts

We want to end this book as we did our first – with a roadmap for the next steps in this research project. We would be more than pleased if readers of this work reach out to us so that we can build a community of interest in this work and develop a network of colleagues who we can investigate, question and challenge our findings more widely furthering our research and knowledge on this and related topics.

The 'Worst of Times'

Before we bring forth this roadmap, we would be remiss if we did not talk about the elephant in the room that has taken place while we have been conducting this research and finishing this project. The pandemic has shone a spotlight onto questions of place, identity, locality, the greater use of technology to connect than ever used before and the cleavages that exist between Rose's (2011) Settlers, Prospectors and Pioneers. We cannot turn the clock back and imagine that the convergence of technology and globalisation is not taking place. However, we can be aware of its consequences and choose to design deep local networks of resilience that join to wider networks, such that people may thrive within digital networks rather than simply be exploited by them. The restrictions imposed by the pandemic created a perfect opportunity to explore how resilience might manifest more widely than the case studies described here. Below are some of the key issues that have emerged as central questions for an emerging public debate about the tensions within the local/global debate.

Education: Because of lockdowns, schools of all types went completely virtual. However, as campuses have opened, universities, in particular, have been reluctant to switch back to entirely face-to-face teaching (Weale & Adams, 2021). If not entirely, then at least partly, motivated by cost, a continuation of so-called hybrid teaching has been loudly opposed by students who hanker for emotional connection and experiential elements of learning (Davis, 2021).

Supply Lines: Global supply chains that caused people such as Thomas Friedman to remark that the world has become 'flat' may have been lean and robust, but their efficiency has been shown to be fragile in the face of unpredictable turbulence and ultimately failed to deliver. Both as a response to shortages and concern over dependence upon, particularly, China. Instead, buying locally has often proved to be more resilient and has become fashionable again (Sneader, 2021) in an implicit repudiation of the just-in-time world that characterises global supply chains.

Living and Working: The pandemic has also shifted our collective sense of 'place' and given rise to significant migration away from major commercial centres. People are starting to think about and relocate to smaller communities (Brown, 2021). Recently, a large and albeit online British bank has committed itself to a four-day work week that can be done virtually. The chief executive of the company stated that the pandemic has 'exploded many of the myths of the modern workplace', including the need to work in an office (Cooban, 2021).

Socio-economic standards: The less-educated and lower-skilled of society, whose incomes are dependent on the traditional in-person service economy, have lost more than even their immediate income – they have lost their relevance. Whilst the discovery that courier drivers, agricultural workers and supermarket staff were 'key workers' (Ellyatt, 2021) animated public debate at the start of the COVID-19 pandemic, a clear divide that was inescapably visible between those who can and cannot afford to live virtually has developed before our very eyes.

Politics: Politicians of all stripes have struggled to deal with the pandemic. At the outset most believed it was, using the Cynefin framework, a complicated problem, when, as we know now, it was, in fact, a complex problem. As governments scrambled to accept that the best they could do was channel emergence through safe-to-fail experiments,[2] reliance upon robust and distant models of governance have been challenged. The hegemony of utilitarian economic logic has come to be increasingly questioned.

Resilience

The pandemic has taught many individuals, firms and governments that resilience is at least as important as robustness. The linear logic that characterises so much of business thinking has, during the COVID-19 pandemic, created personal and systemic vulnerabilities that could not be ignored. A renewed search for identity has led many people, firms and governments to re-evaluate the relationships and purpose that defines their lives.

Local over global: In the area of consumer spending, it is not surprising to find that online shopping increased during the pandemic. Yet there was the shift towards supporting local retailers. In one of many surveys that illustrate this trend, 46% of the American public are shopping closer to their neighbourhood and an even larger number of people – 80% – feel more connected to their communities. An overwhelming 88% of those surveyed expect to maintain these connections once the pandemic ends (Paypal, 2020).

Innovation: A study conducted by McKinsey revealed a surge of new business applications in the third quarter of 2020, which was more than double the level in the same period of 2019 (Sneader, 2021). Furthermore, there was a 50% increase in what is called 'high propensity' businesses. These are the businesses that are most likely to employ additional people, in comparison to a traditional start-up that has one employee.

Charitable giving: In the midst of a pandemic where people were locked inside, millions of jobs were lost and most developed economies shrunk, an almost 10% increase in donations was experienced during this period, with many new donors. The chair of the Fundraising Effectiveness Project, Jon Biedermann, commented that 'what we're seeing is that people remain very generous and continue to support their neighbours, communities and charitable causes when they face crises and hard times' (Fischer, 2020). These trends were also true in the UK, where more money was raised during the pandemic than the year prior to the onset of the virus (May, 2021).

Concluding Thought

We hope that our readers find our model of pioneering stewardship refreshing, invigorating, and interesting, even if they disagree with us on aspects of meaning and conclusion. Complex interdependence may have been a useful approximation of a world where emerging globalisation was driven by multinational companies and political blocs (such as the EU). However, the world we see emerging now, and fast-forwarded by the pandemic, is not only connecting enterprises, consumers and citizens at the scale of individual transactions and exchanges. An emerging search to enrich and deepen local networks through their connection (often digitally) to wider networks is spilling beyond the limitations of place and quietly creeping across boundaries of law, politics and maybe even culture. Whilst the pandemic has created unexpected challenges for us as researchers, in many ways, the timing of our research could not have been more appropriate. The tensions between the global and the local present tantalising opportunities for Pioneers to connect Settler worlds so that no one must choose between their values and their welfare; no one must choose between leaving home or being called a 'scrounger'.

We therefore invite you, the reader, to connect to us in discussing, developing and hopefully challenging us as we take this roadmap and set off on the third leg of our journey to explore how pioneering stewardship is spilling over borders through networks that raise serious challenges to existing models of business, political organisation and international relations.

Notes

1 In 1988, Robert Putnam conceptualised diplomatic negotiations as a two-level game in which national and international politics often collide. In this framework, constituents and interest groups (labour unions, activist groups, etc.) pursue their interests at the national level by pressuring the government to adopt favourable policies. At the international level, governments attempt to meet the pressures

and demands of their domestic constituents while at the same time minimising the possible adverse impact of developments abroad. The interaction between the two levels manifests in the fact that a leader who ignores domestic pressures or who favours domestic politics above international issues will be unable to successfully ratify or negotiate a treaty at the other level. Thus, as Putnam argues, 'the political complexities for the players in this two-level game are staggering'. The flaw in this perspective from the point of view of our work is that Putnam still adheres to a somewhat 'inside/outside' concept, that there is still the domestic and the international, whereas we see the ground substantially shifting through spillover between these two in a manner that we believe is much more complex (Putnam, 1988).

2 Such as the stretching of time between vaccines by the UK government from four to 12 weeks to widen resistance.

References

Argyris, C., 'Teaching Smart People to Learn', *Harvard Business Review*, May–June 1991.

Biddle, J. & Baehler, K., 'Breaking Bad: When Does Polycentricity Lead to Maladaptation Rather Than Adaptation?' *Environmental Policy & Governance* 29(5): 344–359, 2019.

Boisot, M., *Information Space: A Framework for Learning in Organizations, Institutions and Culture*. London: Routledge, 1995.

Brown, J. & Touse, C., 'How the Pandemic Influenced Trends in Domestic Migration Across U.S. Urban Areas', Kansas City Federal Reserve Bank, 2021.

Carlisle, K. & Gruby, R., 'Why the Path to Polycentricity Matters: Evidence from Fisheries Governance in Palau'. *Environmental Policy & Governance* 28(4): 223–235, 2018.

Cooban, A., 'Atom Bank Moves to Four-Day Work Week Without Cutting Pay', *CNN*, Nov 23, 2021.

Crippen, M. & Cortes, A., 'Ecology and Technological Enframement: Cities, Networks, and the COVID-19 Pandemic', in Mutnick D., Cuonzo M., Griffiths C., Leslie T. & Shuttleworth J. (Eds), *The City is an Ecosystem*, London: Routledge, 2022.

Davis, A., 'Students Say They're Being "Scammed into Paying for Glorified Lecture Slides" as Universities Keep Lectures Online', *London Evening Standard*, May 19, 2021.

Ellyatt, H., 'There Are Millions of Jobs, but a Shortage of Workers: Economists Explain Why That's Worrying', *CNBC*, Oct, 2021.

Fischer, M., 'Charitable Giving Up Nearly 8%, Despite Pandemic', *ThinkAdvisor*, Dec 2020.

Hammer, G., 'Reengineering Work: Don't Automate, Obliterate', *Harvard Business Review*, May–June 1990.

Heikkila, Y., Villamayor-Tomas, S. & Garrick, D., 'Bringing Polycentric Systems into Focus for Environmental Governance', *Environmental Policy & Political Networks: The Structural PerspectiveGovernance* 28(4): 2017–2211, 2018.

Iansiti, M. & Lakhani, K., 'Managing Our Hub Economy: Strategy, Ethics and Network Competition in an Age of Digital Superpowers', *Harvard Business Review*, Sept 2017.

Keohane, R. & Nye, J., *Power and Interdependence*. Boston, MA: Little, Brown and Company, 1977.

Mason, P., *Postcapitalism: A Guide to Our Future*. London: Allen Lane, 2015.

May, M, '1.6m Fewer People Gave Last Year – But Average Donation Size Rose', UK Fundraising, Nov 2021.

Morgenthau, H., *Politics Among Nations*. New York: Alfred Knopf, 1985.

Ostrom, E., *Governing the Commons: The Evolution of Institutions for Collective Action*. Cambridge: Cambridge University Press, 2015.

PayPal Editorial Staff, '6 Ways the Pandemic Is Changing Consumer Shopping Habits', Dec 2020.

Putnam, R. D., 'Diplomacy and Domestic Politics: The Logic of Two-Level Games', *International Organization* 42(3): 427–460, 1988.

Rose, C., *What Makes People Tick: The Hidden World of Settler, Prospectors and Pioneers*. Leicester: Matador, 2011.

Sneader, K., 'Trends That Will Define 2021 and Beyond', McKinsey & Company, 2021.

Taylor, A. & Bronstone, A., *People, Place & Global Order: Foundations for A Networked Political Economy*. London: Routledge, 2019.

Walker, R., *Inside/Outside: International Relations as Political Theory*. London: Cambridge University Press, 1992.

Weale, S. & Adams, R., 'Covid Has Been a Big Catalyst': Universities Plan for Post-Pandemic Life', *The Guardian*, July 13, 2021.

Wenger and Snyder, 'Communities of Practice: The Organizational Frontier', *Harvard Business Review*, Jan–Feb 2000.

BIBLIOGRAPHY

Alchain, A. & Demsetz, H., 'The Property Right Paradigm', *Journal of Economic History* 33, March, 1973.

Aldrick, P., 'Huawei Ban Strengthens Britain's Shift Towards Greater Self-Reliance', *The Times*, July 17, 2020.

Alexander, C., 'The New Economy', *Time*, May 30, 1983.

Anderson, C., *The Long Tail: Why the Future of Business Is Selling Less of More*. New York: Hyperion, 2006.

Anthony, S., 'Kodak's Downfall wasn't about Technology', *Harvard Business Review*, July 15, 2016.

Argyris, C., 'Teaching Smart People to Learn', *Harvard Business Review*, May–June, 1991.

Arksey, H. & Knight, P., *Interviewing for Social Scientists*. London: Sage, 1999.

Armstrong, H., 'Community Regional Policy', in Lodge, J., (Ed), *The European Community and the Challenge of the Future*. London: Pinter Publishers, 1989.

Arthur, W. B., 'Increasing Returns and The New World of Business', *Harvard Business Review*, July–Aug, 1996.

Barca, F., McCann, P. & Rodríguez-Pose, A., 'The Case for Regional Development Intervention: Place-Based Versus Place-Neutral Approaches', *Journal of Regional Science* 52(1): 134–152, 2012.

Barro, R. J. & Martin, X., *Economic Growth*. Cambridge: MIT Press, 1999.

Baxter, P., & Jack, S., 'Qualitative Case Study Methodology: Study Design and Implementation for Novice Researchers', *The Qualitative Report* 13(4): 544–559, 2008.

Beardwell, J. & Thompson, A., *Human Resource Management: A Contemporary Approach* (7th ed.). Harlow, UK: Pearson, 2014.

Biddle, J. & Baehler, K., 'Breaking Bad: When Does Polycentricity Lead to Maladaptation Rather than Adaptation?', *Environmental Policy & Governance* 29(5): 344–359, 2019.

Bloodworth, J., *Hired: Six Months Undercover in Low-Wage Britain*. London: Atlantic Books, 2018.

Boisot, M. & Child, J., 'The Iron Law of Fiefs: Bureaucratic Failure and the Problem of Governance in the Chinese Economic Reforms', *Administrative Science Quarterly* 33: 507–527, 1988.

Boisot, M., *Information Space: A Framework for Learning in Organizations, Institutions and Culture*. London, UK: Routledge, 1995.

Bollier, D., *Think Like a Commoner: A Short Introduction to The Commons*. Gabriola Island, Canada: New Society Publishers, 2014.

Bonabeau, E., 'The Perils of the Imitation Age', *Harvard Business Review*, June, 2004.

Bromley, D., *Environment and Economy: Property Rights and Public Policy*. Oxford: Blackwell, 1993.

Bronstone, A., *European Bank for Reconstruction and Development*. Manchester: Manchester University Press, 1999.

Bronwstein, R., 'Red and Blue America Aren't Experiencing the Same Pandemic', *The Atlantic*, 2020.

Brown, J. & Touse, C., 'How the Pandemic Influenced Trends in Domestic Migration across U.S. Urban Areas', Kansas City: Federal Reserve Bank, 2021.

Burlingham, B., *Small Giants: Companies That Choose to be Great Instead of Big* (10th ed.). New York: Portfolio, 2016.

Burton, S., Sheather, S. & Roberts, J., 'Reality or Perception?', *Journal of Service Research*, 5(4): 292–302, 2003.

Business Roundtable, 'Statement on the Purpose of a Corporation', 2019.

Butler, S., 'Great Britain's High Streets Lost More Than 17,500 Chain Store Outlets in 2020', *The Guardian*, March 14, 2021.

Cadbury, D., *Chocolate Wars*. New York: Public Affairs, 2010.

Camagni, R., 'Territorial Capital & Regional Development', in Capello, R. & Nijkamp, P. (Eds), *Handbook of Regional Growth and Development Theories*. Cheltenham, UK: Edward Elger, 2009.

Capello, R. & Nijkamp, P., *Handbook of Regional Growth and Development Theories*. Cheltenham, UK: Edward Elger, 2009.

Carlisle, K. & Gruby, R., 'Why the Path to Polycentricity Matters: Evidence from Fisheries Governance in Palau', *Environmental Policy & Governance* 28(4): 223–235, 2018.

Chesanais, F., 'Technical Cooperation Agreements Between Firms', *STI Review* 4: 52–115, 1988 (Paris: OECD).

CLES (a) 'Community Business and Anchor Institutions', Feb, 2019.

CLES, https://cles.org.uk/what-is-community-wealth-building/the-principles-of-community-wealth-building/, June 22, 2020.

CLES & Preston City Council, 'How We Built Community Wealth in Preston: Achievements and Lessons', 2019.

CLUJ Business, https://clujbusiness.ro/business-support/education/universities/#:~:text=One%20of%20the%20most%20important, 219%20students%2F1.000%20resident%20population.

Clyde-Mitchell, J., *Social Networks in Urban Situations: Analyses of Personal Relationships in Central African Towns*. Manchester: University Press, 1969.

Coase, R., 'The Nature of the Firm', *Economica* 4(16): 386–405, 1937.

Coenen, L. & Morgan, K., 'Evolving Geographies of Innovation: Existing Paradigms, Critiques and Possible Alternatives', *Norwegian Journal of Geography* 11(26): 13–24, 2018.

Collins, D., *Stories for Management Success: The Power of Talk in Organizations*. London: Routledge, 2018.

Collins, D., *The Organizational Storytelling Workbook: How to Harness this Powerful Communication and Management Tool*. London: Routledge, 2021.

Collis, J. & Hussey, R., *Business Research*. Basingstoke, Hampshire: Palgrave Macmillan, 2014.

Cooke, P. & Morgan, K., 'The Network Paradigm: New Departures in Corporate and Regional Development', *Environment and Planning D: Society & Space* 11: 543–564, 1993.

Cowley, J., *Reaching for Utopia: Making Sense of an Age of Upheaval*. Norwich, UK: Salt Publishing, 2018.

Cresswell, J., (ed.), *Research Design Qualitative, Quantitative and Mixed Methods Approaches* (4th ed.). London: Sage, 2014.

Creswell, J., *Qualitative Inquiry & Research Design* (2nd ed.). Thousand Oaks, CA: Sage Publications, 2007.

Crippen, M. & Cortes, A., 'Ecology and Technological Enframement: Cities, Networks, and the COVID-19 Pandemic', in Mutnick D., Cuonzo M., Griffiths C., Leslie T. & Shuttleworth J. (Eds), *The City is an Ecosystem*. London: Routledge, 2022.

Cross, R., Liedtka, J. & Weiss, L. 'A Practical Guide to Social Networks', *Harvard Business Review*, March, 2005.

Curtis-Perry, J., *Singapore: Unlikely Power.* Oxford: Oxford University Press, 2017.

Cuthill, M., Ross, H., Maclean, K., Owens, K. & Witt, B., 'Reporting Social Outcomes of Development: An Analysis of Diverse Approaches', *The International Journal of Interdisciplinary Social Science* 3: 145–158, 2008.

Darwent, D. F., 'Growth Poles and Growth Centers in Regional Planning: A Review', *Environment and Planning* 1(1): 5–31, 1969.

Davis, A., 'Students Say They're Being "Scammed into Paying for Glorified Lecture Slides" as Universities Keep Lectures Online', *London Evening Standard*, May 19, 2021.

Dawkins, 'Regional Development Theory: Conceptual Foundations, Classic Works, and Recent Developments', *Journal of Planning Literature* 18(2): 131–172, 2003.

Day, G., Schoemaker, P. & Snyder, S., *The Network Challenge: Strategy, Profit and Risk in an Interlinked World.* Upper Saddle River, NJ: Prentice Hall, 2009.

Dethan, M., Bremner, C. & Courea, E., 'Macron Gives Britain Ultimatum in Fishing Row', *The Times*, Monday Nov 1, 2021.

Diamond, J., *Collapse: How Societies Choose to Fail or Survive.* London: Penguin, 2006.

Dixon, R. J. & Thirlwall, A., 'A Model of Regional Growth Rate Differences on Kaldorian Lines', *Oxford Economic Papers* 27(2): 201–214, 1975.

Dragan, A., 'Bucharest vs. Cluj-Napoca: The Transylvanian City Tops the Capital in the Main Economic, Social and Demographic Indicators', *The Business Review*, Dec 10, 2018.

Duncan, E., 'Britain Needs More Second-Class Universities', *The Times*, July 9, 2021.

Earle, J., Froud, J., Haslam, C., Sukhdev, J., Moran, M. & Williams, K., 'What Wales Can Do: Asset Based Policies and the Foundational Economy' A CREW/foundationaleconomy.com report, April 22, 2020, 2017.

Easterby-Smith, M., Jaspersen, L., Thorpe, R. & Valizade, D., *Management and Business Research*. London: Sage, 2018.

Electric Castle, https://electriccastle.ro/about viewed Mar 12, 2021.

Ellyatt, H., 'There Are Millions of Jobs, but a Shortage of Workers: Economists Explain Why That's Worrying', *CNBC*, Oct, 2021.

European Union, 'Schuman Declaration' (Schuman declaration May 1950 (europa.eu)), 1950.

European Union, Regional Policy – Major Projects, 2020 (https://ec.europa.eu/regional_policy/en/projects/major/#1), 2020.

Evans, P. & Wurster, S., 'New Economics of Information', *Harvard Business Review*, Sept–Oct, 1997.

Felicetti, A., 'Localism and the Transition Movement', *Policy Studies* 34(5): 559–574, 2013.

Fischer, M., 'Charitable Giving Up Nearly 8%, Despite Pandemic', *ThinkAdvisor*, Dec, 2020.

Fleming, P., 'There's Nothing Good about the Rise in Zero-Hours Contracts – Ban Them Now', *The Guardian*, Sept 7, 2015.

Folke, C., Carpenter, S., Walker, B., Scheffer, M., Elmqvist, T., Gunderson, L. & Holling, C.S., 'Regime Shifts, Resilience, and Biodiversity in Ecosystem Management', *Annual Review of Ecology, Evolution, and Systematics* 35: 557–581, 2004.

Fortech, https://www.fortech.ro/fortech-wins-internal-csr-campaign-of-the-year-award/, March 17, 2021.

Foundational Economy, 'Introducing the Foundational Economy', 2019, https://foundationaleconomy.com/introduction/, June 11, 2020.

Foundational Economy, 'Introduction', https://foundationaleconomy.com/introduction/, May 15, 2020.

Foundational Economy, https://foundationaleconomy.com/introduction/, June 11, 2020.

Fountaine, T., 'Building the AI-Powered Organization: Technology Isn't the Biggest Challenge. Culture Is', *Harvard Business Review*, July–Aug, 2019.

Friedmann, J., *Regional Development Policy: A Case Study of Venezuela*. Cambridge: MIT Press, 1966.

Fuchs, C., *Rereading Marx in the Age of Digital Capitalism*. London: Pluto Press, 2019.

Fukuyama, F., *The End of History and the Last Man*. Free Press: New York, 1992.
Fukuyama, F., *The End of History and the Last Man*. Free Press: New York, 1992.

Gallagher, T., *Theft of a Nation: Romania Since Communism*. London: Hurst, 2005.

Gans, H., *The Urban Villagers: Group and Class in the Life of Italian-Americans*. London: Free Press, 1969.

Gartell, D. & Gartell, J., 'Positivism in Sociological Practice: 1967–1990', *Canadian Review of Sociology* 33(2): 143–158, 1996.

Gavetti, G., 'The New Psychology of Strategic Leadership', *Harvard Business Review*, July–Aug, 2011.

Gillespie, C. & Thomas, J., *Property Rights and the Environment*. London: IEA, 1989.

Gladwell, M., *Blink: The Power of Thinking Without Thinking*. New York: Back Bay Book, 2005.

Goodhart, D., *The Road to Somewhere*. London: Hurst and Company, 2017.

Goodman, R., *The Last Entrepreneurs: America's Regional Wars for Jobs and Dollars*. New York: Simon & Schuster, 1979.

Gray, D., *Doing Research in the Real World*. London: Sage, 2017.

Greenhut, M., *Plant Location in Theory and in Practise: The Economics of Space*. Chapel Hill: University of North Carolina Press, 1956.

Grubb, M. *The Kyoto Protocol: A Guide and Assessment. London*: The Royal Institute of International Affairs, 1999.

Hammer, G., 'Reengineering Work: Don't Automate, Obliterate', *Harvard Business Review* May–June, 1990.

Hammersley, M. & Atkinson, P., *Ethnography: Principles in Practice*. London: Routledge, 1983.

Hammersley, M., 'Ethnography: Problems and Prospects', *Ethnography and Education*, 1(1): 3–14, 1992.

Hammersley, M., *What's Wrong with Ethnography?* London: Routledge, 1992.

Hammond, D., *The Science of Synthesis: Exploring the Social Implications of General Systems Theory*. Louisville, CO: University of Colorado Press, 2010.

Handy, C., *The Elephant and The Flea: New Thinking for a New World*. New York: Random House, 2002.

Harari, Y. N., *Sapiens: A Brief History of Humankind*. London: Vintage, 2011.

Hardin, G., 'The Tragedy of the Commons', *Science* 162(3859): 1243–1248, 1968.

Hassink, R. & Gong, H., 'New Economic Geography', in Orum, A. (Ed), *The Wiley Blackwell Encyclopedia of Urban and Regional Studies*. Oxford: Wiley, 2019.

Heikkila, Y, Villamayor-Tomas, S. & Garrick, D., 'Bringing Polycentric Systems into Focus for Environmental Governance', *Environmental Policy & Political Networks: The Structural Perspective Governance* 28(4): 2017–2211, 2018.

Henwood, D., *After the New Economy*. London: New Press, 2003.

Hiermaier, S., 'Keynote Speech to the Global Resilience Research Network', *Freiburg*, Apr 2019.

Hirschman, A., *The Strategy for Economic Development*. New Haven, CT: Yale University Press, 1958.

Hitchens, D., *Advanced Systems Thinking, Engineering, and Management*, Boston, MA: Artech House, 2013.

Hoover, E., *Location Theory and the Shoe Leather Industries*. Cambridge, MA: Harvard University Press, 1937.

Hoover, E. M., & Giarratani, F., *Introduction to Regional Economics* (3rd ed.). New York: Knopf, 1985.

Hopkins, R., *The Power of Just Doing Stuff: How Local Action Can Change the World*. Cambridge, UK: Green Books, 2013.

Huat Chua, B., *Liberalism Disavowed: Communitarianism and State Capitalism in Singapore*. New York: Cornell University Press, 2017.

Hubbard, P., *The Battle for the High Street: Retail Gentrification, Class and Disgust*. London: Palgrave Macmillan, 2017.

Hutton, W., *How Good We Can Be: Ending the Mercenary Society and Building a Great Country*. London: Little Brown, 2015.

Iansiti, M. & Lakhani, K., 'Managing Our Hub Economy: Strategy, Ethics and Network Competition in an Age of Digital Superpowers', *Harvard Business Review*, Sept, 2017.

Isard, W., Iwan, J. A., Drennan, M., Miller, R., Saltzman, S. & Thorbecke, E., *Methods of Interregional and Regional Analysis*. Brookfield, VT: Ashgate, 1998.

Jackson, M., *Systems Thinking: Creative Holism for Managers*. Chichester, UK: Wiley, 2003.

Jacobs, M., *The Green Economy*. London: Pluto Press, 1991.

Johanson, J., 'Interfirm Networks in Swedish Industry', A Paper presented to the European Commission Conference Europerspective II: Visions and Actions, Namur, April, 1991.

Jolly, A. & Kettaneh, N., *Doing Business in Romania,* London: Kogan Page, 1999

Jones, P., 'Look to Preston for an answer to Labour's – and Britain's – woes', *The Guardian*, Jan 13, 2020.

Jones, T., *Utopian Dreams: In Search of a Good Life.* London: Faber & Faber, 2020.

Kaldor, N., 'The Case for Regional Policies', *Scottish Journal of Political Economy* 17(3): 337–48, 1970.

Kennedy, C., *The Next Big Idea.* London: Cornerstone Digital Press, 2012.

Kennedy, C., *The Merchant Princes.* London: Hutchinson, 2000.

Keohane, R. & Nye, J., *Power and Interdependence.* Boston, MA: Little, Brown and Company, 1977.

Keynes, J. M., 'A Tract on Monetary Reform', December 1923, published in *The Economic Journal* 85(338): 249–271, 1975.

Kingsnorth, P., *Real England.* London: Portobello Books, 2008.

Knickel, K., Brunori, G., Rand, S., Proost, J., 'Towards a Better Conceptual Framework for Innovation Processes in Agriculture and Rural Development: From Linear Models to Systemic Approaches', *The Journal of Agricultural Education and Extension* 15(2): 131–146, 2009.

Knoke, D., *Political Networks: The Structural Perspective.* Cambridge: University Press, 1990.

Kohr, L. *The Breakdown of Nations.* Croydon, UK: Green Books, 2001. Originally published by Routledge & Kegan Paul, 1957.

Krugman, P., *Geography and Trade.* Cambridge: MIT Press, 1991.

Krugman, P. (September 2019) Regional Economics: Understanding the Third Great Transition.https://www.gc.cuny.edu/CUNY_GC/media/LISCenter/pkrugman/REGIONAL-ECONOMICS-3rd-transition.pdf, July 29, 2020.

Krugman, P., 'The Role of Geography in Development', *International Regional Science Review* 22(2): 142–161, 1999.

Kuan Yew, L., *From Third World to First: Singapore and the Asian Economic Boom.* New York: HarperCollins, 2000.

Kvale, S. & Brinkman, S., *Interviews: Learning the Craft of Research Interviewing.* London: Sage, 2009

Larrain, J., *The Concept of Ideology.* London: Hutchinson, 1979.

Leland, J., The Man With the $13 Billion Checkbook', *New York Times*, July 12, 2019.

Leucuta, C., 'Clusters as Innovative Partnerships for Economic Growth and New Jobs in Romania', *The 2nd International Scientific Conference SAMRO 2016 Romania*, Oct, 2016.

Lewin, K., 'Frontiers in Group Dynamics: Concept, Method and Reality in Social Science; Social Equilibria and Social Change', *Human Relations* 1: 5–41, 1947.

Lewis, M., https://thenextsystem.org/sites/default/files/2017-08/MichaelLewis.pdf, 2017.

Liddle, R., 'What If the 'Village Idiots' Are Right About Brexit?', *The Spectator*, May 11, 2019.

Locke, J., *Two Treatises of Government*. London: Dent, 1991.

Lodge, J., (Ed) *The European Community and the Challenge of the Future*. London: Pinter Publishers, 1989.

Lord, C., *The Myth of Europe's Democratic Deficit*. Princeton, NJ: Princeton University, 2017.

Lösch, A., *The Economics of Location*. New Haven, CT: Yale University Press, 1954.

Maani, K. & Cavani, R., *Systems Thinking and Modelling: Understanding Change and Complexity*. London: Prentice Hall, 2000.

Maas, G. & Jones, P. (Eds), *Entrepreneurship Centres: Global Perspectives on Their Contributions to Higher Education Institutions*. Switzerland: Palgrave Macmillan, 2017.

Maas, G., Jones, P. & Lockyer, J., *The Journey to Transformational Entrepreneurship*. New York: Springer, 2019.

Maclean, K., Cuthill, M. & Ross, H. 'Six Attributes of Social Resilience', *Journal of Environmental Planning and Management* 57(1): 144–156, 2014.

Maconie, S., *Long Road from Jarrow: A Journey through Britain Then and Now*. London: Ebury Press, 2017.

Martin, R. L. 'The High Price of Efficiency', *Harvard Business Review*, July/Aug, 2019.

Mason, P., *Postcapitalism: A Guide to Our Future*. London: Allen Lane, 2015.

Massey, D. & Meegan, R., *The Anatomy of Job Loss: The How, Why, and Where of Employment Decline*. London: Methuen, 1982.

May, M, '1.6m Fewer People Gave Last Year – But Average Donation Size Rose', *UK Fundraising*, Nov, 2021.

McGarvey, D., *Poverty Safari: Understanding the Anger of Britain's Underclass*. Edinburgh: Luath Press, 2017.

Merali, Y. & Snowden, D., 'Mastering Complexity in The Networked World: Strategy & Leadership', Cluj, Romania, 2019.

Merali, Y., 'Complexity & Systems', in Taylor, A. (Ed), *Rethinking Leadership for a Green World*. London: Routledge, 2022.

Merali, Y., 'Complexity and Information Systems: The Emergent Domain', *Journal of Information Technology* 21(4): 216–228, 2006.

Moeller, S., Personal Interview, 2021.

Morgan, K. & Coenen, L., 'Evolving Geographies of Innovation: Existing Paradigms, Critiques and Possible Alternatives', *Norwegian Journal of Geography* 74(2): 1–12, 2019.

Morgan, K., https://www.cardiff.ac.uk/people/view/35240-morgan-kevin, June 12, 2020.

Morgenthau, H., *Politics Among Nations*. New York: Alfred Knopf, 1985.

Morris, S., "It Came Out of Adversity': How Treorchy Became UK's Best High Street', *The Guardian*, Jan 24, 2020.

Mudie, K. & Cardy, P., 'How One City is Beating Tory Austerity with 'Radicalism on a Shoestring', *The Daily Mirror*, Nov 4, 2017.

Murray, J., 'Four Charged Over Damage to Colston Statue in Bristol', *The Guardian*, Dec 9, 2020.

Myrdal, G., *Economic Theory and Underdeveloped Regions*. London: Duckworth, 1957.

Newby, H., *Green and Pleasant Land: Social Change in Rural England*. Hounslow, Middlesex, UK: Wildwood, 1985.

Newby, H., *The Countryside in Question*. London: Hutchinson, 1988.

Nonaka, I., 'The Knowledge-Creating Company', *Harvard Business Review*, Nov–Dec, 1991.

North, D., 'Exports and Regional Economic Growth: A Reply', *Journal of Political Economy* 64(2): 165–168, 1956.

North, D., 'Location Theory and Regional Economic Growth', *Journal of Political Economy* 63(3): 243–258, 1955.

OECD, 'Income Inequality' (https://data.oecd.org/inequality/income-inequality.htm), 2021.

Ostrom, E., 'A General Framework for Analyzing Sustainability of Social-Ecological Systems', *Science* 325: 419–422, 2009.

Ostrom, E., *Governing the Commons: The Evolution of Institutions for Collective Action*. Cambridge, UK: Cambridge University Press, 2015.

Ostrom, E., *The Future of The Commons: Beyond Market Failure and Government Regulation*. London: IEA, 2012.

Ostrom, E. *Governing the Commons: The Evolution of Institutions for Collective Action*. Cambridge, UK: Cambridge University Press, 1990.

Ostrom, V., Charles, M. T. & Warren, R., 'The Organization of Government in Metropolitan Areas: A Theoretical Inquiry', *American Political Science Review* 55(4): 831–842, 1961.

Ottaviano, G. & Puga, D., 'Agglomeration in the Global Economy: A Survey of the 'New Economic Geography', *The World Economy* 21(6): 707–731, 2003.

Owens, J., 'The Tech Giants Dominated the Decade. But There's Still Time to Rein Them In', *The Guardian*, Dec, 2019.

Partington, R., 'Preston Named as Most Improved City in UK', *The Guardian*, Nov 1, 2018.

PayPal Editorial Staff, '6 Ways the Pandemic Is Changing Consumer Shopping Habits', Dec, 2020.

Peck, J., 'Putting Banking Back in the Hands of the People – RSA', www.thersa.org. Royal Society of Arts, July 15, 2019.

Peck, T., 'Theresa May Has Delivered an Idiot's Brexit, But the Idiots Will Not Stand For It', *The Independent*, Nov 22, 2020.

Pells, R., 'University 'Safe Space' Policies Leave Academics in Fear of Losing Their Jobs, Claims Professor', *The Independent*, June 20, 2017.

Pentland, A., 'Beyond the Echo Chamber', *Harvard Business Review*, Nov, 2013.

Perroux, F., 'Economic Space: Theory and Applications', *Quarterly Journal of Economics* 64(1): 89–104, 1950.

Petean, M., 'Banca Dacia Felix a vrut un CNN de Cluj', www.hotnews.ro, Sept 25, 2006.

Peterson, D. J., *Troubled Lands: The Legacy of Soviet Environmental Destruction*. London: Westview Press, 1993.

Piore, M. & Sabel, C., *The Second Industrial Divide*. New York: Basic Books, 1984.

Porter, M. & Millar, V., 'How Information Gives You Competitive Advantage', *Harvard Business Review*, July–Aug, 1985.

Porter, M., 'How Competitive Forces Shape Strategy', *Harvard Business Review*, March, 1979.

Porter, M., 'Strategy and the Internet', *Harvard Business Review* 79(3): 62–78, 2001.

Pop, F., 'Povestea Untold 2017 continuă cu 10 milioane de euro. La Cluj vor veni cei mai buni DJ şi cele mai bune voci ale momentului', *Adevărul* (in Romanian), June 22, 2017.

Powell, W., 'Neither Market nor Hierarchy: Network Forms of Organization', in Straw, B. & Cummings, L. (Eds), *Research in Organizational Behaviour* Volume 12. Greenwich, CT: JAI Press, pp. 74–96, 1990.

Prahalad, C. K. & Hamel, G., 'The Core Competence of the Corporation', *Harvard Business Review*, May–June, 1990.

Primaria Cluj-Napoca. https://issuu.com/primariamunicipiuluiclujnapoca/docs/brosura_web

Putnam, R. D., 'Diplomacy and Domestic Politics: The Logic of Two-Level Games', *International Organization* 42(3): 427–460, 1988.

Ramsey, D., 'Philadelphia with Cadbury: Death of a Brand?', *Chocablog*, Jan, 2012.

Restakis, J. (Dec 2016) 'Cooperative Commonwealth & The Partner State' as Part of a Series of Thinker Articles Commissioned for the https://thenextsystem.org website. Retrieved June 22, 2020.

Ricardo, D., *On the Principles of Political Economy and Taxation*. London: John Murray, 1817.

Romania-Insider, 'Wages in Cluj-Napoca Supass Those in Bucharest', *Romania-Insider*, Sept 26, 2019.

Rose, C., *What Makes People Tick: The Hidden World of Settler, Prospectors and Pioneers*. Leicester, UK: Matador, 2011.

Rosenberg, M., 'The 5 Themes of Geography', *ThoughtCo*, Feb 11, 2020, thoughtco.com/five-themes-of-geography-1435624, 2020.

Ryan, A., *Property and Political Theory*. Oxford: Blackwell, 1984.

Saunders, P., *Urban Politics: A Sociological Interpretation*. London: Penguin, 1979.

Saxenian, A., *Regional Advantage: Culture and Competition in Silicon Valley and Route 128*. Cambridge, MA: Harvard University Press, 1994.

Schumacher, E. F., *Small Is Beautiful: A Study of Economics as If People Mattered*. London: Vintage Books.

Schumpeter, J., *Capitalism, Socialism, and Democracy*. New York: Harper, 1947.

Scruton, R. *Green Philosophy: How to Think Seriously About the Planet*. London: Atlantic Books, 2012.

Scruton, R., *Where We Are: The State of Britain Now*. London: Bloomsbury, 2017.

Sekaran, U. & Bougie, R., *Research Methods for Business: A Skills Building Approach*. London: Wiley, 2016.

Senge, P., *The Necessary Revolution: How Individuals and Organizations Are Working Together to Create a Sustainable World*. New York: Doubleday, 2008.

Shah, T., 'Vultures Prey on Bombed-Out Shopping Centres', *The Times*, Dec 30, 2018.

Shaiko, R., 'Religion Politics, and Environmental Concern: A Powerful Mix of Passions', *Social Science Quarterly* 68: 244–262, 1987.

Sheffield, H., 'The Preston Model: UK Takes Lessons in Recovery From Rust-Belt Cleveland', *The Guardian*, April 11, 2017.

Shiva, V., 'One Planet: One Health', *Resurgence & Ecologist* 321: 10–12, 2020.

Silverman, R., 'The British High Street That Became a Ghost Town', *The Telegraph*, July 16, 2019.

Smith, D., 'Fix Our Cities First, or We'll Never Level Up This Country', *The Times*, Nov 28, 2021.

Smith, N., *Uneven Development*. Oxford: Basil Blackwell, 1984.

Smith, S., *The Philosophy of Social Science: An Introduction*. Cambridge: University Press, 1994.

Sneader, K., 'Trends That Will Define 2021 and Beyond', McKinsey & Company, 2021.

Snowden, D. & Boone, M. E. 'A Leader's Framework for Decision Making', *Harvard Business Review*, Nov, 2007.

Snowden, D. & Merali, Y., Complexity in a Networked World. Cluj-Napoca, *Transylvania Executive Education Workshops,* Romania, Nov 16–17, 2019.

Snowden, D., 'The Cynefin Framework', July 2010 ((1) The Cynefin Framework – YouTube).

Snowden, D., "The Origins of Cynefin (part 1)" Cognitive Edge March, 2010.

Solow, R. M., 'A Contribution to the Theory of Economic Growth', *Quarterly Journal of Economics* 70(1): 65–94, 1956.

Stubbington, T. 'Buy Local, Hire Local: Preston Blossoms on Corbynomics', *The Sunday Times* Oct 29, 2017.

Tapscott, D., *Creating Value in the Network Economy*. Boston, MA: Harvard Business School Press, 1999.

Tarko, V., 'Elinor Ostrom's Life and Work', in Ostrom, E. (Ed), *The Future of The Commons: Beyond Market Failure and Government Regulation*. London: IEA, 2012.

Taylor, A., 'Government Cackhandedness in Water Management Policy is Money – and Water – Down the Drain', *Vivid* 63, 2004.

Taylor, A., 'Property Rights and the Differentiating Countryside: A Case Study in South West England', Unpublished Ph.D. thesis, Cardiff, University of Wales College of Cardiff, 1998.

Taylor, A., *Taking Care of Business: Innovation, Ethics & Sustainability*. Cluj-Napoca, Romania: Risoprint, 2013.

Taylor, A., 'Trading Hot Air: Backwards, Forwards or any Which Way You Like', *European Environment* 14: 251–256, 2004.

Taylor, A. & Bronstone, A., *People, Place & Global Order: Foundations for a Networked Political Economy*. London: Routledge, 2019.

Techsylvania, https://techsylvania.com/, March 13, 2021.

Tett, G., *The Silo Effect: The Peril of Expertise and the Promise of Breaking Down Barriers*. London: Simon & Schuster, 2015

The Bishop of Oxford, *Property: Its Rights and Duties*. London: Macmillan, 1913.

The Economist, 'Britain's Decaying Towns', *The Economist*, Oct 12, 2013.

The Economist, 'Preston, Jeremy Corbyn's Model Town', *The Economist*, Oct 17, 2017.

Tiebout, C. M., 'Exports and Regional Economic Growth', *Journal of Political Economy* 64(2): 160–164, 1956.

Tödtling, F. & Trippl, M., 'Regional Innovation Policies for New Path Development – Beyond Neo-Liberal and Traditional Systemic Views', *European Planning Studies* 26(9): 1779–1795, 2018.

Transition Network, https://transitionnetwork.org/about-the-movement/what-is-transition/, June 22, 2020.

Trompenaars, F. & Hampden-Turner, C., *Riding the Waves of Culture* (2nd ed.). New York: McGraw Hill, 1998.

Verdery, K., *The Vanishing Hectare: Property and Value in Postsocialist Transylvania*. Ithaca, NY: Cornell University Press, 2003.

Vernon, R., 'International Investment and International Trade in the Product Cycle', *Quarterly Journal of Economics* 80(2): 190–207, 1966.

Von Bertalanffy, L., 'The Science of Synthesis: Exploring the Social Implications of General Systems Theory', *General Systems Theory* 103, 2010.

Wahl, D., 'Building a New Normal', *Resurgence & Ecologist* 321: 24–28, 2020.
Waldrop, M., *Complexity: The Emerging Science at the Edge of Order and Chaos*. London: Simon and Schuster, 1993.
Walker, B., Holling, C. S., Carpenter, S. R. & Kinzig, A., "Resilience, Adaptability and Transformability in Social–Ecological Systems', *Ecology and Society* 9(2): 5, 2004.
Walker, D., 'The New Gospel of Wealth', *Ford Foundation*, 2015 (https://www.fordfoundation.org/just-matters/just-matters/posts/toward-a-new-gospel-of-wealth/).
Walker, R., *Inside/Outside: International Relations as Political Theory*. London: Cambridge University Press, 1992.
Wang, L. & Buckland M, 'From Fief to Clan: Boisot's Information SpaceModel as a Documentary Theory for Cultural andInstitutional Analysis', *University of Akron Idea Exchange*, Proceedings from the Document Academy, Dec, 2016.
Weale, S. & Adams, R., 'Covid Has Been a Big Catalyst': Universities Plan for Post-Pandemic Life', *The Guardian*, July 13, 2021.
Weaver, M. & Walker, P., 'Government Sacks Roger Scruton after Remarks about Soros and Islamophobia', *The Guardian*, April 10, 2019.
Weber, A., *Theory of the Location of Industries*. Chicago: University of Chicago Press, 1929.
Welby, J., *Reimagining Britain: Foundations for Hope*. London: Bloomsbury, 2018.
Wenger and Snyder, 'Communities of Practice: The Organizational Frontier', *Harvard Business Review*, Jan–Feb, 2000.
Whyte, W., *Street Corner Society: The Social Structure of an Italian Slum*. Chicago: University of Chicago Press, 1943.
Wilkinson, A., 'Leave Voters Are Not All Idiots – Some Londoners Still Don't Get It', *The Guardian*, Feb 14, 2017.
Wolcott, H., *Transforming Qualitative Data*. London: Sage, 1994.
World Population Review, https://worldpopulationreview.com/world-cities/cluj-napoca-population, March 13, 2021.

INDEX

Note: **Bold** page numbers refer to tables; *italic* page numbers refer to figures and page numbers followed by "n" denote endnotes.

For Product Safety Concerns and Information please contact our EU
representative GPSR@taylorandfrancis.com
Taylor & Francis Verlag GmbH, Kaufingerstraße 24, 80331 München, Germany

www.ingramcontent.com/pod-product-compliance
Ingram Content Group UK Ltd.
Pitfield, Milton Keynes, MK11 3LW, UK
UKHW020142200926
475702UK00005B/866
9780367702571